THE BLUE CIVILIZATION
FROM THE AEGEAN TO THE MEDITERRANEAN

THE BLUE CIVILIZATION
FROM THE AEGEAN TO THE MEDITERRANEAN

THE BLUE CIVILIZATION
FROM THE AEGEAN TO THE MEDITERRANEAN

GÜROL SÖZEN

AKBANK

Published by Akbank Department of Art and Culture,
1995 with 3000 copies in Turkish and 2000 in English.

BOOK DESIGN   ERSU PEKİN
TRANSLATION   ADAIR MILL
MAPS   DOĞAN ÜR
COVER PHOTOGRAPH   REŞİT ERZİN

PHOTOGRAPHS   **GÜROL SÖZEN** 8, 10, 11, 24, 25, 28, 34, 37, 45(1), 46(3,4), 47, 48, 49, 50, 51(1,2,3,4), 52, 53, 54, 55, 56, 68, 71(1,2,3), 72(1,2), 74, 83, 96(1,2), 97(1), 100, 117(1), 118, 119(1,2,3), 120(3), 124(1,2), 125, 126, 127, 128(1), 129, 130(1,2), 131(1,2), 134, 136, 141, 143(1,2), 144, 145(1), 147(1,2), 148(1,2), 149, 159, 162, 163(1), 164(1,2), 165, 166, 168, 169, 170(1), 171(1), 173, 174, 175, 176, 178(1,2), 179, 180(1,2), 181(2), 184, 186, 187, 188, 189, 191(5), 193, 194(1,2), 195(2), 197, 199(1,2), 200(1,2), 201(1,2), 202(2,3), 203, 204, 205, 206, 210, 212(2), 213, 215(1,2), 216(2), 217(1,2), 219, 220(1,2,3), 221(2), 223(1,2,3,4), 229, 238(1,2), 239, 242, 243, 250(1,2), 251(1,2,4), 252(1,2,3), 253, 254, 255(1,2), 256, 257, 258(1,2), 260(2), 261(2), 262, 263, 264, 265, 266(1,2), 267, 268, 270(1), 274, 275, 276, 277(1,2), 280(1,2), 282, 283(1,2), 284, 285, 286(1,2,3), 287(1,2), 288(1,2), 289(1,2), 290, 291, 292, 293, 294(2), 296(2), 297, 300(1,2), 301, 302, 304, 305, 307(1,2), 308(1,2), 309, 310, 311(1,2), 313(1,2), 314, 315(1,2,3,4), 316(1,2), 320(2), 323(1), 324, 325, 326(1,2), 327, 328, 329, 330(1), 332, 333, 334, 335, 337, 340(1,2), 341, 342, 344, 345, 346, 347, 348(1,2), 349(1,2), 350, 353, 355(3,4,5), 356, 357, 358, 359(2,3), 360, 361(2,3), 362, 363(2,3,4), 364, 365, 368, 369, 370(1,2), 371, 373(2), 374, 375(1,2,3), 376(1,3), 377(1), 378(1,2,4), 379, 380, 381(1,2), 382, 383(1,2), 384(1,2), 385, 386(1,2), 387, 388(1,2), 389, 390(1,2), 391, 392, 393(1), 395, 396(2), 420, 423, 424, 426, 428(1,2), 429, 431, 432, 434(1,2), 437, 438, 442, 450; **FİRDEVS SAYILAN** 39, 42, 46(1,2), 57, 58, 59(2), 60(1,2), 61(1,2), 65, 67, 70, 75, 76(1,2),77, 78(1,2,3), 79 (1,2), 80, 81, 82, 85, 86(2), 88, 89, 90, 91(2), 93, 97(2), 103, 104(1,2,3), 105, 111(1), 113, 122, 123(1,2), 140(1), 153, 154, 155, 156, 157(1,2), 160, 163(2), 212(1), 230, 233(2), 251(3), 255(3), 260(1), 271, 272(1,2), 294(1), 296(1), 298(1,2), 299, 303, 306, 312(1,2), 317(1,2), 319, 320(1), 323(2), 354(1,2), 355(6), 373(1), 393(2), 394, 396(1), 397, 400(1,2), 401(3,4), 402, 403, 404, 405, 406, 409(1,2), 410, 412(1,2), 413(1,2), 414, 417, 418, 433; **ERDAL AKSOY** 33, 59(1), 64(1,2), 84, 91(1), 102(2), 108, 128(2), 138(1), 167, 170(2), 190(2), 191(1), 198(2), 202(1), 208, 214, 216(1), 218, 221(1), 222, 232, 233(1), 278, 322, 338(1,2), 339, 357; **HADİYE CANGÖKÇE-O. CEM ÇETİN (HEZARFEN)** 19, 20, 26, 27, 43, 44, 86(1), 87, 94, 98, 99(1,2), 102(1), 137,143(3), 145(3), 151, 177, 240, 269, 318, 411, 440;**ARZU KARAMANİ** 140(2), 142(1,2,3), 145(2), 146, 161, 191(2,3,4), 192, 195(1); **REŞİT ERZİN** 9, 31, 35, 38, 45(2), 181(1), 376(2), 378(3), 422; **ŞEMSİ GÜNER** 40, 41,158, 198(1), 330(2), 399, 407, 408; **ALİ KONYALI** 109(1), 114, 117(2), 228, 415, 427; **BODRUM MUSEUM ARCHIVE** 224(1,2), 225, 226, 227; **ERSU PEKİN** 190(1).

COLOUR SEPARATION   MAS MATBAACILIK A.Ş.
PRINTED BY   ANA BASIM A.Ş.
BOUND BY   BAYINDIR CİLT LTD ŞTİ

PAPER   ZANDERS MEGA 135 gr/m²
LINING PAPER   FABRIANO COLORE 200 blue 200 gr/m²
CLOTH   SCHOLCO ELITE 19024

PUBLICATION CODE 92-34-Y.0230.2
ISBN 975-7880-07-8

ISTANBUL 1995

CONTENTS

This book is dedicated to all those who seek refuge in nature, culture and art.

I suppose one of the most difficult things is to convince oneself, even after having written hundreds of pages, that the book is finally complete; especially if it is on the subject of the Aegean and the Mediterranean. All the things you have forgotten to say, all the descriptions and commentaries you have failed to include start to appear one by one in front of you and bring a feeling of emptiness to your heart.

That is why most people add a postscript. After all, isn't a postscript a sort of confession of failure?

It was with this in mind that I added the section entitled "Blue Notes" to the end of my book. But even that didn't suffice. I still keep on remembering things I have forgotten to include.

What really worries me is the vast scope of the subject. The infinite number of unknowns in both the natural and historical background of the Aegean and the Mediterranean, the infinite depths

The various peoples and communities that have bathed in these waters over so many thousands of years have seen so many different civilizations that every further piece of research you carry out into the Aegean and the Mediterranean serves to disprove one or more of even your most firmly held beliefs.

I have attempted to protect myself by writing my book in the form of traveller's notes, without entering in too great detail into the bottomless depths of these seas. In doing so, I have selected passages from writings of the past nine or ten years.

This was a journey of choice. I wrote down what I saw, knew and felt exactly as they affected me in the light of the relevant documents. And I never tried to isolate myself from them. I preferred to stroll among them as one of themselves. As a result, writers and scholars who lived thousands of years ago became my friends and travelling-companions.

In what epoch the various peoples of the Aegean and the Mediterranean that form the subject of my book may have lived is of no concern. The important thing is the outlook on life of those who have lived on Anatolian soil.

I see that people have changed very little in the course of the centuries. However remarkable the works they have created they have always displayed the same passions, desires and contradictions as ourselves. But with one difference: They had a true perception of the Aegean and the Mediterranean. They founded environment-friendly cities on sites that with all our modern facilities we would regard as inaccessible. They adorned life with their poems, their dances, their monumental sculptures and their Spring Festivals.

I would like the people of our own times to possess a more detailed knowledge of this extraordinary cultural wealth and to take lessons from it. Let us work conscientiously on all these various epochs. Let us be worthy of the accumulation of culture and art on Anatolian soil.

What would you say if I were to confess that I am rather doubtful about all this?

And there's another thing I have learned from the Aegean and the Mediterranean Not to belittle nature, or the civilizations that have preceded ours.

I have certainly never belittled anything, but I used to imagine that our own age displayed a marked superiority in interpretative and creative skills.

That is something I can no longer accept.

And that is the reason for the feeling of emptiness within me. There are so many things that have not been written or spoken. And there are so many things that have been written but have never reached me…

But I didn't allow myself to be held back because of sources of which I have still no knowledge. I wanted to share with you, as soon as possible, the beauties I had observed.

In other words, I am happy to have written a book like this.

Blue is not only a colour. It is a civilization.

My friend Ersu Pekin has throughout the whole process played an invaluable role in realizing this project by his work amidst computers, screens, museums and printing-presses.

I should also like to thank Akbank for the publication of the book, and Firdevs Sayılan, Reşit Erzin, Adair Mill, Deniz Yüce, Doğan Ür, Hadiye Cangökçe and Cem Çetin for their contributions to the work.

And now I should like to end by saying, "Have a pleasant journey."

7

I f I were to describe the **Aegean** and the **Mediterranean** as the *"Sea of the Gods"* would it strike you as strange?

It's purely my own personal idea, I realise that. But the foundation on which it rests is every bit as deep as the **Aegean** and the **Mediterranean** seas themselves. In their depth, their colour, their possession of lower and surface currents, there may appear to be no difference between the **Aegean** and **Mediterranean** and any other sea in the world. And it is the same sun that hangs suspended like a pendulum overhead . But don't be deceived.

There is a saying that you can never wash in the same river twice. The same quality of constant change is displayed by these two neighbouring seas, the **Aegean** and the **Mediterranean**. They are distinguished from any other sea by the presence of lower and surface currents, by the light, by the shadows cast by the rocks and by the sometimes green, sometimes yellow colour of the barren mountains on the shore. Otherwise, why should *Poseidon,* the absolute ruler of the seas, have chosen to build his palace in the depths of the *Aigaion* or *Aigaios Pontos,* now known as the **Aegean.**

Evidence for all this is given by the 9th century B.C. poet *Homeros* in a section of the *Iliad:*

> *"The great mountains and forests trembled*
> *Under the feet of the immortal Poseidon.*
> *He took three steps, reached Aigai on the fourth.*
> *He had a famous palace at Aigia, in the depth of the sea,*
> *Completely submerged under the waters, bright and shining,*
> *It never grew old, nothing was lacking."*

In the polytheistic world there is a story for every phenomenon. Which is a good thing, for it was through these stories that the earth and sea prised open the doors of civilisation. These stories form the sources of

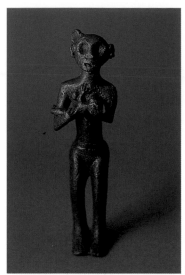

THE ANATOLIAN GODS OF THE POLYTHEISTIC REGIME WHO FOSTERED THE AEGEAN AND THE MEDITERRANEAN

1. Figurine of a bull. Alacahöyük. Early Bronze Age, 2nd half of 3rd millennium B.C.

2. Woman suckling a child. Horoztepe. Early Bronze Age, end of 3rd millennium B.C.

3. Female figurine and woman with pitcher. Terracotta. Early Bronze Age, end of 4th beginning of 3rd millennium B.C. Tarsus Museu.

4. Vase. Gordion. Terra cotta. Phrygian period. End of 8th century, beginning of 7th century B.C.

all the various branches of art. Isn't it the case that the proof of existence lies in the ability to create? So here is a story concerning the derivation of the name **Aegean**...

Let us hear how the poet and writer *Behçet Necatigil* relates the story of *Aigeus,* son of *Pandion,* King of **Athens,** and father of *Theseus:*

"Having grown to be a young man, Theseus set out for Athens. On his way he killed the bandits Sinis, Sciron and Procrustes, as well as the wild sow of Crommyum. Meanwhile, in Athens, prompted by Medeia, King Aegeus realised that the heroic youth was his own son and took steps to prevent his death.

"Theseus slew the mad boar Marathon and offered him as a sacrifice. He was subsequently sent as one of the fourteen victims, seven youths and seven maidens, whom Minos exacted as blood tribute from the Athenians, and who were destined to be devoured by the Cretan monster. On Minos' refusal to believe that Theseus was descended from the god Poseidon, the hero dived into the sea, where he was welcomed and entertained by the goddess Amphitrite, who sent him back with gifts. On Crete, Ariadne, the daughter of King Minos, fell in love with Theseus and gave him a ball of wool so that when he entered the Labyrinth he could unwind the wool as he made his way through its twists and turns, thus making it possible for him to find his way back after killing the monster Minotaur. He then fled from Crete with Ariadne, whom he abandoned on the island of Naxos, where Dionysos found her and subsequently took her as his wife. On approaching Athens, Theseus completely forgot the agreement he had made with his father that in case of success in his enterprise he would hoist white sails in place of the black. The sight of the black sails, which Theseus had failed to replace with the white, led his father Aigeus, who had been watching out for him, to believe that his son was dead, whereupon he threw himself headlong to his death in the sea below, which thus came to be known as the Aigae (Aegean) Sea."

Aren't the heroic deeds, the fears, the hopeless loves, the rebellions and tragic fates that have featured at some time or another in the infinite time span of nature, all part of the life of humanity?

Who can deny that *Theseus'* forgetfulness in failing to hoist the white sail in place of the black forms an inherent part of our own life history?

And who can deny that *Aigeus'* suicide was a perfectly natural human

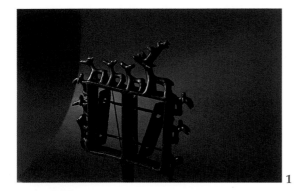

1

2

3

4

reaction on the part of a father, convinced, on seeing the black sail, of the death of his son, however false the belief later proved to be, and finding himself unable to bear the burden of so great a sorrow. ?

Imagine someone looking out one evening over the **Aegean Sea** to the black sails in the distance. What a wonderful subject for a painting!

After such a legend has entered our dreams, how can we ever regard the **Aegean** as just a sea like any other?

The **Aegean** and the **Mediterranean** can also, in a sense, be called the sea of legends. Undoubtedly, this was one of the results of the infinite beauty of nature. In the course of the centuries, man has exploited a large part of this beauty for his own ends. That is why we can observe the constant strength of civilization in both these seas.

Nor should we forget that these waters were the source of all ecstasy and rapture, a fact well known to the powerful gods and goddesses of nature who danced and sang in the revels of *Dionysos* and to all the peoples of the **Aegean** and the **Mediterranean.** They left evidence of all this to posterity, to ourselves in fact, by exploiting their skills to the full in every stone and every piece of marble they carved, in every mural they painted, in every inscription they wrote.

As a matter of fact, as soon as one looks at the written sources one feels like calling on the world of dreams to help us create a completely new legend. In a sense, the waters of the **Aegean** and the **Mediterranean** harbour great friendship, great harmony and perfect balance.

As a result of evaporation, the surface currents that flow from the **Atlantic Ocean** and the Sea of **Marmara** to the **Mediterranean** by way of the Aegean, gradually fall to the bottom, returning through the **Straits of**

THE ANATOLIAN GODS OF THE POLYTHEISTIC REGIME WHO FOSTERED THE AEGEAN AND THE MEDITERRANEAN .

1. Sistrum (instrument used in religious ceremonies). Horoztepe. Early Bronze Age. End of 3rd millennioum B.C.

2. Mountain God. Tarsus. Rock crystal. Hittite Empire. 14th-13th century B.C.

3. Bull's head. Detail of bronze cauldron. Altıntepe. Urartu period, end of 8th century, beginning of 7th century B.C.

4. Four-horse chariot (chariot of the gods). Gordion. Phrygian, end of 8th century, beginning of 7th century B.C.

Gibraltar to the **Atlantic Ocean,** from which they originally came. The surface currents descend to the depths and the lower currents rise to the surface... Like a great traveller who keeps on travelling till the end of his life in an attempt to get to come to terms with himself and the world he lives in. That is why the **Mediterranean** was called the "breathing sea", just as the **Aegean,** because of the great number of its islands, was known as the *"Archipelago".*

Formed two and a half million years ago, the **Mediterranean** is the largest of the world's inland seas. Moreover, it has witnessed the Ice Age. Three times it has subsided and risen again. With such a history behind it, how could it fail to give rise to a legend all of its own?

The waters of the **Mediterranean** are warmer and rather more salty than those of the **Aegean.** For example, in February, the temperature varies from 10° C in the north **Aegean** to 15° C further south; while the temperature varies from 14-15° C in the Western **Mediterranean** to 22-25° C in the Eastern parts.

When the sun is at its height in the month of August the temperature of the waters of the **Aegean** rises to 23° C, while in the **Mediterranean** it is 26-28° C, the temperature of a lukewarm bath.

But to the gods and goddesses such differences were of no importance, for both seas, and their shores, were the birthplace of civilizations. It was all one to them whether they washed in lukewarm water or made their bodies glisten with grains of salt. They had arrived in the world to initiate a passion and enthusiasm that was to survive for thousands of years. Their rule encompassed the whole world from the regions underground to the space above the clouds. It was enough that mankind should be able to enjoy life to the full.

It was inevitable that during a period dominated by the jealousies and self-indulgence of the gods and goddesses wars should break out from time to time. It was inevitable, too, that heroic deaths should be transformed into a symbol of eternity.

The people of the **Aegean** and **Mediterranean** world, who displayed all their skills in poetry, music, dancing, painting and sculpture in their daily lives as well as in the Dionysiac revels, were well aware of the real nature of the world they lived in. Strength was essential for their survival, for the preservation of peace and harmony. That was why they ascribed all power and strength to *Zeus,* the father of the gods, and why they built his palace in the sky, above the clouds.

I hesitate to say it, but it seems to me that they had no alternative. With so many gods and goddesses around who else could exercise effective control? Who else could guide mortals on the true path and assume responsibility for instigating wars that might well end in death? They got out of it very conveniently by placing the whole burden on *Zeus'* shoulders.

Homer, the lyric epic poet who lived in the **Aegean** region two thousand nine hundred years ago, bears witness in the *Iliad* to the part played in all this by almighty *Zeus:*

"Two pitchers stand on the threshold of Zeus,
One filled with evil gifts, the other with good.
Zeus mixes them together, and offers them to mortals,
Mankind receiving due share of the good and the bad.

In short, in every age there has been good and evil people. But the good and the evil they produce are only transitory. Just as nature itself is no bed of roses, the houses, streets and cities created by men possess, like the heart of man, little comfort. And the reason lies in the fact that mankind is responsible for its own creation.

The legends that people relate all over the world reveal, from one point of view, their own basic reality. In seeking a branch they can cling to they have created a legend and woven a whole skein of symbols around it. From these symbols, in which art plays a predominant role, we too have benefited and taken pleasure. Without them, no one would ever have thought of setting out on a voyage through the **Aegean** and the **Mediterranean.**

Careful scrutiny reveals that the creative thinkers of past centuries have always behaved very reasonably, never attempting to foist this or that god on to the people. Just like *Hades,* the god of the underworld, who only interfered when obliged to, as, for example, in the case of Sinis, who would bend down the tops of pine trees until they reached the earth and then tie someone he had captured to the branches and suddenly let go, sending the victim hurtling to his death.

Life is made intolerable by the sort of god who confronts you at every turning and follows you everywhere. We need gods and goddesses who inspire us with a love of life, fill us with passion and enthusiasm, and seek out the voice of the heart in the pursuit of beauty. And we need many such. There are so many gods and goddesses with so many different qualities and characteristics that we cannot help uttering a cry of sheer amazement.

Of *Apollo,* the flying god, the patron of nature, music, science and all the fine arts, the foreteller of the future and mighty archer, they say that *"when he bends his shining bow all the gods leap to their feet".*

Mankind has such a love for *Aphrodite,* the goddess of beauty, who sprang from the foam of the crystalline seas, that ever since the Neolithic Age she has continued to reside on **Anatolian** soil, transforming herself, from one generation to the next, into the Mother Goddess, *Kybele* or *Artemis.* Who could fail to fall in love with *Aphrodite,* born from the foam of the **Aegean** and the **Mediterranean** in the infinity of man's intellect and dreams?...

And *Dionysos?*

I have a particular love for *Dionysos.* That is why I have devoted a special chapter to the source of all ecstasy and rapture in the **Aegean** and **Mediterranean.**

AN INFINITY: DIONYSOS

A storm is about to break.. A vague indigo from the east is descending over the deepening blue of the sea. The white clouds that brought peace and comfort have long disappeared. The cloud masses that shaded the sun, even for a very short period, that brought a certain coolness and allowed the body to breathe, have quietly vanished in the distance. They must have been afraid of the wrath of *Poseidon*, the absolute ruler of the seas, who dared challenge even **Zeus**, the father of the gods....

And what of the birds?.. The birds wheel revelling in circles in the blue of the sky!..
They fly low, skimming the waters. Now and again the leaders turn and look back to see that they are still in touch with their followers.

But he himself remains completely indifferent, reclining on a long narrow sailboat.

The wind fills the snow-white sail.

The stern of the boat has been transformed into the head of a swan. With a crown on his head, a pointed beard and a garment covered with hundreds of stars he fixes his gaze ahead. He is well prepared. So that he need not be continually filling up small glasses he holds a tall goblet in his right hand.

And what about the mast of the boat?

Perhaps you'd better not ask!...

What sort of mast would you associate with a boat carrying Dionysos over the sea with a goblet in his hand capable of holding a whole pitcher of wine

Reckoning that no matter how enormous a goblet may be the wine will

(above) Door-knocker with head of Dionysos. Foça.
(opposite) Dionysos. Afyon. Marble. 1st-2nd century A.D. Istanbul Archaeological Museum.

Inside of goblet. The motif of Dionysos surrounded by dolphins racing the ship was a common source of inspiration for the artists of the ancient world. Vulci. 3rd quarter of 6th century. Munich Museum.

sometime or other be exhausted, he has transformed the mast into a climbing vine whose thick foliage and heavy clusters of grapes veils the the dark blue of the sky itself.

Dolphins leap and gambol around the boat, some of them in the depth of the sea, other wheeling in circles on the surface of the waters.

Another question. Who are these dolphins?... They are pirates of the

Dionysos, god of life, love, enthusiasm and enlightenment.

wine-dark sea who had attempted to seize Dionysos and whom the god had transformed into dolphins, creating good out of evil.

A storm will soon break out... Let it come, who cares!

Exekias, the most celebrated vase-painter in ancient Athens, must have felt the same when he produced a rough sketch of the scene...

A rough sketch of *Dionysos* is also to be found in the *Bacchae*, the tragedy written by the 5th century writer *Euripides. Dionysos* himself describes the task he had been given.

> "I, the god Dionysos, son of Zeus, born of Semele, daughter of Cadmus, in the midst of thunder and lightning, now step on Theban soil. I have divested myself of my godhead and taken on human form... I come from the golden plains of Lydia. I have traversed the sun-parched meadows of Iran, the long defence walls of Bactria, the frozen steppes of Media, the

blessed lands of Arabia Felix, all the Asian countries along the shores of the salt sea, and the splendid cities with fine citadels where Greeks and barbarians live together. I gathered my choruses together there, I taught them my rites and rituals. Now I wish to make myself known to the Hellenes. Thebes is the first city in Hellenic lands which I made ring with the shrill cries of the Bacchantae, clothing the naked bodies of the women with panther skins and placing the thyrsos, the ivy-entwined mace, in their hands."

The chorus of the **Bacchae** sing thus of **Dionysos:**

> *"Dionysos, son of Zeus,*
> *Loves joy and festivities.*
> *Dionysos loves peace*
> *That brings men comfort.*
> *He is the source of the wine that brings*
> *Release from pain to both rich and poor.*
> *Dionysos has no love for the man who cannot take pleasure*
> *From free and generous days and nights.*
> *Take heed of what he says:*
> *Avoid all pride and deep thoughts,*
> *Believe in the faith of the common people,*
> *And live as they live."*

Now do you realise how it was that Dionysos could feel perfectly at ease in the presence of the storms and pirates of the wine-dark seas?..

It was because he was the god of life and love, and passion and virtue and enlightenment.

The Bacchantae in Euripides's tragedy give expression to the love of the people. Dionysos has no love for the man who cannot take pleasure from free and generous days and nights..... Nor has he any love for the proud man who cannot believe in the simple faiths of ordinary mortals..... Of all the virtues he stands for "Peace" comes first.

Peace, passion and profound humanity.

But be careful. Don't say, "These are just myths. There is one God omnipotent. We cannot worship this god or that. It's all a lot of rubbish..." You want to know what will happen? Nothing! But what we must get to know and learn is life itself. Whether we lived thousands of years ago or here and now... Where is the man who doesn't long for peace and passion and profound humanity?... The multiplicity of gods is only a means...

There is a basic truth of which the communities and societies that lived in a polytheistic environment were all very well aware. They never gave themselves up to blind worship. For they knew that they themselves were the creators of the myths, and of the temples and monumental statues constructed around them. It was they themselves who were responsible for the poems and rituals with which they celebrated the spring festivals. Where do I find evidence for all this?.. The answer is given, not by myself,

(opposite) Marble relief for the tragic poet Euripides. Vicinity of Izmir. Late Hellenistic period, 1st century B.C.- 1st century A.D. Istanbul Archaeological Museum.

ΣΚΗΝΗ   ΕΥΡΕΠΙΔΗΣ

but by **Terpandros,** a poet who lived in the 7th century B.C. The poem is entitled *"A Gift to Zeus".*

> *"Zeus, the source of all things,*
> *All-powerful and omnipotent,*
> *Zeus, I bring you a gift:*
> *It was I who began the poem, the song."*

Is the poet **Terpandros** putting Zeus in his place? Not at all!.. He is simply smiling, and declaring what he himself had created on behalf of future generations. And in doing so, employing all his poetic skill...

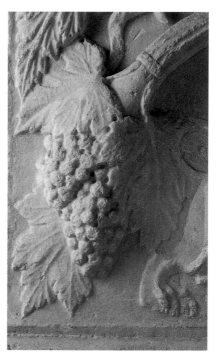

Cluster of grapes. Marble relief. Bergama. Hellenistic period, 2nd century B.C. Istanbul Archaeological Museum.

THE NATURE OF DIONYSOS

D iscussions of identity are not confined to our own age or solely to monotheistic societies. Polytheistic communities also prescribed limits to the supernatural powers they created and defined their attributes. **Dionysos** had many names: *Bakkhos, Bromios, Euhios* and *Dithyrambos.* But he was most commonly known as *Dionysos.*

Here is how *Azra Erhat* describes **Dionysos:**

> *"Dionysos was a stranger god. He was a foreigner quite alien to the Hellenic pantheon. There are many tales and legends clearly reflecting the difficulties that Greece experienced in accepting Dionysos, and the popular resistance to his cult*
>
> *"Dionysos was in every way intimately associated with nature, but he was not so much a nature god as a link between man and nature, a great power that initiated man into the natural mysteries.*
>
> *"Access to the power and the secrets of nature, in other words, the achievement of godhead, is something that mankind longs above all else to attain. Dionysos makes it possible for everyone to reach that goal, through wine and ecstasy. The spread of the vine throughout the world meant that the stage introduced by the cultivation of wheat was now succeeded by a new stage in the development of civilisation, opening a new era in the evolution of humanity, which was now freed from its dependence on agriculture alone. It was only after man had been given the gift of wine that he achieved the power to "work transformations", the power that lies at the root of all creativity.*
>
> *"Dionysos is not a single individual. He is the human condition itself. That is why he is never static, but always in a state of motion and transformation. He is the reflection and creation of universal life, above all through the medium of the human soul and body."*

We should also listen to what *Behçet Necatigil* has to say on the subject:

> *"He was the son of Zeus by the Thebean Semele. Semele asked to see Zeus*

in his true aspect, but this was to be the cause of her death, for Zeus appeared to her in the form of a thunderbolt. Although Semele herself was consumed, Zeus rescued her unborn son Dionysos and sewed him up in his thigh. Later he entrusted him to the nymphs of Mount Nysa, who were made responsible for his upbringing.

"*Dionysos was a Thracian god. His orgiastic cult was celebrated by the frenzied women known as the Bacchae, who had arrived in Greece before the beginning of the historical period. They would dance in the forests and on the mountain, and Dionysos would punish anyone who attempted to obstruct the frenzied rites held in his honour. Finally, Apollo accepted the new god in the oracular temple at Delphi, which was handed over to Dionysos during the winter months, thus ensuring the worship of Dionysos a more orderly form. Satyrs and Sirens joined with Dionysos in the three days of the spring festivals (Anthesteriai) at Athens. It was from the festivities of the masked god, Dionysos Aleuthreus, that Athenian tragedy originated and developed. Dionysos took Ariadne as his wife.*

"*In the work entitled 'Dionysiaka' the Greek epic poet Nonnos, who lived in the 5th century B.C., sings of Dionysos' victorious progress as far as India. In ancient Greek art, Dionysos is portrayed as a man with long hair and beard crowned with ivy and holding a wine-cup in his hand. It is only after the 4th century B.C. that he begins to be depicted as a graceful youth.*"

A closer examination of mythology and the relevant sources will reveal further details of the god of fertility and rapture:

"*Although Dionysos was of Thracian or Phrygian origin, the legends relating to his birth and death and his marriage to the Cretan goddess Ariadne give the impression that the Dionysiac cult was a return to the pre-Greek Minoan nature religion.*

"*The Dyonisiuc festivities spread very rapidly among the women during the post-Mycenaean period. The women participating in his rites were known as Bacchae. His rites were generally regarded with some disfavour by men. According to legend, the Bacchae tore the Theban King Pentheus to pieces for having secretly observed their rites and punished with impotence the Athenian men who had shown disrespect to Dionysos. But as a result of the reaction of the men, the women abandoned their families and took to the mountains, clothing themselves in panther skins and wearing wreaths of ivy on their heads. During the rites, the Bacchae would dance the sacred dance to the accompaniment of flutes and drums in the light of torches, waving thyrsoi consisting of branches of fennel entwined with ivy.*

"*The cult of Dionysos survived for a very long period in Anatolia, particularly in Phrygia and Lydia. The cult is associated with a number of Asiatic gods.*

"*Phallic symbols occupied a very important place in the Dionysiac rites.*"

The events connected with **Dionysos** are not all of them legendary. The theatre buildings erected beside the temples of *Dionysos* formed one of the elements on which human creativity was based. The birth of tragedy and comedy are closely connected with the name of *Dionysos.* The earliest of the Greek theatre buildings took shape during the festivities in his honour. With the arrival of the Dionysiac spring festivals, the previously simple theatre buildings assumed a certain grandeur and magnificence, the inclusion of poetry, speeches, music, votive offerings and dances necessitating a certain modification of the architectural setting.

It is through the operative power of art that aesthetics and the preoccupation with form are introduced to the cities... It was during the festivities of *Dionysos* that the plays of *Euripides, Sophocles, Aeschylus* and *Aristophanes* were produced for the first time in the 5th century B.C.

It was, therefore, as a result of the festivals of *Dionysos* that the earliest theatre buildings, which had consisted of a few rows of wooden seats on the slope of a hill, were replaced by magnificent stone structures...

The **Ionian** philosopher *Thales* tells a story concerning the city of **Teos** (Sığacık) which aspired to become the leader of the twelve cities forming the Ionian league.

> *"The city of Teos boasted the largest temple of Dionysos in the ancient world, and it was at Teos, towards the end of the 3rd century B.C., that the first league of Ionian actors was founded. Though the members of the league gave performances at various places they retained Teos as their centre, and the fact that these actors in the festivals of Dionyos and the houses in which they lived enjoyed inviolability on account of the sacred duty they performed made their residence in the city something to be greatly desired. However, the actors of Dionysos were obliged to move to Ephesus towards the middle of the 2nd century B.C. on account of dissensions that had broken out among them, and, shortly afterwards, King Attalos sent them to Myonnesus because of various activities they had indulged in at Ephesus. The actors were later settled by the Romans in Lebedos, where they took up permanent residence, except for a short period when they were brought to Priene by Mark Antony for the entertainment of Cleopatra."*

Let us glance for a moment at what *Strabo,* the famous geographer who was born in the town of Amasya in the 1st century B.C., has to say concerning the actors taking part in the *Dionysiac* festivities.

> *"All the Dionysiac artists from the Hellespont would gather in the Ionian city of Lebedos (present-day Gümüldür), where they would take part each year in the festivities held in honour of Dionysos. They originally came from Colophon (present-day Değirmendere) and settled in the Ionian city of Teos, whence they fled to Ephesus on the outbreak of an uprising there. When Attalos settled them in Myonnesos, a city situated between Teos and Lebedos, the citizens of Teos sent a deputation to the Romans requesting that permission should not be given for the fortification of Myonnesos against them and at the same time migrated to Lebedos,whose citizens*

warmly welcomed them in view of the sparseness of the local population."
Talking of **Mark Antony** and the actors involved in the festivities of
Dionysos, what about joining in one of the spring festivals to be held in
Ephesus this year?

THE MADNESS OF ANTONY

The arrival of spring is being celebrated on the mountain slopes stretching down to the plains below and the dark blue waters of the **Aegean.**
Torches have been lit on both sides of the colonnaded street in front of the
theatre of **Ephesus.** The day is about to dawn and the audience is watching
the *Dionysiac* actors in rapt enthusiasm. Some are reciting poems praising
the virtues, ecstatic passion and power of *Dionysos.* Others sing songs to
the accompaniment of instruments, while the actors, in their white robes,
perform frenzied dances in the dim light of early morning.
Silence suddenly falls. The actors, poets and musicians withdraw to one
side. Goat-footed **Satyrs** representing the forces of nature leap and whirl
along the marble way.
Meanwhile, the *Bacchae,* the chorus of bare-footed women with their bodies swathed in spotted panther-skins, stand in quiet dignity with wreaths
of ivy on their heads and ivy-entwined **thyrsoi** in their hands. The pine
cones at the end of the long **thyrsoi** glisten in the light of the torches.
One of the royal heralds who has mingled with the throng murmurs in
amazement at what he sees. He will soon hasten to the side of the king and
inform him of what is taking place....

> *"The Bacchae wiped the deep sleep from their eyes. Suddenly all of them,
> young, old or virgin, leaped forward in amazing order and precision. They
> first of all flung their hair over their shoulders, tied and tightened the loos-
> ened nebris and wound the snakes that were licking their cheeks like belts
> around their leopard-skins. Some of them were suckling the deer and wolf
> cubs they were carrying in their arms. These were women who had newly
> given birth and had abandoned their children but whose breasts were full of
> milk. Finally they all placed wreaths of ivy, oak-leaves and blossoms on their
> heads. One of them seized her staff and struck it on a rock, whereupon water
> gushed out as clear as morning dew. Another struck her thyrsos on the
> ground, and the god made a pitcher of wine spring from the earth. There was
> milk for those who wished it. Honey dripped from the ivy-entwined thyrsoi.
> Ah, if only you had been there to see it you would have offered thanks to this
> god in whom you profess no belief."*

The royal herald was bewildered. He too was affected by the enthusiasm of
the crowd. Unable to keep silent he announced to all what he had intended
to say privately to the king:

> *"Your Majesty, whoever this god may be, he is undoubtedly a great god.*

Grant permission for him to enter our city. They say that it is he who gives the wine that dissipates the care of mortal men. Without wine, there would be no love, or anything else..."

And now the herald falls silent. One emerges from the ranks of the Satyrs and Bacchae with a crown of vine-leaves on his head, a thyrsos entwined with vine-leaves in one hand and a gold goblet in the other. His long white garment is fastened with gold brooches. His face is like clear marble. Curly locks fall over his brow.

Can this being who emerges from the ranks of Satyrs and Bacchae be the god *Dionysos* himself?

The people shout out in ecstasy: "All glory to you, the new god *Dionysos*, all glory to your festival!"

"Who is that?", the herald asks someone next to him.

"Mark Antony..." he replies.

DIONYSOS, WINE AND LIFE ITSELF

It was not for nothing that the people hailed *Marcus Antonius*, the Roman lover of the 'New Aphrodite', *Cleopatra*, as the 'new Dionysos'. The event that took place at **Ephesus** is described by some as a symptom of madness. But for others it was life itself.

However that may be, *Dionysos* led countless communities from west to east and from east to west... From the **Aegean** to **Anatol**ia, and from **Anatolia** as far as the **Indian** continent ...

According to the legends handed down from one generation to the next, and changed and modified in the telling, *Dionysos* enjoyed a very happy childhood. He would scamper hither and thither in an infinity of green and blue. After all, he was the son of *Zeus*, a child *Zeus* had concealed in his thigh.

He was a skilled hunter. But as well as being a skilled hunter he was also said to be an expert in the taming of wild animals. That was probably why, wherever he went in the forest, he was always accompanied by two tigers he himelf had tamed.

For man, nature was utterly virgin... Everything that *Dionysos* touched sprouted and blossomed and gave fruit! One day he saw hundreds of clusters of grapes among the leaves. Each cluster was heavy with rich fruit. Some were dark purple, others a sort of red. They all hung above his head. The sunlight played on the ripe, juicy fruit.

Dionysos was unable to resist. He ate one of them and, relishing the taste, ate several of the rich warm clusters. He couldn't stop. He squeezed some of the fuit and drank the juice. Then he fell asleep. When he woke up at the return of day he drank some of the juice that remained, and immediately experienced an indescribable pleasure.

He ran, urging everyone he met, on mountain or plain, to drink some of the juice from these grapes. And whoever he met, on mountain or plain,

Mask with ram's horns used in festivities.
Terra cotta. 3rd-2nd century B.C.

fell into an ecstasy. They began to dance and sing. They went everywhere, on mountain and plain. The people of the city of **Miletus** welcomed them with joy. They immediately began to cultivate vines and to make the wine that produced such ecstasy.

Dionysos picked up his pitcher and set out for the East. He went as far as **India**. On his return journey through Anatolia he visited *King Midas* of Phrygia. You remember *Midas*, *Midas* with the donkey's ears! *King Midas* had made Phrygia the wealthiest of countries. In the good old Anatolian tradition he refused to allow the ecstatic *Dionysos* to leave, and entertained him for days and nights on end.

But this was *Dionysos*. No one knew what might issue from his lips during his periods of ecstasy. Apparently he announced, *"May whatever you touch turn to gold!"* And from that moment onwards everything that *King Midas* touched actually turned to pure gold. Whatever and whoever he touched was transformed into bright glistening gold.

> *"Almighty god of nature,"* he cried, *"master of ecstasy, I beg you to have pity on me, let me enjoy my food as the poor and destitute are able to do!"*

Forerunners of irony in the theatre. Kültepe. Terracotta. 1st half of 2nd millennium. Ankara Museum of Anatolian Civilizations.

Dionysos told him to bathe in the river, and *Midas* bathed in the river as *Dionysos* had told him. And, from that day to this, small particles of gold can be seen glistening in the river of **Lydia** and **Phrygia**.

Born of *Semele* by *Zeus*... Though it isn't really true to say that he was born of *Semele*, since she lost her child after he had been only seven months in her womb. After that he was sewn up in *Zeus*'s thigh, to mature there for two months longer. *Zeus*, the father of the gods, was, in a sense, both his father and, for two months, his mother!

But let us not spoil the tradition: *Dionysos*, son of *Zeus*, born of *Semele*, drew everyone after him all over the world. Whoever was in pursuit of ecstasy came to him. Whoever wished to exploit the powers of nature followed him in his path...

At first he was an inexperienced youth who would scatter perfume on his fair curly locks, while purple stained cheeks framed eyes that looked out with all the mystery of *Aphrodite*...

In this, I am only repeating what *King Pentheus* said. In the *Bacchae* of *Euripides* the **Theban King Pentheus** is driven by wrath to describe *Dionysos* in this way. Just look at what he says. May God preserve us from such imputations!..

> *"While I have been away, the city has been visited by a strange calamity. Our women have deserted their homes to take part in the rites of Bacchos. In groves and on barren mountains they worship a new god called*

Dionysos, a god I have never heard of. Everywhere there are pitchers full of wine. The women hide in corners and throw themselves into the laps of the men. They claim that this was the way the Maenads worshipped, but i twould appear to be Aphrodite, rather than Bacchos, with whom these women are infatuated!"

King **Pentheus** was livid with rage. Just listen to what he said to **Cadmos**, the founder of the city of **Thebes**!

"Don't touch me! Go, join in the Bacchanalian orgies! Don't try to infect me with their frenzy!"

But let us not get involved in such nonsense. Let us return to reality.

Dionysos was depicted as a beautiful, curly-haired, well-built youth. He wore a wreath of ivy. In his right hand he held a wine cup and in his left a thyrsos. A tamed tiger would lie at his feet.

Half a century later, as we approach the end of the age of **Pericles**, the 5th century artists who had depicted him thus in painting or sculpture began to add jewels to his hair, along with a garment of the finest gauze and a goat or panther skin thrown over his shoulder.... His chariot was drawn by the lynxes and tigers he had hunted in India. In some of the paintings and sculptures we find chattering magpies, whether as heralds of **Dionysos** or flatterers I wouldn't know. But the inclusion among his attributes of the fig and the oak-tree alongside the vine leaf and the pine cone shows that they were accepted as part of the Dionysiac cult.

The **Dionysos** with the long beard and the long garment and the spotted leopard skin over his shoulder was a source of inspiration for the artists of the 6th to 4th centuries B.C. The ivy wreath on his head, the long thyrsos and the wine cup in his hand were characteristic attributes. It would appear that **Dionysos** had devotees from every generation, with the result that everyone chose a **Dionysos** of his own age. And rightly so... What has age to do with ecstasy, dance and the bonds linking mankind to nature!

Who could find any objection to deriving *tragedy*, which means 'goat', with a **Dionysos** who sprang from the union of **Semele**, meaning 'spring' and **Zeus** the father of the gods?

Weren't the festivals of **Dionysos**, in which the **Bacchae**, the actors in their multi-coloured masks, the **Satyrs**, the dancers, the poets and thousands of ordinary people all took part and wine was drunk for six days on end, practically identical with the carnivals of the present day?

So we can see that the custom of holding such festivities has continued uninterrupted from the time of **Dionysos** to this.

He was the object of such love and affection that people living thousands of years ago would name their children after him:

(above) Tragic mask. Trelles (Aydın). Marble, Early Roman, 1st century B.C. (opposite) Statuette of comic actor. Aydın. Marble, Roman period, 2nd century A.D. Istanbul Archaeological Museum.

• In the 5th century B.C. we find a *Dionysos* teaching history in **Ephesus**, another *Dionysos* working in the Library of **Alexandria** and a third *Dionysos* an orator in **Miletus.**

• In the 4th century B.C. there was poet from *Sinop* with the name *Dionysos.*

• There was a grammarian by the name of *Dionysos* who was born around 170 B.C. and died in 90 B.C.

• There was *Dionysos of Alexandria,* an archbishop who lived in the 3rd century A.D.

• There was also a sculptor called *Dionysos* who lived in **Argos** in the 5th century B.C.

And these are only a few of the tens of thousands of examples. According to *Azra Erhat,*

> *"The spread of vine cultivation over the world brought about the next stage in human development after that introduced by the cultivation of wheat. It also opened an epoch in which human evolution was no longer linked solely to agriculture. It was only after the invention of wine that men achieved the power of transformation that lies at the basis of all creativity. Dionysos is an expression of this truth as both a natural and a supernatural phenomenon."*

Ecstasy is the source of all art. And the power of the artist is the power of nature.

It would be no exaggeration to say that there is a little of *Dionysos* in everything produced and everything created.

There is a very close resemblance between ourselves and the people that lived here thousands of years ago. The only real difference lies in the way we dress. We drink our water and our wine from the same type of cup. We plant the same flowers and trees in our gardens, not to mention the blue sky we gaze at in common, and the rushing torrents or still waters. And I don't count the grape, that comprises every form of plenty and abundance.

Do you ask why?

Because then the **Hittites,** the **Phrygians,** the **Urartians** and the other masters of the **Anatolian** soil will emerge with goblets and a cluster of grapes in their hands!..

As Shakespeare says, *"What's past is prologue.."*

FROM DARDANOS TO THE AEGEAN

I don't know why, but every journey on sea or land leads me to the mysteries of the past, perhaps because of my unwillingness to rest content with dry history books. There is also the fact that on these journeys I hear the voice of joys and sorrows much more profoundly.

A tree, a secluded harbour, a fluted column lying by the water's edge, the endless pattern of a *meander* motif, each of them exerts a certain fascination over me. Everything is in motion there, like the word *motif* itself. Even the water that appears so still and stagnant...

Civilizations have come and gone. Their languages have passed away, like their people. They were constantly at war, but they were also constantly creating works of art. You have only to examine one carefully for so many stories to emerge that you can't simply ignore them.

War may be inevitable, but war itself isn't eternal. The secret behind *Alexander the Great's* success, in his short life, in fighting his way from Greece to India, is not to be sought solely in his brilliance as a general. His bloody conquests were transcended by the lessons in philosophy he had received from *Aristotle*, his admiration for science and art, the inspiration he received from *Homer.* It may have been this aspect of *Alexander the Great,* who claimed a godhead for himself, that exp[ains his success in creating a new world. The many great and flourishing cities in the civilizations he founded remain as proof of this.

That is the way of humanity. After months of winter and storms, filled with poverty, pain and death, we have only to see the blossoms opening on the boughs and hear the birds singing in the trees to forget it all. Our hearts are filled once more with joy and hope.

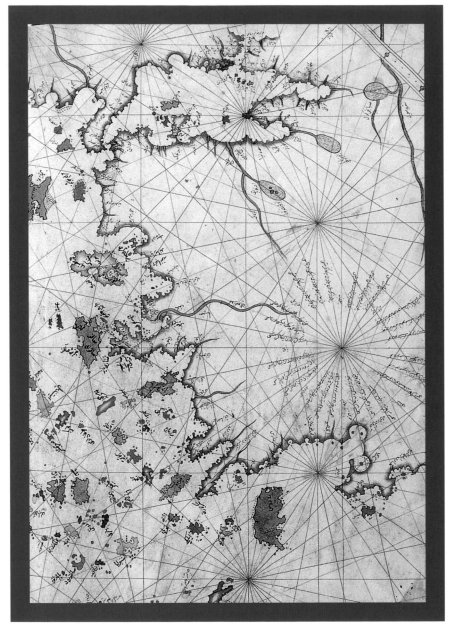

16th century map of the Aegean and Western Anatolia. Atlas of Ali Macar Reis.
(opposite) The voyage through deep, blue seas began from the Dardanelles.

Perhaps it is because I don't want to forget. I have no rose-coloured spectacles, but one thing is certain: when making a journey, I prefer the skill of man produced in collaboration with nature.

It may be an unusual wish, but I hope and trust that each one of us will be sustained by the power of art and knowledge.

I look at the sea of **Marmara**, as it sends its waters into the **Aegean** in the upper currents flowing through the **Dardanelles**. They are full of restless life, eager to reach the open sea as quickly as possible. First the **Aegean** and then the **Mediterranean**.

So much for the motion of the waters. But what about the sky!.. Neither of them are under our control. Only *Zeus* and *Poseidon* are in command. No one can interfere! And I have no intention of voicing an objection. I know my place....

Quite apart from the sea and the sky, there are so many things of which we know nothing in the thousands of years of past history, and as for the things we know, no one wants to learn from them. It isn't a very pleasant experience when someone seizes one excuse or another to offer you advice. But there's one thing that intrigues me. What do you do on one of these journeys when you are suddenly confronted with a marble slab with strange writings on it or a polychrome fish on a fragment of a broken pot?

If you say "I couldn't do anything about the marble slab, but I would slip the sherd with the fish on it into my pocket without letting anyone see." you are ruining the whole magic of the trip right from the start.

Actually, the **Aegean** and the **Mediterranean** we see today are no more than the remains from past plunder.

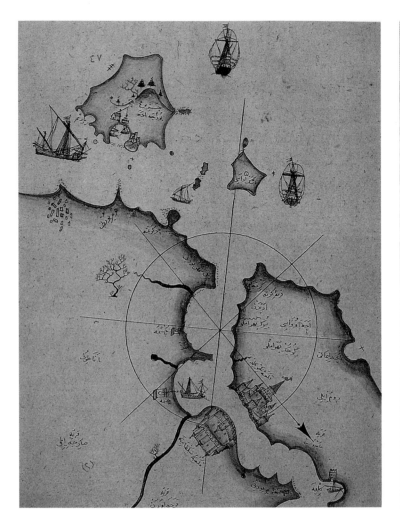

Chart of the Dardanelles. The opening into the Aegean. "Kal'a-i Bahr-i Kilid" and, opposite, "Kala-i Sultaniye". The island of İmroz in the Aegean. "Kitâb-ı Bahriye", Piri Reis, Ayasofya Library.

I am not addressing people with those particular professional interests...Quite frankly, I am not mad about the history of art. But I am interested in the skills that encompass nature, earth and water. For me, the fish on the pot and the inscription on the marble, with its message for the present day, are both mysteries. As they are, I am sure, for most of us...

In sending its water along the the surface currents on its long journey to the **Aegean,** the **Marmara** makes use of the **Dardanelles.**

Finding a way into the **Aegean** is no easy matter.

To make even a short journey we must solve the mystery of the **Dardanelles**.

We must first of all open the geographical gates. And after that, the gate of legend, poetry and civilization that confronts us everywhere.... This voyage is, after all, a voyage of pleasure. Don't worry if a small wave throws us on to the shores and all the history associated with them...

According to documentary sources **Gallipoli** is separated from the

The Dardanelles. 19th century engraving.

Çardak Feneri opposite by a distance of 32 km. **Kum Burnu** or its lighthouse is 94 km. from **Çardak Feneri**, and a distance of 3.6 km separates **Kum Burnu** from **Ilyas Burnu** immediately opposite.

The narrowest section of the straits is the 1.2 km between **Çanakkale** and **Kilitbahir.**

The surface and lower currents make this the most fertile fishing-grounds in Turkey with a migrant population of *istavrit, camgöz, seabass, orkinos. bonito, bluefish, chub mackerel and dülger.* If they are not caught by a fisherman's line or emmeshed in a net they will go on happily swimming hither and thither. Their only worry is the pollution they will encounter in the **Iznik** and **Gemlik Gulf.**

As you sail through the **Dardanelles** you may not find the appearance of both shores equally interesting. But a little knowledge of history and mythology will endow the apparent dullness of the shores with a truly thrilling fascination. For it was through these straits that the *Argonauts* sailed, long before the story of **Troy.**

Sunflowers between the Marmara and the Aegean. The joy of life.

Argo, which means 'swift', was the name of the boat that carried the ancient heroes from **Thessaly** through the **Dardanelles** and the **Black Sea** to **Colchis** in their search for the *'Golden Fleece'.*

In the 3rd millennium B.C. **Troy** was already a highly civilized city located at the entrance to the **Aegean.** It was a city composed of a series of superimposed layers that had survived centuries of wars and conflagrations.

After this came a number of other cities, one of them being **Elaious,** or "wild olive tree", a city situated at the southern end of the **Gallipoli Peninsula.**

Elaious was founded in the 6th century B.C. by migrants from Athens.

Sunset in the Dardanelles.

From the day of its foundation onwards it was never free from war, right up to 1915 and 1916..

The First World War was a war of honour, full of tragedy and heroism, fought out in the **Dardanelles,** in the "land of the wild olive". Over four hundred thousand young men now lie under the *Gallipoli Memorial* that rears its majestic bulk up to the sky.

If you have time before entering the **Aegean** and you wish, without feeling any nostalgia for war, to become fully conscious of the birth of a nation, I should advise you to visit the place, to stroll around the'*National Park*' into which the area has now been converted.

I have no idea what *Hades*, the god of the underworld, the "invisible", would have said of such noble deaths, but *Poseidon* speaks as follows:

> *"The world was divided into three, and each of us received his share,*
> *We drew lots, the foaming sea fell to my portion,*
> *Hades received the land of mist and darkness..."*

Looking across from the soil on which *Hades* trod, you will see **Dardanos** on the opposite shore. A great deal can be said of **Dardanos,** but *Homer* is more qualified than myself to talk of it. The following is an extract from the *Iliad...*

"Zeus of the storm-clouds was father to Dardanos
And Dardanos founded Dardania.
At that time sacred Ilium was not yet in existence,
The mortals had no great city on the plain.
The Dardanians settled on the slopes of Ida of the many springs.
Dardanos begat Erichthonios, who became king.
The wealthiest of all mortals.
He grazed ten thousand mares on his pastures.
Rejoicing to see the fresh young foals.
Boreas saw them as they grazed, and was smitten with love,
He transformed himself into a black-maned stallion and mounted the
mares,

The mares became pregnant and bore twelve foals
That skipped and gambolled on the fertile fields,
They ran over the wheat ears, injuring none of them.
They raced hither and thither over the surface of the vast seas,
They raced hither and thither on the myriad-coloured foam.
Erichthonios begat Tros, the King of the Trojans.

We will be accompanied throughout our voyage by the geographer *Strabo*, who was born in **Amasya** in 64 or 63 B.C. He will be constantly at our side. We are deeply indebted to him for our knowledge of **Dardanos** and the civilizations that succeeded those described in the *Iliad* of *Homer*. One of these will be that of the *Trojans.* Moreover, he is an **Anatolian,** and so can be reckoned a compatriot of ours...

"According to Plato, there were three stages in the civilization that fol-
lowed the Great Flood. The first, which developed on the tops of the moun-
tains, was rough and primitive. Men feared the waters that still covered
the plains. In the second civilization, which formed on the slopes of the
mountains, men gradually gained confidence as the waters began to
recede. The third civilization was centred on the plain. There was also a
fourth, a fifth and even more, but the principal civilization was the one
established on the plains and sea-shore by men who had finally rid them-
selves of all fear. The greater or lesser amount of courage they displayed in
gradually drawing nearer to the sea is an indication of the various stages
in behaviour and civilization - like the qualities of primitiveness or refine-
ment on which the milder nature of the second stage was based. There is a
certain feature that distinguishes the second stage. I am referring to the
contrast between the primitive, the semi-primitive and the civilized. For
example, They began to add suffixes to the new names, thus revealing a
certain refinement and superior culture, while at the same time an
improvement can be seen in their behaviour, accompanied by changes in
their dwellings and way of life. According to Plato, When Homer
described the Cyclops as dwelling in caves on the tops of the mountains

and living on the wild fruits they gathered without "sowing or reaping" he was referring to the first stage of civilization. Homer declares that "they had no assemblies or codes of laws, they lived in caves on the tops of the mountains with each man exercising sole authority over his wife and children."

He takes the age of **Dardanos** as an example of the way of life in the second stage of civilization. "*The mortals founded the city of Dardania and dwelt on the foothills of Ida of the many springs.*"

As an example of the third stage of civilization he takes life on the plain in the time of **Ilos**, the legendary, eponymous founder of the city. It seems reasonable to assume that **Ilos**, the first to have had courage enough to settle in the plain, was also buried there.

"And they raced past the wild fig tree in the middle of the plain where Ilos, son of Dardanos, was buried. Ilos lacked the courage to found the city on its present site, preferring a site now known as 'the town of the Ilionians' on higher ground thirty stadia towards the east, towards Mount Ida and Dardania. But the present-day inhabitants of Ilium, wishing to identify their city with the famous old city of Ilium, claim that some of the events described in Homer's epic are untrue, since their own city is thus made to appear a different city from that of Homer. Some claim that the city has changed its site several times and that it came to occupy the present site around the time of Croesus. I have no hesitation in accepting that the change from higher to lower sites in these periods points to various stages in the progress of civilization and way of life, but the whole question will be examined at another, later date."

The colours of the Marmara in a Şarköy kilim.

I hope, as we move out into the waters of the **Aegean,** that you will forgive my padding out the subject of **Dardanos** with quotations in this way. It may be I want to avoid the sort of association so often found at the present day - on tins of fish for example. But I am all in favour of employing names of old cities or civilizations. In one way or another, it takes us back thousands of years. One day, perhaps, the name will

The Dardanelles and the Çanakkale War
. Memorial. Life and death side by side.

induce someone to turn to the past and carry out research on the subject. After all, this is a very strange world!...

But in choosing this quotation, what interested me most was the way *Strabo,* who was born in 64 or 63 B.C., notes the observations made by *Homer,* who was writing 750-760 years before that date. *"This is the information given by Homer on the subject of Dardanos,"* he writes, *but I shall look into it myself."* Just like an everyday conversation, but stressing the importance of knowledge and scholarship.

That is one reason for the beauty of these deep, blue waters.

DEATH IN TROY

The end of the **Gallipoli Peninsula** and the whole area of the **Dardanelles** would appear to have been specially chosen throughout the whole of history as a site of war and conflict.

That is why, before sailing out into the open sea, we must make a stop in front of **Troy**.

The reason is very simple. **Troy**, or **Truva**, as is it is called in Turkish, is only 30 km. from **Çanakkale**, and only 6 km. from the shore of the **Aegean** into which the Strait of the **Dardanelles** opens out. Whoever happened to settle in this area were forced to engage in war. This is the only sea route leading into the **Marmara** and the **Black Sea**.

Homer had good reason to write:

"Man wearies of everything, of everything on earth,
Of sleep, of love, of sweet songs and dances.
But all these are to be preferred to war.
Yet the Trojans could never have their fill of fighting."

The great city was destroyed nine times and nine times rebuilt. After all, it was situated on the main trade route. One cannot expect a source of such immense profit to be ignored. It was not for nothing that so many historians and poets, Homer at their head, wrote epics on a city that had been nine times destroyed and nine times rebuilt.

The written sources refer to *Dardanos* as the ancestor of the kings of **Troy**, and when we look at the royal pedigree we find that *Dardanos* was the son of *Electra* and the god *Zeus*. The child of such parents could hardly expect to live free from war, especially if his city is founded on one of the main trade routes. But the wars were accompanied by something utterly different - lyric epics commemmorating all the death and destruction.

The nine cities built one on top of the other comprised nine civilizations and nine culture layers. The history of these nine cities began in the 3rd millennium B.C. The period between the 3rd and the 2nd millennia represents the highest peak achieved by the agricultural communities, and it was also a period of great importance from the point of view of cultural accumulation. The city later came under the hegemony of the *Persians, Alexander the Great*, the *Seleucians*, the **Kingdom of Pergamon** and the *Romans.*

The local inhabitants carried on the story of **Ilium** until 330 A.D., after which it gradually faded into oblivion, and was finally erased from the pages of history.

Think of it! A siege that lasted ten years. And look at the combatants! *Hera, Poseidon* and *Athena* on the side of the Greeks, and *Apollo, Ares* and *Aphrodite*, the goddess of beauty, on the side of the Trojans!

I am not very sure what *Aphrodite's* role was supposed to have been in all this, but in view of the fact that they were able to keep the opposite side at bay for ten whole years her conquetry would appear to have been employed to good effect!...

The Trojan Horse.

I have no intention of entering into the details of the war and the legends surrounding it. Each one is a subject of study in itself. But as far as literary influence is concerned, the epics woven around the Trojan war formed the prototype of lyric epics that appeared many centuries later. The legend of **Troy** was passed from hand to hand in 13th century **Sicily** and 16th century **Burgundy**.

The sources refer to the existence of seventeen different manuscript

Remains of walls of various periods in the Troy excavations and the Odeon (opposite, above).

copies in the **Burgundian** palace. Even today, the legends of **Troy** preserve their truth and validity.

It was by taking these legends as the basis for his research, together with certain written sources and suggestions made by the Consul Franz Calvert, that *Schliemann* finally, in 1868, discovered the **Hisarlık** mound. Five excavations were conducted here under his direction in 1870-73 and 1878-79, and a further two excavations after 1882.

Professor Dr. *Ekrem Akurgal* offers the following information on the **Troy** excavations:

Troy. Well and altars in the sanctuary.

"The discovery and excavation of the Trojan citadel is one of the most important events in the history of archaeology. Troy was excavated by Schliemann, Dörpfeld and Blegen. It had long been Schliemann's ambition to find the Troy of Priam and the Homeric epics. He set to work in 1870 by digging a large north-south trench, thus revealing a burnt stratum belonging to the 2nd building layer. Schliemann was under the impression that he had found traces of the city that forms the subject of the story of the Trojan War and that the gold finds yielded by this layer formed part of the treasure of Priam. Schliemann's later cooperation with Wilhelm Dörpfeld, an archaeologist who had gained extremely valuable experience from his work with the Olympia excavation team, initiated the most productive phase in the excavation work in Troy Nine different building layers were identified, and these layers were confirmed and further excavated by a team of American archaeologists who conducted excavations in Troy under Carl W. Blegen.from 1932 to 1938. Though basing their work on *the archaeological progress made in the previous period, the Americans adopted a more scientific technique and a more detailed manner of research, further dividing Dörpfeld's nine culture layers into nearly thirty habitation layers."*

A strange story is told of **Troy** and of those involved in the work there, including *Schliemann* himself... According to the encyclopedias he was

"the son of a poor pastor. An illustration of Troy in flames in a history book his father gave him at the age of seven remained indelibly imprinted on his memory and fostered a firm conviction that Homer's epic rested on a historical foundation. In 1868 he set out on a journey through Greece and Anatolia to visit the places mentioned in Homer.

"The American consul, F. Calvert, had already done some excavating at Hisarlık, and in 1971 Schliemann himself began work on the large mound. Believing that the city of Troy referred to by Homer was to be found in the lower layers of the mound, he dug through the upper layers without giving them very much importance. In 1873 he came upon several fragments of the defence walls and found a hoard of gold objects between the walls. Believing that the hoard was the treasure of Priam he felt convinced that he had discovered Homer's Troy. Later, with the help of his wife, he succeeded in smuggling the treasure abroad.

According to the written sources he applied to the Ottoman authorities for permission to conduct further excavations in 1874. However, not only was he refused permission but an inquiry was instituted into his activities. Nevertheless, he was able to resume excavations on the site in 1878.

Whatever the nature of the legend and the truth of the various events, the finds served to direct attention to a completely new phenomenon. Researchers who had been working on the civilizations of **Greece, Rome, Egypt, Babylonia** and **Syria** were now confronted with a wholly new civilization: the **Bronze Age** civilization of *Homer's* **Troy.**

Moreover, the Trojan finds constituted some of the most extraordinary products of Anatolian civilization.

The **Trojan** potters had made full use of the potters' wheel. They had produced three-legged pots, two-handled bowls, beak-spouted jars and pitchers, shallow dishes and idols in crimson, tile-red, lead-coloured and glazed clay.

The pots answered an obvious need, but what of the decoration?..

What of the human face on a jar discovered in the third **Trojan** layer and now exhibited in the **Istanbul Archaeological Museum?**

The face is rendered with such skill and abstraction that it seems to be directing questions at you from thousands of years ago. The ears, eyes, eyebrows, mouth and hands are utterly modern in their style and treatment...

One cannot help being amazed at the treatment of form displayed in both the human figures and the abstract pottery. And there is so much

Female head, terracotta, Troy-Hisarlık. Hellenistic period, 1st century B.C. Istanbul Archaeological Museum.

else from this period: ear-rings, necklaces, bracelets, hairpins, brooches.. Every object ever created is based on natural or human beauty. But the artistic skill displayed by the gold jewellery unearthed by *Schliemann* is inspired solely by nature.

The Trojans displayed great skill in fashioning metal. They were also masters of the art of creating figurines of the *Mother Goddess.*

Present-day **Troy** is packed with the unknown. If you should make a trip to the region be sure to include a visit to the excavation area and the archaeological park with its symbolic *Wooden Horse* .

Whether you are interested or not, pay a visit to the excavations. See how full utilization has been made of every detail. *Manfred Korfmann,* the head of the excavation team, is a fervent archaeologist. He never tires of telling you all there is to know about every find. Moreover, he is working with leading experts. He can explain a scientific phenomenon in very simple terms, encouraging the listener to get to know his own country. Maps of the region, sketches, plans and elevations, photographs, documentary films, etc. etc.

These all provide a cross-section of the thousands of years of history of a city that was infatuated with war but was unable to avoid ultimate destruction and conflagration.

Had it not been for the *Iliad* of **Homer** we should have known nothing of the legends of this nation. Had it not been for the legends, we should never have learned anything of the heights that poetry and imagination can attain. Had it not been for the enterprising spirit of the archaeologists we should have known nothing of the communities that lived on this soil and were to bequeath us such skill and refinement in both culture and art. It cannot be dismissed as merely a piece of waste ground. Moreover, the story is still continuing. There will be plenty of work for future generations on this soil...

In **Troy** we find life and death bound inextricably together.

Dancer, terracotta. Troy.
Hellenistic period.
Istanbul Archaeological Museum.

ISLANDS AND VINEYARDS

You have a choice here!... You can go up to the main road 5 km from **Troy,** and then make your way to **Assos** via **Ezine** and **Ayvacık**... If you take this route you will travel through pine forests for most of the way.

But there's another route, if you should feel like a breath of sea air. But this "sea air" may be a little deceptive. You had better think of it as "some sea, and some grapes, wine and fish".

I don't know about you, but I myself but would never think of setting foot in the **Aegean** region, specially in grape time, without calling in at **Bozcaada**...

Approaching Bozcaada.

Bozcaada harbour and castle.

1

2

3

1. *Bozcaada. View from the castle.*
2. *House in Bozcaada.*
3. *Church.*
4. *Door-knocker on an island house.*
5. *Bozcaada. Interior of church.*

4

All you have to do in order to get there from **Troy** is to make your way through **Taştepe, Pınarbaşı, Kumburun, Geyikli** to **Odunluk** landing-stage. In the old days (and today too) there were boats plying from the harbour here. Your car would make make its way over two planks, along with yourself, poultry and food. It's a tricky operation, but so far, as far as I know, no one hs ever fallen into the sea.

Before setting off for **Bozcaada**, which you can already see in the distance, you can make a stop at **Odunluk Iskelesi** and have a cup of tea in the coffee-house by the shore. The boat plying at the moment looks to me like a modified landing-craft, rather like one of the car ferries belonging to the Turkish Maritime Lines cut in two. On stormy days you may have to wait on the mainland. The inhabitants of the islands are quite happy with that sort of weather. It saves them from the hordes of visitors that throng the island on *bayrams* and holidays. For a great deal of interest is being taken in the island nowadays. More and more people are thinking of building a vineyard house here as soon as they can.

I am afraid I don't understand the passion for a vineyard house on the part of people who can't even drink wine properly.

The old name of **Bozcaada** was **Tenedos**, from **Tenes,** the name of an

Vineyards on Bozcaada.

ancient hero. The relevant story is not very attractive or inspiring.

Tenes' mother-in-law accused him of having tried to rape her and locked *Tenes* and his sister in a chest and set them adrift on the sea. However, *Poseidon* came to the rescue and washed them on to the shore of **Tenedos** (Bozcaada). Still under the influence of his mother-in-law's calumnies, *Tenes* cut the cables of his father's boat and drove him from the island.

Tenedos was occupied in turn by the **Persians, Romans, Byzantines, Venetians, Aydınoğulları** and **Ottomans**. There used to be two harbours but now there is only the one beside the castle facing **Kumburun**. The castle itself dates from the **Venetian** period.

The harbour is surrounded by fishermen's restaurants, a market, wine shops, a bakery and a few guest-houses. Besides the mosque and the church, which have lost nothing of their original character, there are a number of old Greek houses now included in a conservation area that extends as far as the vineyards in the rear of the island.

Bozcaada. The Sulubahçe shores.

The restaurants in the **Bozcaada** harbour serve sea bream, red mullet and lobster, though the choice of fish is not limited to just these. You can choose in accordance with the season and the wine you are drinking. But if you miss the *"Çavuş grape"* season you will have missed the real flavour of **Bozcaada.**

You can hire a taxi from the harbour and drive through the vineyards to **Sulubahçe**, stopping on the way to sample a small cluster of grapes as a traveller's privilege. But be careful. The *Çavuş* grapes are the large yellowish grapes with the thin skins. The others are for wine. If anyone objects just tell him that you have *"a friend that bought half an acre of land here twenty years ago, and so far he has eaten a couple of boxes. Take that into account"*... The friend in question is myself...

Sulubahçe opens on to a beach with fine sand and marvellous sea. If you can escape from the building cooperatives you will be able to spend at least a short time enjoying the vineyards, the sea and the fish.

You will find the water very hard, as it is in all islands (except **Gökçeada,** as far as I remember). If, as soon as you soap your hair, it becomes hopelessly matted, don't worry, the islanders are used to matted hair. As a matter of fact they take badly with properly combed hair!.

If being an islander has special associations for you, then take a note of **Gökçeada**, formerly known as **İmroz.**

If you have a boat, you can sail from **Tenedos,** where *Poseidon* rested his horses, across the water to **İmroz.**

You can also get to **Gökçeada** by ferry from **Çanakkale**, and in the sum-

Fruit and vegetable stall on İmroz (Gökçeada).

mer months there is a ferry between **Gökçeada** and **Kabatepe.**

As on Bozcaada, the streets and the houses with gardens around the harbour preserve the old island tradition.

Once inhabited by the *Lelegians* and *Carians,* it has opened its doors to many different peoples - **Achaeans, Dorians, Persians** and **Athenians.**

A member of the *Delian Confederacy* In the 5th century B.C., the island was later taken over by the **Romans** and **Byzantines.** Nor were the **Genoese** and **Venetians** far behind. They held sway in the island for a very long period, finally to be succeeded by the **Ottomans.**

You probably know it already but I'll tell you all the same. The *Delian Confederacy* was a league founded at **Delos** in 478 B.C. under the leadership of **Athens.** Each of the **Aegean** cities had an equal vote. The main aim of union, which survived as a power to be reckoned with until 338 B.C., was the prevention of further **Persian** expansion.

For your first impression of the city founded on the ruins of ancient **Panagia** you must enter the street of the church of **Aya Panaia** near the harbour. The church itself is set amidst pink and white oleanders, roses and geraniums.

If you arrive here in the melon season you are sure to come across street-vendors under the old mulberry tree, which you will find decked out in carnaval fashion with strings of red peppers. A little further on, under the pine trees, you will find the house of the **Metropolitan.**

If you include the villages of **Dereköy** (Sinudi), **Uğurluköy, Kaleköy** (Kastro), **Zeytinliköy** (Aya Todori), **Bademliköy** (Gliki) and **Tepeköy** (Ağridiya) the island has a population of around ten thousand. If you feel like visiting these villages I should advise you to start off with **Tepeköy.**

Like other villages you may come across on the **Aegean** shores, **Tepeköy** is composed of wood and stone houses surrounded by olive, fig, almond and mulberry trees. An atmosphere of solitude reigns in the small square with its church and its coffee-house, surrounded by a network of narrow streets overhung with vines, while the view over the red-tiled roofs and the valleys beyond just as day begins to dawn is particularly inspiring.

1 İmroz (Gökçeada). Church of Aya Panaia.
2. Bozcaada, House that has preserved its original fabric.
3. Square in Tepeköy.
4. Imroz. Paved streets in Tepeköy.

It was fortunate they decided to protect themselves from pirates by choosing the summits of the hills for the site of their settlements, for this has allowed the ancient city to survive unspoilt.
I spent a day on the island during the celebrations held in August when

51

Tepeköy.

people come from **Greece** and the other islands to exchange holiday greetings with their relatives here. I also sampled the home-made wine.

There is an interesting story about **Tepeköy** in a little book on **İmroz Island** entitled *Gökçeada-İmbroz* by *Erol Saygı.*

> *"After the battle of Preveze in 1538, the Ottoman fleet, under the command of Barbaros Hayrettin Pasha, took refuge from a storm in the bay beneath Tepeköy. Calliope, one of Barbaros Hayrettin's favourites, died during their stay there. Her body was carried to Tepeköy where the local population gave her a magnificent funeral. On the fleet's return to Istanbul, Barbaros asked Sultan Süleyman the Magnificent to reward the inhabitants of İmroz for the interest and respect they had shown on that occasion, whereupon the Sultan declared the island a royal foundation and exempted the inhabitants from all taxation. The people then proclaimed the dead girl who had brought them such good fortune a saint and built a monastery dedicated to Aya Calliope."*

The comprehensive introduction to the island presented by *Erol Saygı* includes the following very interesting piece of information:

Tepeköy. Street with mulberry tree.

"The inhabitants of İmroz and Lemnos were regarded as citizens of Athens as well as citizens of either İmroz or Lemnos, a privilege handed down from father to son. In this way the new immigrants from Athens who settled in either of these islands retained their rights as Athenian citizens, a right that was exploited to the full by the inhabitants.

"For example, a citizen of İmroz who committed a crime in Athens could

House in İmroz (Gökçeada).

refuse to attend the court and, on being seized, could escape punishment by asserting that on the date when the crime was committed he was in İmroz.

"This right of dual nationality was exploited to such excess by the inhabitants of the island that the term 'İmrozlu' (citizen of İmroz) entered Athenian legal literature with the meaning 'artful dodger - justice evader'. The term is still used in Greek at the present day."

It would be hard to find any sailor or traveller who has not paid a visit to the island at some time or another. *Piri Reis,* the famous 16th century seaman, gives the following description of the island:

"The castle is situated in the north-west of the island on a high rock over-

looking the sea. Beneath the castle there is a small bay in front of some vineyards and it is in this bay that soldiers arriving at the castle disembark. It is an open place, and cannot take large ships. The island, which is in the form of a long ridge,.is some fifty miles in circumference.

Azra Erhat, who visited the island with some friends while on a *'Blue Voyage'* trip, remarks on the warmth and friendliness of the people:

> *"In the evening, when our meal was served at our table in the Barba Manol restaurant in Tepeköy, the tables around us were all full. The women were sitting knitting or doing embroidery and singing away at the same time. What lovely Greek and Turkish songs these women were singing! And there wasn't a trace of self-consciousness. They sang whatever we asked and we applauded with real warmth and enthusiasm."*

İmroz. House of the Metropolitan.

At a distance of 3.5 km from the central district, formerly known as **Panayia**, you arrive at the village of **Zeytinliköy** (Aya Todori) which, with its typical streets and houses, is every bit as interesting as **Tepeköy** (Ağridiya) itself.

A coffee made from freshly ground beans in the wooden coffee-house known as 'Madam's coffee-house' is an essential preliminary to a tour of **Zeytinliköy**. It is a real distinction to be a native of the island. An islander possesses a characteristic type of personality and his own individual way of life. Who would expect, when ordering a coffee, that instead of a brew of ready-ground coffee you will get very special coffee made from freshly ground beans!.. Probably that is why Madam's coffee-house has such a high reputation. When you leave with the flavour of ground coffee on your palate you realize that that is quite enough to explain **Zeytinköy**'s popularity.

Another village that visitors to **İmroz** should certainly visit is **Bademliköy** (Gliki) 4 km from the centre. If only its inhabitants hadn't abandoned it for one reason or another. The village, with its houses, streets, churches and trees, lies almost completely deserted. It is home now to only forty or fifty people.

One of the most striking features of the population of **İmroz,** like the population on the other islands, is the way the Turkish and Greek communities live together in perfect peace and harmony, without any prejudice or discrimination. The same community feeling is evidenced in the local newspapers. They are well aware that dissension would be of little advantage to themselves. Everything they own, they own together in a common partnership...

And this is a partnership typical of the whole of the **Aegean** region.

THE ASSOS REALITY,
MT IDA AND SARI KIZ

In my opinion, there is a very special quality about the **Aegean** and the **Mediterranean** that is to be found nowhere else in the whole world. It is this peculiar quality that allowed art and trade to flourish side by side throughout the thousands of years of polytheistic civilization.

It is not only the life-style that forms a common feature of the different islands. Both nations bathe and sun-bathe in the **Aegean**. In the same way as the currents intermingle in its depths...

Let me give you a striking example: I have a friend in Athens. He was a student at the Technical University in Istanbul. His name is *Stathis L. Trimis.*

One rather hectic night, a friend read me a letter from *Trimis.* On a sudden impulse, I signed a copy of the catalogue for an exhibition of mine that had just opened and sent it to *Trimis,* with a reference to the Istanbul in which we had both lived.

A reply arrived through my friend.

In the catalogue to the exhibition I had concluded some thoughts on my art as follows:

"...to whatever it was that endowed me with the gift of art, whether god or mortal or nature or the old civilizations by which I have been inspired, I owe a deep debt of gratitude.

"Otherwise I would long ago have been burnt to ashes in this hell."

Trimis quoted this passage and added his own feelings:

"...You say "...to whatever it was that endowed me with art (only art?).....I owe a deep debt of gratitude.

"In other words, Yunus Emre, Mevlâna and Francis of Assisi are also ours, but we are all great-grandsons of our (the word 'our' is underlined)

Assos. The harbour.

Gregorius Palamas who, although he is also one of us, is, sad to say, quite unknown to you.
"...
"The pounds sterling of lords are poor, powerless and barren compared with the nectar in the wine-cup of Dionysos.
"So come, saki, let us drink from the wine-filled cup, in reason and raison raisonante. Let us rejoice and be merry that, thanks to Dionysos, we have avoided ruin and devastation, and still preserve the civilization and humanity (underlined) that great Anatolia has bequeathed us."

I have never met *Trimis*, but he has become a true pen-friend.
I feel sure that one day we shall meet in the **Aegean** or in Istanbul. I know that we shall drink the wine of Dionysos from the same bottle.
The mystery of the **Aegean** rests in such friends and friendship...
The olive groves, vineyards and wines of **Gökçeada** and **Bozcaada** form the true source of civilization. We shall enjoy its savour throughout our voyages in the waters of the **Aegean** and **Mediterranean**, as we talk continuously of their cool, blue waters...

57

Let us sail right past the islands to the shores of Anatolia, landing at **Odunluk Iskelesi** opposite **Bozcaada**. We find ourselves here on the **Biga Peninsula.** Never, at any time throughout the ages, has the .peninsula remained empty. Legends, civilizations and conflicts have been handed down from one generation to the next. But is it only human beings who have exerted dominion over the peninsula? Hasn't nature played its part?

Murad III Bridge on the road to Behramkale.

Is it possible to imagine a community that does not depend on nature or benefit from its riches?
Out of the question!...
Fish, olives and grapes provide a sufficient foundation for the nourishment of a civilization. Fish, olives and grapes form an integral part of life, and are each a natural source of legend, poetry and passion.
Throughout this journey, we shall sometimes talk of the olive tree we pass without noticing as we enter a city of civilizations, and the fish as well; not to mention the grape, which for thousands of years has remained with mankind as a source of rapture and enthusiasm...
And now is the time for the quotation.
Actually, I have just been waiting for an excuse.
Don't ask what the 12th century philosopher *Ömer Khayyam* is doing in the **Aegean.** Just listen to what he has to say:

> *We have given our heart to wine, the source of all ecstasy;*
> *We are filled with exhilaration: we leave the earth for the heavens;*
> *In the end we are stripped of the body and the flesh;*
> *We came from earth, and to earth we return*

There are olives in the **Aegean** and there is also fish. And wherever these two are found together you are sure to find grapes and wine. They form a friendly trio! The olive that contributes a drop to the mixture is the most important of the common ingredients. Fish needs oil, and so does wine... Perhaps you will say, "Fish we understand, but what has olive oil to do with wine?" Olive oil was used for centuries to prevent air getting into the wine.
The short journey from **Odunluk Iskelesi** to **Biga Peninsula** will bring you to **Neandria**, the present-day town of **Ezine.** If you examine the

(above) Assos. Acropolis. Charles Texier, "Description de l'Asie Mineure", 2nd half of 19th century.
(opposite) Behramkale/Assos today.

(above) Gürpınar. Temple of Apollo Smintheus.
(below) Stone relief.

ruins of **Neandria**, 13 km south of **Troy,** and the carved decoration to be found upon its stones, you will find vine leaves included among the vegetal motifs. Clear evidence of the existence of viniculture!

The ruins of **Neandria** include 3200 m of defence walls, a temple and an archaic acropolis. The city walls are thought to have been constructed in the 5th century B.C., the archaic temple in the 6th. *Prof. Ekrem L. Akurgal* describes the temple as *"the most important monument in Neandria..."* The column capitals from this temple are now preserved in the **Istanbul Archaeological Museum.**

Before rounding **Babakale Point** there is another ancient city - **Khryse,** meaning "gold" - the remains of which can only be reached by the **Ayvacık-Gürpınar** road. The most imporant monument to be found here is the temple dedicated to **Apollo Smintheus.** The name "Smintheus" means "mouse". Don't belittle the mouse. You can see the figure of a mouse at Apollo's feet on the Trojan coins. *Strabo* tells us all this in his *"Geography"*....

We never know what any particular community may choose to worship. Isn't money the symbol of the one God omnipotent of the modern age?.. But what sort of coin?... That's a moot point. As long as the coin passes muster, does it matter in the slightest whether it is inscribed with a mouse or a lion?

Just beyond **Baba Point** there is another interesting city - the most magnificent city on the whole coast, and very popular at present. If you go by sea you will find a small harbour used mainly by fishermen... On one occasion, as my friends and I landed here some time after midnight, the fishermen had just returned from their catch and were picking hundreds of bonito from their nets by the light of a lantern. We bought one and had it grilled over charcoal in the teacher Mustafa Yüce's **Assos Restaurant** right on the shore. Logs were thrown on the fire, wine-bottles were opened and huge quantities of "shepherd's salad" prepared. We were sleeping in the rooms upstairs so we could drink as much as we liked. Moreover, this is the city of *Aristotle*. Wine opens up infinite vistas of poetry and philosophy...

Assos. Fragments in the ruins.

Although it's something I'd really rather forget, this harbour once proved our salvation. On one of our trips from the **Mediterranean** to the **Aegean** we were caught in a storm off the island of Mytilene. It often returns to me now as a sheer nightmare. I tremble just to think of it...

At first the sea was as smooth as a mill pond, but as dusk fell it began to rise It was practically the first voyage my friend's **Bodrum** type yacht had ever made and we were still not too familiar with its moods and temperament.

At first we began to feel cool drops of water on our faces. It was quite pleasant. Then it grew very dark. So dark we couldn't even see the sea. The radar was our only guide. I kept my eyes glued to the screen as if I knew something about it! I told the captain that the dark spot that appeared in the compass window was probably **Assos**.

The captain was singing away to himself to give us confidence, but the fact that the words made no sense at all made it only too obvious that he was just as scared as we were. There was no other boat anywhere in the vicinity. The heavy teak dining-table in the stern kept lunging backwards and forwards from one side of the ship to the other. I kept glancing at the radar but the distance didn't change. It always registered between eight and nine miles. We thought of turning back and taking refuge in Mitylene. At least we would have the waves behind us. But that would be quite another kettle of fish.

I thought of the two boats that sank in the waters off **Gelidonia** and **Kaş-Uluburun** in ancient times. A lot of boats have sunk in storms and why I should have thought of these two in particular I really don't know.

At last we caught sight of the lighthouse at **Assos** harbour, whereupon my friend took it into his head to say *"Don't be too confident Boats have sunk within three hundred yards of the shore!"* And one couldn't just ignore him. His father had been one of the general directors in the **Turkish Maritime Lines** and he had spent most of his childhood at sea!

It was on that trip that I came face to face with the strange border that separates life and death. The sensation of sheer terror lasted over an hour. A blind, dark terror... On hearing the voice of the official on shore answering our signal from out of the darkness I immediately imagined myself a real sailor and began rushing hither and thither all over the deck. To hear the splash of the anchor in the water was utter bliss.

After that adventure, whatever the seas, we thought nothing of making a voyage in the dark. At midnight, in all the disorder and confusion of the ship's galley, we would find a bottle of wine and celebrate our achievement in reaching the last stop on our voyage of terror...

That night I slept the deepest sleep I have ever known. When day dawned, the cormorants were skimming over the smooth waters out of **Assos** harbour...

During this trip I experienced to the full the strange frontier between life and death, and made a sketch of the journey after the storm.

There's also another road you could take. If you go to **Assos** via **Ezine** you pass through magnificent pine forests. It is 18 km from **Ayvacık** to **Behramkale**, and 1 km from **Behramkale** to **Assos**.

The **Assos** reality is **Behramkale**. The mystery behind the stones spreads out from the narrow streets and houses and castle of **Behramkale** down to the meadows below and the vast sea beyond.

Historians tell us that the city of **Assos** was founded by **Aeolians** from the city of **Methymna** on the island of **Lesbos** (Mytilene) and that it was under **Lydian** rule from 560 to 547 B.C. and **Persian** rule from 547 -479 B.C., later gaining its independence and becoming a member of the Athenian naval league.

In 405 B.C. an oligarchic government was formed in **Assos.** In 336 B.C., when the **Phrygian** satrap *Ariobarzanes* rebelled against the **Persian** king, the wealthy banker and businessman *Eubolus* joined *Ariobarzanes* in his occupation of the whole of the region from **Atarneus** to **Assos.**

In 350 B.C. the government of **Assos** was taken over by one *Hermieas*, so I'd better give you a few details about the man. He was a eunuch slave

The gate of Assos and the reconstruction of the Doric temple of Athena. Charles Texier, "Description de l'Asie Mineure".

belonging to *Eubolus,* who sent him to Athens for his education. There he became one of *Plato*'s students and struck up a friendship with *Aristotle.* On his return from Athens he collaborated with *Eubolus* in the government of the state.

Hermeias later presented the city of **Assos** to **Erastos** and **Koriskos**, who had been students of **Plato.** (This is the real crux of the matter.) They also taught philosophy there.

On *Plato*'s death, *Hermeias* invited *Aristotle* to **Assos**. *Aristotle,* who was soon to become related to *Hermeias* through his marriage to a girl from *Hermeias'* family, arrived in **Assos** accompanied by *Xenocrates,* and together they founded a school of philosophy there. *Aristotle* remained in **Assos** from 347 to 345 B.C.

Surely the arrival of *Aristotle* is quite sufficient reason for the name of **Assos** to be registered in the annals of scholarship...

The temple of *Athena,* the theatre, the gymnasium, the agora and the ruins of **Behramkale** all combine to form a culture entirely of their own.

Or has it all disappeared beneath the black stones?

Obviously, it would be somewhat of an exaggeration to say that the voice of *Aristotle* still echoes in the village of **Behramkale,** but we can justly claim that the wind of **Mediteranean** civilization still blows through the theatre and agora of **Assos**. Aren't the pitcher shaped chimney tops on the houses sufficient evidence of this?

Magic, prophecy and sacrifice may require sorcerers. They can place sacred stones side by side and produce prescriptions for our age. But when *Hermeias* decided to leave war and conflict behind him, together with the deep blue sea of **Assos**, to study philosophy in **Athens**, it must have been in pursuit of something very profound...

And the same is true for *Aristotle's* three years' stay in **Assos**.

And there must also be some reason for the fact that *Cleanthes*, the second master of the **Stoic** school which adopted as it basic principle that *"it is nature that chooses most wisely, acts most patiently and distributes most fairly and justly.."* was born in **Assos**.

Assos is now a heap of stones. As is also **Behramkale**.

The harbour stones from past civilizations are now submerged in the blue waters. The narrow strip of shore, with its stone houses, contains fishermen's restaurants, guest-houses and a small fountain. That is all there is for the visitors to **Assos** and the inhabitants of **Assos** themselves. Everything preserves its own individual character. No damage has been done either to the natural environment or the legacy of past civilizations.

But before turning to the ruins themselves I should like to quote a passage from the geographer **Strabo,** who was born in **Amasya** in 64 or 63 B.C. After all, he is of very special importance as an eye-witness!

"Assos was fortified by both nature and man. From the side towards the sea,

Assos. Excavations in the necropolis.

access to the town is given by a long, very steep road. The lyre-player Scratincos says very aptly, "If you want your death sentence to be expedited, go to Assos." The harbour is protected by a large breakwater. Zenon was succeeded by the Stoic philosopher Cleanthes, a native of Assos, as head of the school, who was in turn succeeded by Chrysippos of Soli. Aristotle remained here as a result of his becoming related by marriage to the tyrant Hermeias, a eunuch, and the slave of a money-lender. During his stay in Athens Hermeias had been the student of both Plato and Aristotle. On his return to his own country he shared the office of tyrant with his old master, who had occupied the whole of the provinces of Atarneos and Assos. On succeeding the tyrant, Hermeias sent invitations to both Aristotle and Xenocrates, taking them both under his own protection and at the same time marrying his brother's daughter to Aristotle. Just then, Memnon of Rhodes, a general in the service of the Persians, pretended friendship to Hermeias and invited him on the pretext of both business and pleasure. On his arrival he arrested him and sent him to the king , who had him hanged. The philosophers fled from the captured provinces mentioned above and so managed to escape."

The passage quoted by **Strabo** from **Stratonicos** the lyre player *(If you want your death sentence to be expedited, go to Assos.")* may have been inspired by the fate of *Hermeias.*

In every age there are people who cannot abide others' scholarship and ability. I don't use the word 'envy', because envy is a natural part of life. The urge to actually destroy is something quite different!

Just think! *Hermeias* was a slave, and a eunuch to boot. And yet he was able to study under *Plato* and *Aristotle* in **Athens.** Then he came to **Assos**, where he not only ruled the country wisely and well but also introduced the study of philosophy and suceeded in attracting *Aristotle* to the city. At the same time he sought to make the appointment permanent by making his brother's daughter *Aristotle's* wife. And after that?... After that, a sentence of death...

Perhaps it hasn't got much to do with it but I am reminded of the short story *"John dory"* by **Sait Faik**, a native of the island of **Burgaz.**

As far as I can remember, the John dory had done a great deal of travelling around in the seas. There wasn't a hook he hadn't seen and tested. He would examine the hooks hanging down into the depths and make a careful evaluation of them all. His only desire was to end his life on the hook of a really expert fisherman. After a great deal of roaming around he saw a hook that he decided "must certainly belong to an expert fisherman". With great pleasure he fixed his teeth into the chosen hook, but when he was hoisted squirming into the boat he realised that the fisherman at the other end of the line was a raw beginner. Moreoever, his only aim was to catch fish. He had no interest in the art.

The story of *Hermeias* is somewhat similar.

I haven't gone into any great detail and I haven't examined the matter too closely but while writing about the **Aegean** and the **Mediterranean** I got really very angry with the **Persians**. Whenever I carry out any research into any city I find myself confronted with these **Persians**. Nothing but war and slaughter...

I may be mistaken in my judgment. I sincerely hope I am. But why play such a dirty trick on *Hermeias,* who, in spite of being a slave and having had part of his anatomy removed, devoted himself to life and philsophy, founded a city and ruled it with great skill, while at the same time patronising scholarship and learning? I imagine they were too afraid to attempt to kill him in battle. So they murdered him by an act of treachery.

Today **Assos** is chosen, not for a sentence of death, but for days of pleasure and romance. But not in the heat of July and August, naturally! If you choose, not just **Assos** perhaps, but anywhere in the **Aegean** or the **Mediterranean** in July or August, I can do nothing to stop you! It doesn't matter what the reason may be, whether it be love or passion. It is enough that your heart is with the sea and the sky...

What is there to be found at **Assos**?

Probably nothing. I am not one to exaggerate the value of ancient cities.

Assos, Doric columns in the Temple of Athena.

Assos harbour.

They plunge me right down into a depression. But I have taken **Assos** as an example of a city of scholars. If you are really interested in the history of art and archaeology we shall open the windows a little..

The city defence walls belong to the 4th century B.C. The **Temple of Athena** was built in 530 B.C., the market and agora in the 3rd or 2nd century B.C., the Agora Temple in the 2nd century B.C., the gymnasium also in the 2nd century B.C. and the theatre in the 3rd century B.C. There is also a 14th century Turkish mosque and a Turkish bridge. The necropolis dates from the Hellenistic and Roman periods.

Excavations in Assos, conducted by an American team under J.T.Clarke and F.H.Bacon in 1881-1883, were resumed in 1982 under the direction of Professor Ümit Serdaroğlu. The 3 km defence wall surrounding an acropolis founded on the summit of a hill dominating both sea and land, is one of the best preserved walls in the Hellenic world."

This information is taken from the book entitled *Anadolu Uygarlıkarı* (Anatolian Civilizations) by *Professor Dr. Ekrem Akurgal*, a Turkish scholar remarkable for his research, his revealing commentary, his points of view, his lively style of writing and the smartness of his personal appearance.

I have no intention of entering into a detailed archaeological description of the ancient city of **Assos.**

Making one's way down the sharp bends and turns leading from **Behramkale** to the sea, one can see the city defence wall of the ancient city on one's left and the phosphorescent sea on your right. What associations may be suggested by these beautifully constructed walls, the witness to past centuries, and the deep blue waters, and how you decide to spend the day, is entirely up to you. The choice is yours... If you love wine and the sea, surrender yourself to the cool waters. But never forget that this is the same sea *Aristotle* and *Hermeias* bathed in. I am sure the Persians had little love for the sea! If they had, they would have been aware of the colour, the depth of the sea and the value of scholarship and learning...

I said that out of sheer bad temper. I haven't really the right to condem a whole community. Look what old *Herodotus* has to say about the **Persians:**

> *"To urinate or spit or wash their hands in running water is something they never do themselves and will never allow others to do, for they have the most profound respect for rivers."*

Should one perhaps make a distinction between the people and the rulers?

If you like archaeology, you can make your way up the winding road early in the morning and stroll around amongst the grey and brown stones on the summit of the hill.

This is **Assos.** The city that gave *Aristotle* his bride!....

This is **Assos,** but there is another side to its reality. **Assos** can be regarded as the foothills of the **Kaz Mts.** And the **Kaz Mts.** are strange, rather eary places! In olden times they were known as **Mt Ida,** and legends about them are still current at the present day...

"You want to know what **Mt Ida** is?"

It is the home of *Kybele*, the goddess of fertility.

"You want to know who *Kybele* is?"

Ask *Aphrodite!*

Herodotus and *Strabo* frequently refer to this mountain. It was a mountain of great fertility overlooking the **Gulf of Edremit.** According to *Strabo,* the mountain contains the sources of three rivers, the **Scamander,** the **Granicus** and the **Aisepos.** *Homer* refers to the *Aisepos* in poetic vein:

> *"Achilles and Hector sped along.... and so came to the two lovely springs that are the source of Scamander's eddying stream. In one of these the water comes up hot; steam rises from it and hangs about like smoke above a blazing fire. But the other, even in summer, gushes up as cold as hail or freezing snow or water that has turned to ice."*

In his *Geography,* **Strabo** politely offers a correction to *Homer's* description. After all, he arrived eight hundred years after Homer. After a thou-

(above) Assos. The harbour wall.
(opposite) Trees and flowers on Mt Ida.

sand years not only the springs but Mt Ida itself might well have disappeared. ***Strabo's*** emendation is as follows:

> *"Nowadays there is no hot spring here and the source of the Scamander is not here, it is in the mountains. The hot spring would thus seem to have disappeared, while the cold spring either empties into the river through an underground stream or is only thought to be the source of the Scamander because of its proximity to the river. For people tend to point to several different springs as sources of one and the same river."*

The important thing for us is undoubtedly the story of the people who shared the same soil and the same mountains thousands of years ago. Otherwise, would **Mt Ida** still form the setting of the legends around the figure of *'Sarı Kız' (the fair-haired girl)?...* The story has been told by the *'Fisherman of Halicarnassus'*, the wonderful story-teller of the **Aegean** and its shores.

> *'Sarı Kız was carried off by a young man named Selman from Kafdağ to Kazdağ, i.e. Mt Ida, where he built her a palace on Sarıkız peak. There he lived with Sarı Kız for twenty-one days, but after twenty-one days Sarı Kız vanished, and Selman grew old and finally disappeared.'*

The legend is not as brief as all that. There are many more details. But if I

once got involved in the beauties of the details I should never get away from the **Gulf of Edremit** and **Mt Ida.** The cool waters of the **Aegean** and the **Mediterranean** would remain no more than a dream...

But if I don't touch upon some features of the *Sarı Kız* legend that still exist at the present day I should be omitting some of the essential reality of **Assos**. For the *Sarı Kız* festivities are still held today, after thousands of years.

Let me continue with the quotation from the *Fisherman of Halicarnassus:*

"*For the Takhtajy Turcomans the goose is a sacred animal, and the diagonal pattern of a goose's foot is to be seen embroidered in a triangle on the collars and shoulders of their garments.as a symbol of good luck and plenty. A goose's foot has three claws The amulets are triangular. It is therefore quite natural that the*

Chepnis (one of the twenty-four clans of the Oghuz tribe) should have called Mt Ida "Goose Mountain" (Kazdag). But there is more to it than that.

"One hundred and fifty years ago, the Chepnis withdrew into remote forests and valleys in order to preserve the secrets of their religious sect. By government decree, the Chepnis were forced to abandon their nomadic habits and adopt a sedentary way of life"

Let me break off the quotation from the *Fisherman of Halicarnassus* at this point and add a note of my own. According to the **Ilhanid** historian *Reşideddin*, the name **Chepni** means "ready to fight wherever there is an enemy". The same explanation is to be found in the various sources. One section of the Chepni clans settled in the **Aegean** region in the 18th

Relaxing in Assos.

century. There are long stories about them. Some of them, perhaps exhausted by the long wars, chose **Mt Ida.** Now let us return to the *Fisherman of Halicarnassus:*

"On one of the peaks of Kazdağ, amidst heaps of stones, stands the seven-doored abode of Sarı Kız. There are said to be seventeen other abodes elsewhere. But the Chepnis and the Turcoman women and girls of the same faith believe that the real abode of Sarı Kız is the one on the highest peak of Kazdağ. Every year, in a certain season and on a certain day, they bring votive offerings and make wishes. If it is impossible to visit the spot each year, it is absolutely essential that a visit should be paid every seven years."

Mt Ida has been home to many, from *Kybele,* the goddess of fertility, to *Aphrodite.* The tradition is continued in the legend of *Sarı Kız.*

Another interesting point is that the skirt worn by the various goddesses of beauty are made up of three panels. These three-piece robes are still worn by the Turcomans at the present day. It was also a sacred dress for *Sarı Kız.*

Every legend reflects an event, and every event a different phenomenon.... For example, the fact that *Sarı Kız* lives in an abode with seven doors, and the existence of seventeen abodes..

İsmet Zeki Eyüboğlu, well known for his contribution to Anatolian culture through his personality, his wide knowledge and his research, has produced a book entitled *"Anadolu İnançları" (Anatolian Beliefs)* iin which he gives some detailed information on the topic of "sevens".

> *The belief that the number seven bears a sacred significance is to be found in both Anatolia and the neighbouring countries. This number occupied a very special place in the minds of Egyptians, Sumerians, Iranians, Akkadians, Indians, Hittites and, later, Greeks and Romans. The sacred significance of this number has a fundamental link with various events and ceremonies, in short with all the various aspects of everyday life.*
>
> *"For example, we find the concept of 'seven heavens' in ancient Babylon, Sumeria and Anatolia. There is also the concept of 'seven layers below ground'. This belief later crossed to Anatolia where it fused with local beliefs and produced a new synthesis."*

The tradition may well be continued at the present day in "7 up"

FROM CUNDA ISLAND TO BERGAMA, THE MOST IMPORTANT CITY OF THE HELLENISTIC PERIOD

To enter the **Gulf of Edremit** by boat is not a particularly enjoyable experience. I should strongly advise you to approach it by land.

Every journey has its own particular charm. The traveller can be captivated by sea-shores just as much as by the mystery of mountain peaks. The **Kazdağları** for example...I myself am following a route traced out by nature and legend. I'm not particularly interested in sun and sea. Lie and roast and then into the sea. Out of the sea and lie and roast!..

Shallow waters and strips of land have never interested me. You see a piece of barren soil. If you have sufficient interest and means of research and you can uncover in some part of that barren soil a story dating back thousands of years, then that is a different matter. Those who have bequeathed civilizations to the communities that succeeded them will surely have something to offer you.

The route I have traced out is not determined by the topography of the region. I may well branch off to visit any piece of land or water that looks beautiful or interesting enough. My journey through the **Aegean** and the **Mediterranean** is thus a journey of many options. If there should be any places I don't mention or don't dwell upon - and there certainly will be - you can add them to your own notes.

The **Aegean** and **Mediterranean** regions are at the same time the richest in gods and goddesses. The peoples that have lived throughout the millennia have worshipped now one god and now, when finding themselves in difficulties, another... The most important thing is not to offend them.

(opposite) A street in Ayvalık.

For myself, I have chosen **Dionysos!**
And what does that mean exactly?
It means that I never know where I shall spend the night and where I shall wake up!.. I am neither a **Herodotus** nor a **Strabo**! I have never at any time in my life been a systematic, programmed traveller.
You wonder what I'm getting at?
 What I'm trying to say is that when I enter a subject I tend to leap around like a grasshopper. But **Herodotus**, the father of history, **Strabo** and **Homer** will always be at my side. I never take a step without them!
The streams from **Mt Ida** flow into the **Gulf of Edremit.** The gulf is full of streams great and small. It is no mistake to say that it is the region

(left) House in Ayvalık.
(right) Church on Cunda Island.
(opposite) Interior of church.

richest in olives and olive oil. It is also rich in pines, oaks, beech, chestnut and lime trees. It is also famous for its hot-water springs.
Akçay and **Ören** are tourist resorts. There are also the ancient cities of **Adramyttion** near **Ören** and **Antandros** near **Altınoluk.** Those who like crowds, sun and sand can begin the day with various types of olive at breakfast.
A journey of 40-50 km along the **Edremit-Burhaniye** road will bring you to the town of **Ayvalık.** Sheltered from the cold north winds by **Kaz Dağ** mountain, various typically **Mediterranean** products are cultivated here.

Ayvalık, like **Edremit** itself, is famous for its olives and olive oil. The row of old **Ayvalık** houses by the harbour is the loveliest part of the whole shore. Here, a boat is absolutely essential. A sort of archipelago is formed by **Cunda,** the loveliest island of the region, together with the small islands of **Kız, Poyraz, Maden, Pınar, Çıplak** and **Güneş.**

Cunda is now known as **Alibey Island.** As a matter of fact it is no longer a real island, having been converted into a peninsula by a road connecting it with the mainland. The word 'road' is not always synonomous with 'civilization'. The tendency to identify ease of communication with roads has resulted in the destruction of the whole charm of **Cunda** island. On summer days the lovely island is absolutely packed with cars. In the 19th and early 20th century most of the **Aegean** houses were located on **Cunda**. The whole place was strikingly beautiful, with its gardens, courtyards, shuttered shops, fishermen's restaurants, high-ceiling coffee-houses and palm trees.

The joy of getting into a boat in **Ayvalık** and sailing out to the island for a fish meal is a thing of the past. You can still take a motor-boat to the

1. *Cunda. Balcony console.*
2. *Street in Cunda.*
3. *House in Cunda.*
4-5. *Old buildings in Bergama.*

island but be prepared for a chorus of car horns. And whatever you do, come back to the mainland by boat...

The islands to the south of the province of **Mysia** lie very near the island of **Midilli** (Mytilene), formerly known as **Lesbos**. As a matter of fact the two islands are so close to one another that you can exchange *hors-d'oeu-*

4

5

Cunda Island. The coffee-house.

vres with people on one island as you sit drinking *rakı* on the other. As long, that is, that the authorities don't interfere! When they do interfere, **Cunda Island, Alibey Island is** immediately transformed from an island into a peninsula. But even the *hors-d'oeuvres* served in the two islands are the same. What is known as *"cacık'* in Anatolia is known as *'cacıkaki"* in **Midilli.**

No one ever used to worry about cultural variety in Anatolian history. If they had, think of the task that **Herodotus,** the father of history, and **Strabo**, the author of *Geography,* would have had to face! While writing their books they would have had to rummage around in all sorts of places and regions.

And we are not the only ones to rummage around in this way.. But the reason for this confusioon lies in the continual quarrels between neighbouring peoples, and their inability to stay still.

Ayvalık. The inland sea from Şeytan Sofrası (The Devil's Table).

To the north of the province of **Mysia** there were the **Trojans.** On their right, the **Phrygia** of **King Midas**, and below them the **Lydians.** So far so good, except that they were in continual bickering and strife. According to **Strabo:**

> *"The poets, and particularly the tragic poets, confuse the Trojans, Mysians and Lydians by calling them all Phrygians, while at the same time they describe the Lycians as Carians."*

In such a mix-up and confusion what can one expect the poets to do?...
If you intend to continue by road via **Ayvalık** don't pay any attention to what I say. Spend a night there whatever happens, cross over to **Cunda**

Cunda. Interior of the old coffee-house.

by boat and find the *Günay Restaurant*. Enjoy the salad and fish that are the specialities of the island and, if you have time, climb up to the **Devil's Table** to watch the sunset.

Nature conceals all ills.

The next day you will have a journey of about 42-45 km via **Ayvalık.** As soon as you see the **Bergama** sign turn left, and you will arrive there after about 8 km.

Even if I didn't say anything you would be sure to stop in **Bergama.** And I am sure you would spend two or three days there, the information and signs given in the guide or map you are holding in your hand being quite enough to arouse your interest. Three names are enough: **Bergama, Asclepion** and the **Acropolis...**

Believe me, when I come to this point, my heart begins to flutter. I lose control of my arms and legs.... I feel as if I were entering a dark, dusty, musty old shop. Red, blue and white spots twitch and turn like fireflies in the half-darkness. This must be a **Bergama Carpet.**

I go out into the cobbled street. In the distance, through the mist, I can see monumental structures nestling against the **Bergama** slopes. I torment myself. I obstinately refuse to look at the notes and plans in my hand. That's my way of visiting ancient cities. I like to walk along without worrying about order or precedence. There is a mystery in beauty. Beauty in no way resembles magnificent food served on silver plates. It is something to be first of all savoured on the palate. You must make them ask you questions. And then you should get up and go.

Ours is an age of speed. We don't want to make any effort in the presence of beauty. We have got used to the idea of "out of the freezer and into the microwave".

The old civilizations were in no hurry. For thousands of years they watched the progress of spring, summer and winter on the same plot of land. They were used to all sorts of weather. They were always prepared to wait... In other words, they never offered you beauty without allowing you to savour it on your palate and slowly swallow and digest it....

I stroll through the market. Kilims and carpets are spread out on the ground or hung over the walls. On **Bank Street**, just beside the police station, you can find the **Pergamon Pension.** It's an old building with a courtyard with a pool in the middle. The courtyard is an ideal place to spend the evening. We leave our things here. Water plants and tortoises from the streams and reed-beds in the vicinity float around in the pool.

The **Bakır,** one of the streams flowing into the **Çandarlı Gulf,** has transformed the surrounding country into a fertile plain. And be sure to have a look at the kilims and carpets woven in the **Kozak Yayla** and **Yağcı Bedir** villages. Carpets and kilims have been woven for hundreds of years on handlooms on the **Bergama** uplands.

The geometric design known as *Zili* or *Sili* would have made the painter *Mondrian* green with envy, if. that is, he had ever had the opportunity of seeing it.

These kilims present a riot of colour in which crimson, indigo and white predominate but in which other colours also play their part. The most striking feature is the use of stylized vegetal motifs of every colour. *Mondrian's* paintings, particularly those produced in the 1930s and 1940s, are composed of coloured squares and rectangles, whereas the *zilis* consist of incredibly involved squares, diagonals and hooks, with dots scattered here and there like daisies in a field. In the one, discipline prevails, in the other, both discipline and abandon.

But let me say right away: I have no intention of making a comparison between a well-known artist and the anonymous craftsmen of quite different qualities and identities, and of judging this to be good, that bad. I simply wanted to stress the power of interpretation of those driven by the same winds of nature.

As in many another Anatolian kilim, this abandon appears in **Bergama** *zilis* in the motley coloured fringes studded with blue beads

Zili is a type of weave dating back to the 14th or 15th

Bergama kilim (detail).

83

Bergama Bridge at the end of the 19th century. Charles Texier, "Description de l'Asie Mineure".

century. It is often to be found in both the **Aegean** and **Central Anatolia**. There are various types of *zili* - **Düz zili** (plain zili), **Çapraz Zili** (oblique zili), **Seyrek Zili** (loose zili), **Damalı Zili** (checked zili) and **Konturlu Zili** (contoured zili).

And what about **Bergama** carpets?

If a city can survive wholly on the quality of its kilims and carpets there must really be something to it.

The geometric design, the indigo, crimson, white and green that characterize the kilims are also to be found in the carpets. The free abandon of the kilims appears in the carpet in a more elegant and more disciplined form. There are also octagons and lozenge designs reminiscent of the 17th century. But **Bergama** carpets are characterized first and foremost by the light and gay abandon of the **Aegean** region.

In this city, you will find yourself in a dream world in which you are suddenly carried off into the most unexpected times and places. You will find the motifs in these kilims and carpets in stone carvings from the **Kingdom of Bergama** thousands of years ago.

Isn't life itself a dream world? You can trace a connection with the **Phrygians** that once included this city within their borders, or the **Lydians,** or the magnificent statues of the **Hellenistic** culture. Someone will be sure to come out with a "That's absolutely impossible!" Actually nothing could be more reasonable? But instead of getting involved in futile arguments, you can at least discuss civilizations and their products. And what's more, you have so much material at your disposal!

Is it conceivable that the **Phrygians, Lydians, Persians. Hellenes, Byzantines,** the **Caresians** from the Emirate period and the **Ottomans** could possibly have occupied the same region, one after the other, only to make their exit from the world's stage without exerting any influence on each other!... Obviously not!

Even nomads who pitch their tents on the same spot and then continue on their way exert some mutual influence.

So?... Any objections?

And now here's a school for you. You want to know what sort of school?

The **Bergama School of Sculpture.** This school, founded in **Bergama** during the **Hellenistic** period was later to influence the **Roman** city of **Aphrodisias.** I'm sure you already know that **Aphrodisias** was the most important centre of sculpture in Anatolia.

But before visiting the **Bergama Archaeological Museum** take a seat in a carpet shop or a coffee-house in the Bergama market and enjoy a cup of Turkish coffee prepared exactly to your taste. I recommend an *orta* or an *az şekerli* (medium sweet or with very little sugar). And a glass of lukewarm water to go with it...

The exuberance to be found in **Bergama** kilims and carpets has its

Horse and cart in the Bergama Market.

(above) Statue of Nike. Bergama.
Marble. Hellenistic period, end of 2nd
century B.C. Istanbul Archaeological
Museum.
(above right) Female statue. Bergama.
Marble. Roman period, 1st century A.D.
Bergama Museum.
(opposite page) Head of Alexander the
Great. Bergama. Marble. Hellenistic
period, 1st half of 2nd century B.C.
Istanbul Archaeological Museum.

source. in the school of **Bergama** sculpture which reached its peak in the 2nd century B.C. This particular style of sculpture was characterized by the great importance given to light and shade and the display of great emotion and sensitivity. Let me give you an example. The head of **Alexander the Great** in the **Istanbul Archaeological Museum.**
This head of **Alexander the Great of Macedon** was found in excavations of the agora in **Pergamon (Bergama).** Whenever I go to the Istanbul Archaeological Museum I first of all gaze on the head of **Alexander** from a distance, then I go up nearer to it, like someone performing a ritual dance around a votive altar. The head, slightly inclined towards the left, with its smiling lips and tousled hair, is not the head of a fierce warrior. It is more a symbol of civilization.

(above) Finial from Bergama. Bergama Museum.
(opposite page) Statue of Hadrian. Bergama School of Sculpture. Bergama Museum.

Mention must surely be made here of the sculptor **Lysippos**, who carved the head of **Alexander the Great** in marble in the 4th century B.C., for it was **Lysippos'** sculpture that inspired the head of **Alexander** in the Istanbul museum, produced by the **Bergama School of Sculpture** 150 years later.

But examples of the **Bergama School of Sculpture** are not confined to the head of Alexander. Other products of the school include a statuette of a winged *Nike,* the goddess *Aphrodite,* a *centaur* in the **Bergama Museum** and a relief of a winged god.

And there's something else we shouldn't forget: that a distinguishing feature of the kings of **Bergama** was their ambition to raise **Bergama** to the cultural level attained by the **Athens** of the classical period... And they succeeded... One reason for their success lay in the policies they adopted... The kings of **Bergama**, finding it difficult to achieve peace in the region and ravaged by constant wars decided to act in close association with the **Romans.**

The catalogue for the *Exhibition of Anatolian Civilizations* that opened in **Istanbul** in 1983 contained the following note:

> *"The reason for Bergama's extraordinary expansion is to be sought in its close cooperation with Rome in Aegean politics and the support which it received. in return.*
>
> *"Finally, the last king of Bergama, in his will, bequeathed his kingdom to Rome, with the result that on his death in 133 B.C. the Romans peacefully acquired the whole of Western Anatolia and converted it into a Roman province. The Romanization of Anatolia was thus achieved through a peaceful process rather than by force of arms, and Hellenistic culture was able to survive into the Roman period."*

Those who belittle culture and art have little to hope for in the future. These examples provide the most cogent proof. And that remark is perfectly valid for our present rulers.

And let me give you another example. You know, of course, that it was the **Egyptians** who invented *papyrus.*

And *parchment?*

The name points to its origin: **Pergamon** or **Bergama**. There is said to have been two hundred thousand parchment scrolls in the Bergama library during the kingdom's most brilliant period in the 2nd century B.C. And obviously these scrolls of parchment were not blank.

One could take a just pride in merely having placed two hundred thousand scrolls of parchment in the **Bergama Library**. But the kings of **Bergama** were not content with that. They saw to it that a space of 50 cm was left behind the shelves so as to allow ventilation and protect the scrolls from damp. The **Library of Celsus** at **Ephesus** profited from this example and installed the same type of ventilation system. Present-day architects, please take note!..

Love, they say, is blind. And the **Bergama Library** found the saying to be only too true. In around 30 B.C. **Erotes** were fluttering around **Mark Antony's** head. He had fallen head over heels in love with **Cleopatra,** the Queen of **Egypt.**

And so, intoxicated with amorous passion, he takes the parchments in the **Bergama Library** and presents them to the **Library of Alexandria...** If **Antony** had been ugly it would be understandable. But as far as we know from the written evidence he was a perfectly normal, well-built individual. Historians tell us nothing as to whether this presentation of books served any useful purpose!.. The only consolation is that it was all for love! I can understand the role played by love in the books affair, but I cannot understand the transfer of the **Altar of Zeus** to **Berlin.**

It was **Sultan Abdülhamit II** who granted the permission.... Perhaps there may somewhere be written evidence as to why he indulged in an act of such extraordinary generosity...

I don't know the reason, but the Turkish scholars who have written on the subject of the **Altar of Zeus** have never dwelt on this topic. If it hadn't been for the campaign begun in recent years for the return of the altar to its original site their 'state of slumber' could have continued totally undisturbed.

But I feel it is high time I started to consult the written sources. I am beginning to waffle a bit without realising it. The reason for that is the coming of dusk. A drink invites me. And there's the smell of aubergine *kebap* in my nostrils.

While on the subject of the importance of the city there's just one more point I'd like to make. While making its plans for expansion into

Anatolia Christianity chose **Bergama** as the first step. Which goes to prove that for all communities and civilizations **Bergama** was for one reason or another indispensable. But what really bowls me over is the use of line and colour in kilim and carpet that has continued over so many centuries.

Tonight will be given over to my dreams... Tomorrow, I shall bequeath to my friends whatever remains of the **Bergama Library**! First of all, I shall arrange a festival of **Dionysos** in my name in the ten-thousand seated theatre on the slopes of the mountain, and after the festivities are over I shall hand over the theatre to my friends. But on one point I haven't been able to come to a decision. Should we arrange camel-wrestling to the accompaniment of drums and *zurnas!*... Or should we instal loudspeakers all around and present what commonly passes for music by singers and folklorists in glistening, transparent costumes studded with spangles?...

But I have made up my mind. I shall certainly give something to some-

Begama. Altar of Zeus.

one tomorrow. To avoid gossip, I shan't give anything to my wife or daughter! But I must certainly give something to someone! That is all part of the **Bergama** tradition! After all, what's the difference between me and **Mark Antony** and **Abdühamit II**?

But that's tomorrow!...

And how shall *tomorrow* appear in this book?

Today I am a decent, law-abiding traveller...

I woke up just as day was breaking. But my dreams continue!...

I feel I have been cured of my delirium. Only one image remains in front of my eyes. The image of steps, tiers of steps on a slope...

The eighty steps surrounded by a vegetation that keeps itself very much to itself and descends very, very gently to the stage... As if the king were watching the players and the chorus all by himself. And as if the ten thousand spectators behind the king were watching the festivity without a king at all.

This is something that the architects of our own age should attempt. Such magnificent constructions would suit them down to the ground! But I realise that they have no time to spare from their discussions, debates, panels and other social activities!..

Very well, but who on earth was it who arranged ten thousand people on a slope in such a way that they would be able to hear every word from the chorus on the stage while gazing out at the blue of the plain beyond?

They can't tell us his name. Probably because they didn't attach enough importance to it!

(above) Bergama, the Red Church. Charles Texier, "Description de L'Asie Mineure". (below) The Red Church today.

Perhaps all this is just the effect of my dreams, or of **Dionysos,** who tempts me with wine!...

I turn to *Ekrem Akurgal,* who talks of **Dionysiac** festivities lasting the whole day; festivities comprising poetry, music, literature and dance. Every master vying with his fellow.

Only one problem remains. And that problem has nothing to do with the architect who can erect his building without lacerating nature; or the person who can house an audience of ten thousand and still hear the voice of man or nature and still see the view; or the actor who can hold the attention of ten thousand spectators throughout the whole of a festivity.

I have only one problem: How was it that a people who experienced the same festivities and the same orgiastic madness for over 150 years from the 3rd century B.C. onwards, came to feel the need for architectural monuments of this type?

As we coast along the shores of the **Aegean** and the **Mediterranean** we shall very often encounter the masters of a culture firmly founded on nature.

As I write this they are firing blank shots in the streets. There is the incessant blare of motor-horns... Someone must have won a match. The fans are celebrating.. I can't see them from my house. They are hidden by the judas trees and the laurels. The acacias are in bloom. There are wild violets on my window sills....

Who said we could stay in **Bergama** for two or three days? Was it me that was so generous four or five pages ago? Do whatever you like, but leave me in **Bergama**. Perhaps I could register as a monk in a monastery! After all, the **Byzantines** built a monastery here! No, I've changed my mind. I could never be a monk. Better leave me in the market!..

To tell you the truth I am hopelessly mixed up... I open **Strabo's** *Geography*. What sort of a geographer is this? He talks about books!

> *"As far as I know, Theophrastos was a book collector. Aristotle bequeathed his library and his school to Theophrastos and, as far as I know, this man was the first to collect books, and the first to teach the kings of Egypt how to build up a library."*

Just think of it! A bookworm in the middle of the 4th century B.C. Never mind the **Aegean** and its provinces, he tells the king of **Egypt** how to build a library! Quite apart from giving information he acts as teacher to the king.

Bergama theatre nestling on the slopes.

If only someone would recommend a book to the educated administrators of our own day, something besides economic bulletins and computer notes! He could at least recommend some "Tales for Adults"!...

Strabo refuses to digress. He goes on with his story. *Theophrastos* was a bibliophile, and he left his own private library to **Neleos.** It would appear that when **Neleos** grew old he left it to someone or other by the name of **Scepsis**.

From my experience a father leaves his son or daughter money. At least, that's what we are taught to regard as the normal procedure at the present day .

But **Scepsis'** heirs, being just ordinary, unscholarly people, buried the books in a damp place underground because of a rumour going around

Athena, Goddess of War. Marble.
Roman period, end of 5th century B.C.
Istanbul Archaelogical Museum.

that the kings of the **Attalos** dynasty were on the lookout for books for the **Bergama Library.**

The story doesn't end here. And don't forget, it isn't a story. It's a fact..

They saw that the books that had once belonged to **Aristotle** and **Theophrastos** were beginning to rot. So they dug them up and sold them to **Apellikon** of **Teos,** an ancient city on the **Sığacık Gulf** a little way south of **Izmir.**

Strabo, as the author of a *Geography,* takes an objective view of the whole thing. He tells us that *"Apellikon of Teos was a bibliophile rather than a philosopher, and, finding the texts defective in many places ,filled in the gaps, quite erroneously, in accordance with his own ideas,"*

So we find ourselves confronted once again with the **Bergama Library.** In **Strabo's** notes, the height of the interior of the library built by *Eumenes II* is given as 6 m. According to *Akurgal:*

> *"Manuscripts consisted mainly of dressed leather and were arranged upright on the shelves either folded or in the form of the modern book. Even if we take it that the shelves were 4-5 metres high, the room could not have held more than 15-20 thousand papyrus or parchment manuscripts.*
>
> *"As the ancient writers declare that the Bergama Library contained 200,000 volumes, we must assume that the rest of the manuscripts were housed in the other three rooms and in other places."*

A theatre with ten thousand seats, and a library with 200,000 books!.. Surely that is enough to prove that more than half the population of the city was intimately involved with art and culture. Some wise guy of the present day would probably tell us that that was because they had nothing else to do!

I love people that make remarks like that! I think it would be useful to offer these smart alecs, who have never read anything except a newspaper and who have their computers indexed to the currency rates, the example of an ancient king or administrator.

Euemenes II, the king who built the library, fought with the **Seleucids,**

the **Galatians** and the **Macedonians,** and immediately after the conclusion of hostilities he built the **Temple of Athena**. You know, the temple that slipped away to Berlin! Yes, that's the one!...

According to the plan, this temple was to be located immediately behind the library. It bears the following inscription: *"From King Eumenes to **Athena**, the bringer of victory.*

Athena was a goddess of war. It was King *Eumenes* who won the victory, but the king declares that it was not he himself, but the goddess *Athena* who won it, or at least arranged that it should be won. So like the modest rulers of our own day!...

It never ends.... *Eumenes II* also built the city defence wall, as well as the **Altar of Zeus.**

The sculptors of the city had not been idle. The victories won by *Attalos I* and *Eumenes II* were depicted by sculptors such as *Epigonos, Pyromachios, Stratonikos* and *Antigonos.*

Akurgal has an interesting point to make concerning the **Bergamese** sculptors: *"Instead of exalting the soldiers of Bergama who won the war they depicted, with great sensitivity, the defeated Galatians who had fought so heroically."*

This expert in war was undoubtedly also an expert in art. It is no wonder that the citizens of Bergama regarded *Eumenes II* as a god....

Bergama is remarkable not only for its library, its **Temple of Athena** and its theatre. It also displays the distinguishing characteristics of a great city in its houses, its agora, its Heroon, the temple of Dionysos and its gymnasium.

A city does not consist merely of rows of houses and streets bisecting each other at various odd places. A city is a way of life. Particularly in ancient cities, where priority was given in the houses to light, the way they were set to the wind, the water supply and infrastructure. Throughout the whole of the **Hellenistic** period **Bergama** was, from the architectural point of view, a model city.

Eumenes II, who built the city of **Bergama,** the most beautiful and most powerful city of the **Hellenistic** age, on a foundation of war, peace, culture and art, was only thirty-eight years old when he died. In other words he must have been fully mature by the age of twenty. An age when our own youth are just beginning to venture out to discotheques.

That *Alexander the Great* should have died at the age of thirty-three is, perhaps, even more amazing. But that shouldn't lead us to belittle the achievements of *Eumenes II,* born one hundred and twenty-six years after *Alexander*. After all, *Alexander the Great* is rather an exception!...

Alexander the Great was twenty when he succeeded to the throne. At the age of sixteen he had already led the **Macedonian** army to victory.

I tend to ascribe everything to culture, knowledge and art, and I ascribe the *Alexander the Great* phenomenon to the same factors. **Alexander** was already taking lessons from *Aristotle* at the age of thirteen.

95

(above) *Bergama Asclepieion. North gallery.*
(below) *Bergama Asclepieion. Tiers in the theatre.*

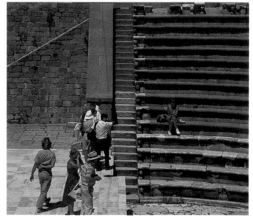

I am very happy that *Alexander the Great* will be accompanying us for much of the way on this journey of ours. Not because he was a great warrior, but because of his fascinating personality.

And now it's the turn of the **Asclepieion.**

I have no idea how you intend to programme this visit, but in **Bergama** you must certainly walk along the colonnaded marble way.

This is the main street of the **Asclepieion.** To be more explicit, to see what was founded in the name of *Asclepios*, the physician god, is good for health! He is also said to have been a good surgeon. I wouldn't swear to the fact that he could resurrect the dead. What if he resurrected people whose places could be reckoned 'vacant' even when they were still alive?

The sacred way leading from the city of **Bergama** to the **Asclepieion** is

about a kilometre long. There is also a library here. After passing the remains of a temple dating back to around 150 B.C. you will arrive at a fountain, which is still in use, and immediately behind the fountain lie the patients' rooms, of which only the foundations now remain. If you go into the tunnel under these foundations on a hot summer day you will feel refreshed by the delicious coolness. I imagine this tunnel must have formed part of the therapy. There is also a mud bath and a pool for ablutions round about the same place.

Immediately opposite you will find a theatre for 3500 built in the Roman period with a row of **Ionic** columns beside it that constitutes one of the most magnificent features of the **Asclepieion**.

You can sit on the steps of the theatre and take a glimpse into the world of dreams. But on one condition. The sun shouldn't be blazing at its zenith overhead.

But to return to my dreams...

In the cool of the morning or the evening, you must walk along the sacred colonnaded way to the monumental gate.

This monumental gate opens on to a courtyard surrounded by spirally fluted **Ionic** columns. You may, if you wish, stop in at the library on the right and glance through the pages of a manuscript book, or you can cool off by the roofed fountain in the shade of a tree and drink a glass of cool fresh water.

The rites of **Dionysos** are about to begin. Make sure of your seat in the theatre. You can choose the beauties of **Bergama** that imitate the goddesses with their long fair hair, their long, full white dresses and their necks and bare arms tanned by the **Aegean** sun. Just act naturally. But there's one thing you mustn't do. You mustn't tell anyone that you have come to be treated by the god **Asclepios**. The best thing is to say that you have brought a sick friend for therapy!..

(left) Underground passage thought to have been used in the treatment of the patients.
(below) Funerary stele. Bergama Museum.

97

Choose one of them as your companion, and as the actors leave the stage you will turn towards the colonnaded street. You wonder what you will talk about?

That's entirely up to you!

I have only one piece of advice to give you. Be careful not to choose July or August, or the noonday heat, for your glimpse into the dream world of archaeology. Otherwise even **Asclepios** will not be able to save you!...

But I have one last piece of advice: Before leaving the city go up to the **Acropolis** and, as you leave the theatre, go into the temple of *Dionysos,* and turn round and look for the last time at the theatre nestling gently on the slope of the hill and the infinity beyond...

(opposite) Asclepios and Hygenia. Marble relief. Bergama School of Sculpture. Istanbul Archaeological Museum.
(left) Asclepios, the god of health, and his son Telesphorus. Miletus. Marble, Roman period, 2nd century A.D. Istanbul Archaeological Museum.
(above) Detail.

The journey from **Bergama** to **Izmir** is quite a short one, but there are places like **Gryneion, Myrina** and **Kyme** that you can call at in between. The ancient city of **Pitane** near **Çandarlı,** with its Genoese castle dating from the 13th and 14th centuries, may be rather out of your way, but finds from there can be seen in the archaeological museums in **Bergama, Izmir** and **Istanbul**. Meanwhile, you can easily pay a visit to **Myrina** and **Kyme**, where the *terracotta* figurines in the **Louvre, Istanbul** Archaeological Museum and the **Bergama** Museum collections were produced. Both these places are on your way.

At this point, we should have another glance at **Strabo's** *Geography*. And then we can turn to the **Lydians** who lived in the province of **Izmir.**

Like **Mysia** to the north, **Lydia** was a completely distinct civilization. *Strabo* quotes from *Plato* on this point:

> *"According to Plato, the flood was followed by three stages of civilization. The first, which arose on the summits of the hills, was coarse and brutish. Men still feared the waters that covered the plain. In the second, which arose on the slopes of the mountains, men, seeing the waters recede from the plains, gradually gathered courage. The third arose on the plains. We could also speak of a fourth, a fifth and even more, but the essential point is that men finally rid themselves entirely of their fears and established their civilizations on the plains and seashores."*

The fears of these men of so many thousands of years ago were by no means groundless. Many a powerful community and brilliant civilization had been annihilated by earthquakes in the **Aegean** and its islands, a fact to which the islands of **Crete, Rhodes, Chios** and **Santorini** can all bear witness.

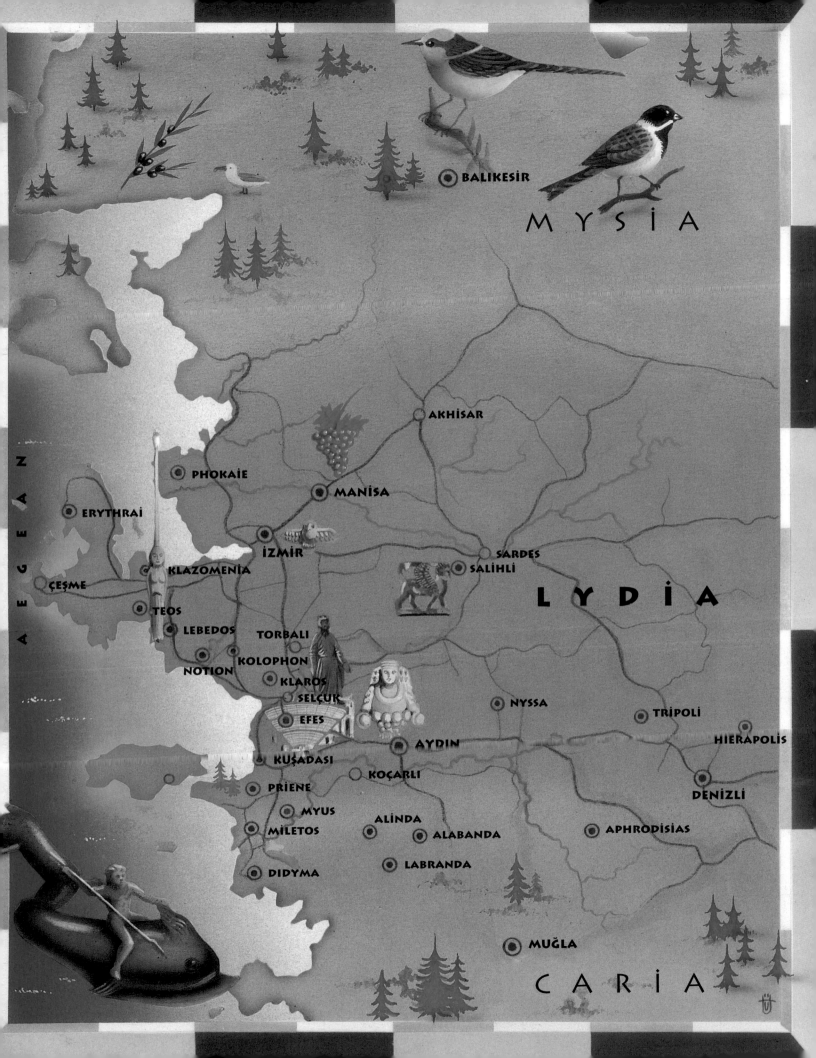

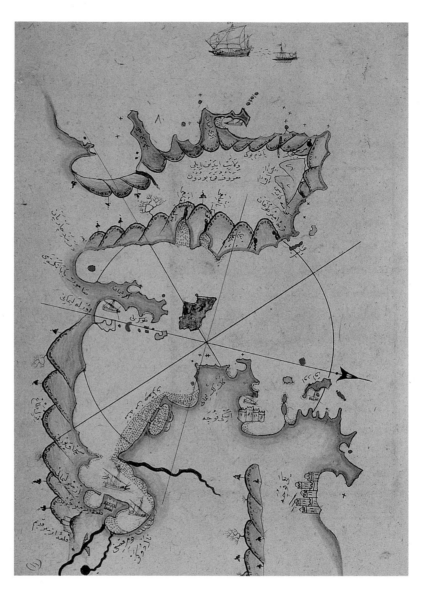

(above) Aphrodite drying her hair. Myrina. Terracotta. Late Hellenistic period, 1st century B.C. Istanbul Archaeological Museum.
(above right) Old and new Foça, İzmir. Chart of Urla harbour. Piri Reis. "Kitâb-ı Bahriye". Ayasofya Library.
(opposite) House in Foça.

In 1500 B.C. the island of **Crete** was the home of the most powerful nation in the **Aegean**. This belonged to the civilization known as the **Minoan,** which possessed a strong tradition dating back to the **Bronze Age.** The end of the **Middle Minoan** period coincided with the complete annihilation of the **Minoan** civilization as a result of the eruption of the volcano on the island of **Santorini**. According to geologists, debris from the explosion was flung 30 km into the air, extended over a distance of 300 km and devastated an area of 200 km².

Although this was obviously not the "flood" referred to by *Plato.* there is still a basis of truth in his account. Great civilizations have always arisen on seashores or rivers, and we thus cannot afford to ignore the civilizations on the shores of the **Aegean** and the **Mediterranean**.

Strangely enough, the volcano on the island of **Santorini**, which annihilated several civilizations at the peak of their power, now, thousands of years later, proffers its services to tourism. Far above the redhot rocks below ground, we now find white-washed, blue-shuttered houses and blue domed churches, each challenging the deep indigo blue of the sea. Mankind stubbornly clings to each fragment of land in the **Aegean** and the **Mediterranean.** Though perhaps the term "stubbornly clings" is a bit strong. For thousands of years a mild climate has been created here by a combination of the blue of the **Aegean** and the **Mediterranean,** the north wind that tempers the summer heat and disperses the fogs and mists, and the south wind that brings the rain. And to all this we must not forget to add the fertility of the soil.

Who would hesitate to settle in such a region, with its mild climate, fertile soil and deep waters?

The exhibits you will see on your visits to museums in the Aegean and the Mediterranean consist mainly of decorated and figured jars, goblets, drinking-mugs, wide-mouthed bowls, statues and ornamental accessories.. These are all, undoubtedly, symptomatic of a high standard of well-being. Wars and conflicts arose from a desire to seize a share of this prosperity and abundance, but, in the intervals between wars, let there be grapes, wine and rejoicing!

Even a cursory examination of the island of **Crete** and the **Palace of Knossos** is quite sufficient proof of this. The frescoes, pottery, statues and interior and exterior decoration are all based on nature. Wild animals, flowers, leaves, birds and beautiful women constitute the basic source of inspiration for their artists. The bath in the **Palace of Knossos** is

more like a reception room. But the eruption of the volcano on the island of **Santorini** brought this whole civilization to an end. And this was followed, as in every age, by looting and pillage carried out by their neighbours...

But let us turn back to our journey through **Lydia**.

If, after a brief look at **Kyme,** you continue on your way, you will soon see the sign pointing out the way to **Foça.** From here it is about 25 km.

Foça, or **Phokaia,** as it was known in ancient times, is now a holiday resort. The city was presented to the **Phokaians** by the citizens of **Kyme.** The excavations here were conducted by *Prof. Dr. Ekrem Akurgal.*

Strabo traces the Ionian frontiers as follows:

"A journey along the coast of Ionia is one of three thousand four hundred stadia. [All the sources I have referred to describe this as 'a unit employed for the measurement of the distance between two places'. But what is this unit? Unfortunately, no one gives the modern equivalent of this unit of length.... But at last I found it. 1 stadia = about 185 metres!] *The reason for this very great length is the number of gulfs and inlets and the extraordinary length of the peninsula. The contours of the Ionian coasts can be traced from the Poseidion of the Miletians and the borders of Caria as far as Phokaia and the river Hermos, and these were to continue to form the demarcation line in later periods."*

Akurgal describes the ***Phokaians*** as expert seamen, and adds:

> *"In place of large cargo ships they employed boats with fifty oarsmen capable of very high speeds and able to carry up to five hundred passengers... Besides being seamen, merchants and colonists, the Phokaians were famous for their coins of electrum (a mixture of gold and silver) which were eagerly sought on the market. Phokaia was also famous for its indigo dye."*

The ***Ionians*** mentioned by ***Strabo*** built up a very brilliant civilization. In the words of ***Herodotus:***

> *"The Ionians founded the most beautiful cities in the world and in the most beautiful climate. Neither the regions further to the north nor those further to the south can be compared with Ionia, not even those to the east or west, for some of these are cold and wet, some of them hot and dry."*

4

1. *Foça harbour.*
2,3,4. *Details of old Foça.*

For the moment, let us postpone discussion of the way of life and the scholarship of the ***Ionians,*** who founded new colonies in the **Aegean, Marmara** and **Black Sea.** It might only confuse you..

To tell the truth, I myself got into such a state of confusion during this research that I found it difficult to find answers to questions concerning exactly where each city began and where it ended; where its frontiers lay and the period during which it flourished.

The **Aegean** coastline is like a family with a great many children. After the tenth, it becomes difficult to remember their names. And if these children get married and start a family, get yourself out of that one if you can!...

Let us take the easiest path. Before we go on to **Foça** let us have a bit of gossip about the ***Lydians***, on whose lands we now find ourselves. The source of our gossip is ***Herodotus:***

> *"Unlike the other provinces, Lydia possesses nothing of very great note. There is only the golden sand carried down from Tmolos [Bozdağ in the neighbourhood of Manisa].*
>
> *"The customs and usages of the Lydians closely resemble those of the Greeks. One important difference, however, is that the Lydians give their female offspring over to prostitution. As far as we know, they were the first to issue and employ gold and silver coins, and they were also the first to engage in small commercial enterprises...*
>
> *"All the girls of ordinary families sell themselves until they marry, using*

the proceeds of this trade to purchase their trousseaus. As a matter of fact, the husbands can only retain these girls by their sides if the girls themselves so desire."

Herodotus was born in **Halicarnassus,** probably around 490 B.C. which makes him around sixty-five when he died in 425..... He therefore lived during the period of Persian hegemony in **Lydia** and must have been very familiar with that particular aspect of Lydian social history. If he ever saw those girls in their old age it may well have sent him completely out of his mind!...

The *Lydians* were the first to issue gold and silver coins. At the same time **Sardis**, their most important city, was a centre of textile production. Natural dyes were produced on the foothills of the **Tmolos** (Bozdağ) mountains mentioned by *Herodotus.*

All this must have constituted the basis for the carpet-weaving for which **Bergama** and **Gördes** are still renowned today.

The region is also famous for its wine, and for the cultivation not only of grapes, but also of pomegranates, apples, chestnuts, hazel-nuts, walnuts, tobacco and cotton. The soil is extremely fertile and very fine perfumes are made from the saffron gathered on the mountain slopes. In ancient times these perfumes were the most marketable of their commodities.

With all that wealth it is pretty difficult to retain your sanity!... *Herodotus* was quite right!..

Silver, gold and the arsenic used in the production of dyes were to be found on the **Tmolos** mountains. The finest quality mercury was also extracted from this soil.

Now I can understand why the *Lydians* were so crazy. When you are as rich as that it is difficult to restrain yourself!

But I can't really make any comment on the free and easy attitudes of the *Lydian* girls!

At the present day, **Foça** lies in an arc traced by the **Gediz** river. It is a conservation area, but the passion for concrete construction is ringing the death-knell for the whole district. The Ottoman domestic architecture and the **Greek** houses that were a distinguishing feature of the region are fast disappearing. And it is not only the houses that are disappearing. The centuries' old olive groves are also falling victim to the fury of the jerry-builders. Nevertheless, the **Foça** coast still plays host to a very important sea creature known as the *Mediterranean seal.*

Sea bass and bream swim among the ruins of the **Genoese Castle** submerged in the sea. As for the summer houses, guest-houses, holiday villages, hotels, motels.... the *Lydians'* ancient city of **Phokaia,** the first city to issue gold and silver coins, is now besieged on all sides by cheats and swindlers.

These cheats and swindlers have no interest whatever in the history, nature and civilizations behind them, but they are past masters at the art of constructing holiday homes with two bedrooms, a sitting-room and a *de luxe* bathroom!

Something I don't, and never will, understand is why people of today give so little importance to the wealth of history and the natural heritage presented to them by this truly magnificent peninsula!

Let us assume that a property owner, for the sake of the profit to be gained, takes it into his head to cut down an olive grove and heap up a mass of concrete over the remains of the ancient city of **Phokaia:** a "villa apartment" with one floor for himself, one floor for his daughter, one floor for his son and, if possible, one for a tenant to bring in a bit of income.

What are we to make of the type of architect who approves such projects and prepares the plans?

For an answer to this question let us turn to the *De Architectura*, a treatise in ten books by *Vitruvius,* an architect who lived between 90-20 B.C. *Vitruvius,* like *Homer, Herodotus* and *Strabo,* is one of our most distinguished guests on this journey. It is under their guidance and advice that we shall get the most out of our visit to the **Aegean** and the **Mediterranean.**

In the introduction to his book, *Vitruvius* sets out the qualities with which an architect should be equipped:

"An architect should be properly trained, he should be able to write well, he must be skilled in geometry, he should know history, he should be familiar with the philosophers, he should understand music and he should also have some knowledge of medicine. He should also know something of legal matters and be acquainted with astrology and astronomy."

Vitruvius is going a little too far! He himself must have foreseen such a reaction for he goes on to make certain reservations on the subject:

"An architect need not be a grammarian like Aristarchus, indeed he cannot be. But he should not be ignorant. He cannot be a musician like Aristoxenus, but he should not be entirely ignorant of the science of music. He cannot be expected to be a painter like Apelles, a sculptor like Myron or Polyclitus or a physician like Hippocrates; but nevertheless an architect should know something of drawing, the plastic arts and medicine."

Vitruvius obviously brooks no compromise in his recommendations. I come to realise the reason for this much better as I tour the **Aegean** and **Mediterranean** coasts. For example, how is it possible for a spectator in the very back row of the **Bergama Theatre**, which could hold an audience of ten thousand, to hear the soft tones of a lyre? And if he can hear the sound of a lyre from the very back row there must be a very good reason for it! When *Vitruvius* says that an architect should know something of music he meant that he didn't want the spectator in the back row to feel frustrated.

Vitruvius' treatise also contains a section on *"Sound jars in the theatre"* in which he describes in great detail exactly where these "bronze jars", intended to attract the sound and reflect it without distortion, are to be placed on the steps of the auditorium.

He forgets only one thing: the strident clamour of the drum and *zurna* echoing through the theatre!.. But the way things are going now, and when we think of what is now being produced in the name of music, we may soon feel nostalgic for the sounds of the drum and *zurna* ...

I am not asking my architect friends not to take offence at the frequent references I am making (and will continue to make) to *Vitruvius.* They are merely victims of the age! Or rather, since it is they who have put their signatures to each of these buildings, it is we who are the victims...

In my view, the best solution would be to post *Vitruvius'* recommendations on the door of every local authority office along the **Aegean** and **Mediterranean** coasts. But there's one drawback. If the architect fulfils the musical education requirement by taking up the recorder, what shall we do then?

The best solution is to think of great Ionian cities like **Phokaia** thousands of years ago. But if you are someone who gives no great importance to the old harmony that once existed between buildings and the natural environment you can stay in **Foça** for a little longer while we continue on our way. But I can't promise very much for the **Izmir** we'll be arriving at in an hour's time.

What really gets me down in a journey along the **Aegean** coast is the entrance into **Izmir.** I am not referring to the traffic or the hot, arid appearance. Unfortunately, it is our nose that first lets us know we are

entering **Izmir.** You immediately close the car windows. But the smell still seeps in. A whole mountain covered with stone buildings. It's no good talking. It's no good looking. **Izmir** is a perfect example of the complete destruction of a city.

You needn't tell me! I know **Venice** smells. But the last thirteen centuries have witnessed the construction of not a single building out of harmony with the city's architecture. In **Venice** the human voice prevails, along with houses along the edge of the canals, buildings with courtyards, squares, bridges and statues.

In **Izmir** I feel completely at a loss. And I also confuse my friend, who is driving the car. By the time I say, *"Let's just bypass Izmir. Let's not go into it."* we are already in the thick of the traffic.

The best way to visit **Izmir** is by rummaging through old postcards, and looking at photographs and engravings of a hundred or a hundred fifty years ago.

The **Konak Square** in 1930. The **Clock Tower** in the foreground, the **Government Building** behind... Steps leading up to an arched entrance. Beside it the small **Yalı Mosque** with its single minaret. The **Sarı Barracks** a little further off. In another postcard we can see the **Turkish Hearth** building in neo-classical style. The photograph also shows construction work in progress along the shore...

Izmir contains two very important and very famous districts: the **Kordonboyu** (Esplanade) and **Karşıyaka**... Smartly dressed people can be seen promenading along the seafront on the **Kordonboyu.** All the

(opposite) Izmir, La Borde, "Voyage de l'Asie Mineure".
(above) Aeolian capital. Old Izmir (Bayraklı). Temple of Athena, 600 B.C. Foça stone, Izmir Archaeological Museum.
(left) Ship. Piri Reis.

ladies and gentlemen with hats. The house entrances, the recessed balconies and bay windows are all masterpieces of architecture. Each building has two or three floors. The other district, **Karşıyaka,** is adorned with mansions set amidst palms and tall trees, with the houses reflected in the crystal clear waters of the bay.

Let me tell you right away. It isn't the old districts and the old state of affairs I miss. What I miss is the ability for the eye and the heart to breathe freely in the environment in which I live; the pleasure afforded by the healthy old cities of before my time with their sound architecture and truly natural environment.

Happiness in human life is not connected solely with the contemporary scene. We are fully conscious of no more than some thirty-five or forty years in the course of our lives. But the people who shared the same soil thousands of years ago also play a part at the present day, just as I myself will play a part in the centuries to come. They didn't leave me a traffic-

1

2

3

4

1. *Izmir harbour in the 19th century.*
2. *Imaginary engraving of the port of İzmir in the 19th century.*
3. *Izmir. Primitive stone relief.*
4. *19th century Izmir street.*

Two old photographs.
(above) The Izmir Esplanade, where smart ladies and gentlemen would promenade.
(below) Karşıyaka, with its high trees and palms.

jammed city and a stinking sea, and, leaving future generations aside for the moment, I ought to be able to leave an environment suitable for the age in which I live. And it's no good bringing up excuses like, "But the population etc. etc...."!

Vitruvius wrote a book on town planning and architectural method. I should like to produce a similar work containing what I have been able to gather on the subject of "shoddiness, ugliness, vulgarity, ignorance, incompetence and the practice of deliberate self-deception".

But I have no love for talk and advice with no practical result, and I think I am probably becoming a bit of a bore.

The best thing is to listen to what *Akurgal* has to say about **Izmir,** or **Smyrna,** as it used to be known.

Weaving kilims in Kaleiçi, İzmir.

"If you cast a glance over the Western Anatolian shores, you will see that almost all the Aeolian, Ionian and Dorian cities founded after the Trojan war, dozens of cities like Çandarlı, Foça, Izmir, Clazomenae, Miletus and Iasos, were built on a very small peninsula. The choice of location undoubtedly arose from the fact that the Hellenes were seamen and that in this way they were protected against attacks from both sea and land. Another reason for choosing a peninsula for settlement was that they could make use of two harbours. In the case of one of the harbours being affected by unfavourable weather conditions, sailing ships could use the other. Bayraklı Mound is one of the finest examples of the utilization of a small peninsula of this kind. Its location on the northeast corner of the gulf, with the steep slopes of Mt. Yamanlar rising behind it, provided a very effective defence against attacks from the land. Moreover, it was open in front to the cool wind from the sea known as the 'imbat'. It was for this reason that for three thousand years the ancient city of Izmir was located on this peninsula, and it was only as a result of the great population explosion that took place in the second half of the 4th century B.C. that the site was transferred to the skirts of Kadifekale."

Smyrna, the old name for **Izmir**, a city that has lived through the **Bronze Age**, and the **Hellenistic, Roman, Byzantine, Seljuk** and **Ottoman** periods, is of Anatolian derivation.

According to *Strabo*, the best wine was once produced here, and he also has great praise for the actual layout of the city:

"The city's division into streets is carried out in a very special way. They are all placed as far as possible perpendicular to each other and are paved with stone. They are flanked by wide two-storeyed porticos (i.e. covered galleries open in front)."

But praise soon gives way to criticism.

"But the city has one by no means inconsiderable fault. This fault arises

Çeşme harbour.

from the work of the engineers. When they paved the streets they omitted to construct a drainage system underneath them. The dirty water thus spreads over the surface and in rainy weather the streets are flooded."

In other words, nothing has changed very much from that day to this. And the city's sewage still empties into the gulf.

The same is true of the island of **Samos**. We were strolling quite happily along the shore when we suddenly noticed that the city's sewage and the waste water from the toilets in the restaurants along the shore was all emptied into the sea. We immediately leaped onto our yacht and left **Samos as** far as possible behind us. And yet, in the darkness of the previous night, we had drunk our rakı there, and strolled through **Vathi**, which, in its streets along the harbour ridge and its old houses with their bay windows, so strongly resembles the old **Kaleiçi** district of **Antalya.**

Let me mention another interesting event in the history of **Izmir**, or, if you prefer, **Smyrna**. It was in this city that *Trebonius*, one of the conspirators who assassinated *Caesar,* was seized and put to death.

Bayraklı Mound, on the Karşıyaka road, is, in one sense, the pride of Izmir. According to *Akurgal,* the ancient road and the **Temple of Athena** dating from the 6th and 7th centuries B.C. are *"the oldest architectural monuments of Eastern Hellenic art."*

Akurgal also adds the following:

> *"The oldest example in the Hellenic world of a multi-roomed house is to be found in Old Izmir. Indeed, the double megaron, with its two storeys, five rooms and front courtyard, dating from the second half of the 7th century B.C., is the oldest known house to have several rooms under a single roof. Greek houses previous to that date consisted of a number of megarons arranged side by side. In the second half of the 7th century B.C. the streets of Old Izmir were already arranged on a grid plan, running either north to south or east to west, with the houses generally facing the south... The Bayraklı urban plan is the earliest example of this type of arrangement in the Western world. It was also in Old Izmir that the oldest paved road in the Ionian civilization was unearthed."*

I hope you'll forgive me, but that's all I have to say, and anyway it's high time we left Izmir...

It is 81 km from **Izmir** to **Çeşme.**

Çeşme, like **Foça**, is a tourist resort. In other words, in magazine and advertisment language, an "outstanding place of recreation and amusement" with holiday villages, huge hotels and places of entertainment.

But I am afraid I don't care for "outstanding" places. If a place is so obvious right from the start the whole magic disappears. So as soon as I see signs like "Full board", "Super Luxury", "Package Tour", "All Sports Facilities" I immediately take to my heels.

But of course, if tourism had been applied in accordance with my own personal tastes every single resort would have gone bankrupt long ago.

You can find all these in **Çeşme.** But I mustn't be unfair to the place. If you put up there you will be able to see some very interesting sights, as well as streets and houses from the beginning of the 20th century.

Another special feature is that you can sail round the peninsula by boat... And the fact that there are so many mooring-places for your boat is also very important. **Gülbahçe Bay, Paşa Harbour, Sakızlı Cove** and the private harbour at **Altın Yunus** all invite you to make the journey by sea. But for our own part, we shall continue our journey by land, because from **Urla** onwards a number of old and new settlements are to be found in close proximity to one another.

I shan't say anything about the **Gulf of Sığacık** under the peninsula. It was from **Sığacık** I took my bearings when I set out to sea! Just to get my own back on the **Gulf of Izmir** and its harbour!

Day trips to **Erythrai, Çeşme** and **Alaçatı** are particularly enjoyable. And this time I have several reference books to hand. What I like about the peninsula is that I am not caught in a trap. There are plenty of places where you can escape to from the rows of identical holiday houses and the dull, wearisome prospects...

Çeşme lies immediately across from **Sakız Adası**, the island of **Chios**. The crossing by boat is rather like a sail down a strait. That's probably why, in the 14th century, the *Genoese* built a castle at **Çeşme**. The present castle was built by *Bayezid II* at the beginning of the 16th century and is to be found indicated on the map prepared by the bold seaman *Piri Reis.* The following information is given by *Evliya Çelebi,* who visited the castle in 1671:

> *"The castle is built on a square plan, with stone walls, all totally Turkish in construction. It measures 200 paces [127 m] lengthwise from east to west, and 150 paces [86 m] across. As the western side is directly on the sea there is no moat. The castle contains a garrison of one hundred and eighty five, of whom fifty are soldiers and the rest auxiliary personel. There are twenty-seven cannon, two of them large bore and twenty two small bore."*

Our eloquent *Evliya Çelebi* is a past master in giving information on every place and every event on Anatolian and Ottoman soil. I can just see him with his turban and his robe, holding a notebook and a ruler in his hand. And there would almost certainly be a horse and groom standing at the door!

If modern fax and telephone facilities had been available to him what an extraordinary amount of information *Evliya Çelebi* would have been able to send to the Ottoman capital in Istanbul! He was a spendthrift who acted here as war correspondent, there as art historian and architect, here as a gossip writer and there simply as a gourmet and pleasure-seeker. Sometimes he was simply a chronicler in the shadow of the Sultan...

Çeşme Castle is now open as a museum. If you can succeed in battling your way through the crowds in the long **Çeşme** market without losing your wife or your companion you may, if you are lucky, finally arrive at the castle.

Although castles like this were used primarily for military purposes they no doubt also possessed a commercial function. According to the old sources, the construction of the castle was followed by a significant increase in revenue from trade and harbour dues. This is shown by the five-fold increase in the values recorded in the income registers.

Nowadays you will never find anyone who visits a holiday resort without visiting the castle, if there happens to be one. For a castle means being able to get a bird's eye view of the city. If there are a few bastions, you can climb up to the highest one and imagine yourself an airline pilot or at least the commander of the garrison! The only people that don't climb up the castle bastions are the young lovers, who prefer to

(above) Çeşme Castle, now a museum.
(below) Çeşme beach.

Natural sculptures at Foça.

salmon and grey mullet, and they had plans for breeding lobster. Great care is taken with regard to temperature, fish food, pollution and disease. Size is also carefully observed.

There's a story for everything in life!.

I wonder what set me off on this one? Actually, they were talking about it at the fish farm, beside a pool containing tens of thousands of young fish. The fish measured 1-1.5 cm. They were fed at certain times every day. One day they noticed that the tiny fry weren't eating. They tried every-thing, but it was no good. The whole thing later solved itself. The keepers

that usually fed them had gone on two or three days' leave. When they came back the little fish immediately swarmed around them.

"It's really incredible," the keeper remarked, *"Tiny little fish like that can recognize me, and they are really devoted to me!"*

The same keeper also told me that there were special pools for the large, full-grown fish. They were kept aside for breeding. But the fertility levels among these fish is rather limited. They are very big, but not very fertile.

"So what happens to them afterwards?

"They are taken off to the restaurants. They look fine in the show cases. Then they are brought with great ceremony to customers who have ordered a fish dish but really know nothing about fish and who have already drunk whisky and eaten all sorts of things into the bargain. It's like sticking a lettuce in your mouth. The customer is very pleased that the fish brought to the people at the next table is much more expensive. But actually this fish is absolutely tasteless."

I ought to point out, however, that these remarks don't apply to large fish like *sinarit, orfoz, grida* and *levrek*. It refers only to medium sized fish. ..

In any case, the best fish restaurants are the ramshackle but spotlessly clean fish restaurants on the shores where the fish are actually caught. It's the rule in these places to serve only fish and salad (perhaps with a little white cheese thrown in). Whatever fish you eat the flavour should linger on your palate...

But now, if you have finished your coffee, let's set out.

To get to **Alaçatı** from **Ildır** you have to go back by the **Çeşme** road. But you can bypass **Çeşme** itself. The **Ildır-Reisdere** road is shorter.

Relaxing in Alaçatı, and detail from a house facade.

Alaçatı is not yet completely spoilt by tourism. You can still find local herbs and fruit, cucumbers and carobs being sold in the market. If you make this journey in spring you will see yellow flowers and mimosa by the roadsides. In any case you will be attracted by the fragrance. Mastic trees are a special feature of the region. That's all very well, but aren't there any other varieties of vegetation? Of course there are! You'll find broom, jasmine, honeysuckle, begonia and geraniums growing all over the place.

I suggest you go through the **Alaçatı** market and into the streets behind it. Make your way by the two or three-storey stone houses, some of them built side by side, some with courtyards, some with bay windows. If you like, you can gaze at the decoration on the buildings, the animal figures and the dates of construction. If a coffee-house should catch your eye in one of the side streets you can take a chair and sit by the side of the road. One of the features of these coffee-houses is the way they use the road as a private courtyard.

If you like a chat (and even if you don't) an old man is sure to come over and start talking about everything under the sun. He'll tell you all about his house, his sons and his daughters-in-law. It's a common feature of the **Aegean** and the **Mediterranean** It is a characteristic of people that live on the shore. In big cities they would be regarded as "idiots" but in the **Aegean** and the **Mediterranean** they're the "salt of the earth"! In the great cities where men are caught in the cogs of a machine conversation only gets going after a few drinks. Then they talk all sorts of nonsense about politics, corruption, forecasts, traffic, employer-worker relations

Alaçatı market.

etc.... If they are encouraged they will give you a list of all the trickery and deceit indulged in by the administration!..

Whereas here, on this shore and in these streets, there's nothing to tie you. There are only short conversations on the way. And you'll sure to find some interesting details. Who used to live in these streets or these houses. What flowers they grew in their gardens....

Alaçatı has another interesting feature - the natural formations at the end of **Çark Beach** and **Piyale Bay.** They obviously can't compare with **Göreme** and **Ihlara Valley**, but the shapes into which the winds have fashioned the calcareous rock are of a quite amazing beauty.

BEYOND TEOS, AND THE MAGNIFICENT WORLD OF THE IONIANS

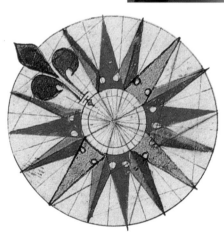

On arriving at this section I gave a great deal of thought to the matter. My heart is with the *Ionians* and *Ionian* civilization. And I have such an accumulation of notes and documents!

And yet I just can't begin. Perhaps I'm tired. I think of all that I have already written and published.

Perhaps the best thing would be to put my notes in proper order!

Perhaps the best thing would be to base myself on other writers and scholars!

Perhaps the best thing would be to make a selection from the whole!

Perhaps the best thing would be to set out from **Alaçatı**, the place I wrote about in the last section, and make my way to **Sığacık Bay**. After all, didn't I say that it was from from **Sığacık Bay** that I was going to set out on my voyage?

Or perhaps the best thing would be to appeal for help to *Herodotus*. Let's leave it to him to tell us about the *Ionians*. Yes, the best thing would be to leave it to *Herodotus*.

And now I come back to myself again; for the world of the *Ionians* is so magnificent that there must have been something very special about them!

For doesn't *Herodotus* write that *"The Ionians built their cities under the most beautiful sky in the whole world and in the most beautiful climate"*?

"They don't all speak the same language. There are four different languages. Beginning from the south, the first city is Miletos. Immediately after that come Myus and Priene. These cities are located in Caria and

(opposite) "The Ionians built their cities under the most beautiful sky in the whole world and in the most beautiful climate". Homer.

speak the same local language. In Lydia we find Ephesos, Lebedos, Teos, Klazomenai and Phokaia. There they speak a language common to the whole region, which is quite different from the one spoken in the cities mentioned above. Apart from these there are three other Ionian cities, two of them being on the islands of Samos and Chios. The third, Erithrai, is on the mainland. Of these cities, Chios and Erithrai speak the same regional language, whereas the Samians speak a language of their own."

"Thus there are four quite distinct regional languages."

But now let us draw up a list of the cities mentioned by *Herodotus*, together with their modern names.

Miletos (Milet), **Myos** (Afşartepe), **Priene** (Turunçlar), **Ephesos** (Efes), **Colophon** (Değirmendere), **Lebedos** and **Teos** (Sığacık Bay and its environs), **Klazomenai** (Urla), **Phokaia** (Foça) and **Erythrai** (Ildır). Then there are the two islands: **Samos** (Sisam) and **Chios** (Sakız).

You will notice that all twelve of the city-colonies of the *Ionians* were located on the shore of the **Aegean**. Nor did they forget the islands opposite. They converted the **Aegean** into a common sea in the full sense of the word.

Of these cities, **Phokaia** (Foça) and **Erythrai** (Ildır) have already been treated in a previous chapter.

According to *Herodotus*, the Athenians disliked being referred to as *Ionians*. *"They would blush at the suggestion."* And he adds, *"But when I listed the twelve cities they felt proud on hearing their names."*

In *Bertrand Russel's* opinion it is not at all surprising that the **Ionia** that produced *Homer* should at the same time have been the source of scientific discoveries and learning. It is only natural that scientific speculation should have free reign in places relatively free of mysticism.

We have only to mention some of the names besides *Homer* connected with *Bertrand Russel's Ionian world* to understand the reason for the envy of which they were the object. In **Miletos** we find the geometrician, mathematician and astronomer *Thales. Hippodamos*, who introduced the grid system into urban planning, was born in **Miletos,** and other citizens of **Miletos** included *Anaximander, Anaximenes, Hecataeus* and *Leucippe... Pythagoras* was a native of **Samos.**

Another description of *Ionian* civilization is given by *Akurgal:*

> *"The most brilliant period of the Ionian cities began after the foundation of the colonies in the second half of the 7th century B.C. and reached its climax in the golden age of the years 600-545 when the leadership of the ancient cultural world passed from the Middle East to the Ionian centres. The Ionia of this period was the leader, not only in the positive sciences, but also in the arts of sculpture and architecture."*

Thales and the others will be considered together with their own particular cities.

Ionia found a staunch defender in the *Fisherman of Halicarnassus,* who

(opposite) Teos (Sığacık) harbour.
(above) Teos fishermen, from the castle.
(below) Teos in the 19th century. La Borde, "Voyage de l'Asie Mineure".

(above left) Teos. Marble carving displaying highly skilled workmanship.
(above right) Teos. Temple of Dionysos.

wrote of **Ionia** with great passion and enthusiasm.

"The Ionians had no moralistic gods, nor were they governed by divine commands and prohibitions forbidding this and that. They had no thought of life after death, and so they were completely free from selfish hopes and fears concerning the other world. The dead had no eyes, and couldn't see, they had no ears, and couldn't hear. They were simply referred to as 'shades'."

Now let **Strabon** take over:

"Teos is located on a peninsula and possesses a harbour. The lyric poet Anacreon was a native of Teos. It was during his lifetime that the citizens of Teos, unable to bear the insolence of the Persians, abandoned

their own city to migrate to the Thracian city of Abdera, and it was after this that Abdera is to be found referred to as "Abdera, the beautiful colony of the Teians". But some of them later returned. As I have already mentioned, Apellicon was also a Teian, as was also the historian Hecataeus."

It was just as well that the Athenians denied that they were **Ionians**. The **Ionians** had plenty of people eager to spring to their defence! Actually, the whole question of defence was purely academic. The choice of such a marvellous location on the **Aegean,** combined with the power of art and science, bound them firmly to the site and the soil. To put it more bluntly, the **Ionians** had their feet firmly planted on the ground. What I find most appealing is their having produced so many men of learning. At a period when neighbouring

(above) Teos. Stone carving inspired by nature.
(below) Teos. Some of the ruins.

peoples were obsessed by a world dominated by death, the **Ionians** were founding cities that would remain as objects of wonder and admiration to future generations.

And not content with that, scholars like *Thales* studied the heavens at the risk of their own lives.

They engaged in a detailed study of the art of architecture and invented a style that has ever since been known by their own name: the *Ionic order*.

The column has twenty-four flutings, with a height nine times the diameter of the lower part of a column. But their finest achievement was to create a column capital of much greater simplicity and purity of line than the **Egyptian, Doric** or **Corinthian.**

For tall, slender lines are symbols of continuity and perpetuity. If you cut them at any point the magic is dispelled.

The *Egyptians* cut them off short with rough, coarse capitals. That was the type of architecture the age demanded.

The *Doric* order was the continuation of *Egyptian angst.*

The creators of the *Corinthian* column and capital finally threw off all restraint and indulged in an extravagant composition of boughs and leaves. The same sort of thing occurs when you gather a group of school kids in the stadium, make them walk past the king in strict formation and then blow the whistle and shout "You're free!". And immediately they're all over the place!.

The *Ionic* capital is a continuation of the line in the form of a curve.

It's as simple as that.

Simple?... Well, perhaps not!

Strabo was the the last of the writers who commented on **Ionian** civilization. He also mentioned **Teos.**

Now let us turn to the next city after **Alaçatı.**

And that is **Teos...** Or **Sığacık**, if you prefer the modern name.

To get to **Teos**, you should leave the main **Izmir** road and make your way towards **Güzelbahçe**. In other words, go along the **Çeşme** road.

You can make a stop at **Çeşme,** and then it's 60 km to **Seferhisar.** You will reach the harbour 9-10 km after **Seferhisar.** But don't forget, if you go at the right time of the year you can pick oranges and tangarines from branches hanging down over the walls on either side of the road for the whole of this 9 or 10 kilometres! But just a taste! Don't forget. You aren't on one of *Alexander the Great's* campaigns!

I don't advise you to lay in a week's stock of fruit!...

It's a really lovely experience to enter a town along a road lined with lemon, orange and tangarine trees

What's more, you land up at the sea-side... A small square... A medieval castle on your right... In front of you, fishermen's boats, guest-houses and restaurants...

But there's one thing I must keep on reminding you. Never do this trip in July or August. If you do, I take back everything I've said. So that you won't be disappointed.

Teos; but don't be taken in. To reach the ancient remains you have to go round the harbour and cross the ridge. It's an asphalt road. You always have the sea on your right. When you finally, after groping around in the vegetation, come across marble decoration, you will know that you are now in **Teos**. The temple directly opposite was dedicated to *Dionysos*. Originally a temple with thirty-six columns dating back to the 2nd century B.C., only a portion of it is now standing.

Making your way over cultivated fields and through wild vegetation you will finally come to a theatre nestling against the slope of the ridge, with pine trees growing out of its steps. This is also a product of the 2nd century B.C.

The dangers threatening every ancient settlement are also, unfortunately, present here. The shores of **Teos** are being invaded by new building construction work. A few more houses, a few more motels, a few more building cooperatives and **Teos** will be left sitting like a flowerpot in the middle. People can't leave things as they are. For most of them, ancient finds are things to be preserved in glass cases in a museum. Or displayed in the courtyards or salons of fashionable houses.

Take a theatre or a temple located beside a plum or a mulberry tree. Pick up a sack of wheat. The seeds you scatter around in a circle will become houses, motels, restaurants and places of entertainment.

Developments of that kind are not usually the work of the local inhabitants. How they pick up the scent I don't know, but it's always people from the great cities that find these places. They arouse the interest of the local authorities by holding out the bait of "profit", and get permission to construct the houses of their dreams.

The local inhabitants build barns and stables beside their houses. The fugitives from the cities are more interested in fire-places and a barbecue. People used to use brasiers for grilling meat. They used to be able to carry the brasier from one place to another. Now we have transformed the brasier into a monumental edifice.

> *"There's absolutely nothing like a fireplace! Invite all your friends and gather around it!"*

I've never once come across a fireplace that the owner of the house was able to light without filling the room with smoke. Either the wood is wet, or the chimney is merely decorative and doesn't draw properly or the host's scientific approach to lighting wood doesn't stand up to actual practice.

May the temple of *Dionysos* give protection to **Teos** and its ruins!

Prof. Ekrem Akurgal describes the ancient city as follows:

> *"The citizens of Teos depended mainly on commerce for their livelihood. Around 600 B.C. Thales proposed that Teos should be chosen as leader of the twelve Ionian cities because of its location in the very centre of Ionia. His proposal was not, however, accepted.*

> *"Alexander the Great planned to build a canal connecting Teos to the Gulf of Izmir.*

> *"...The Ionian branch of the Artists of Dionysos was founded at Teos at the end of the 3rd century B.C. but, although resident in Teos, the Artists gave performances in various other places. The fact that the Artists of Dionysos made Teos their centre was of great importance for the city, for their participation in the festivals of Dionysos was regarded as a sacred duty which endowed both their persons and their place of residence with inviolability....*

> *"One of the most celebrated citizens of Teos was the lyric poet Anacreon,*

The theatre at Teos.

who lived in the 6th century B.C. The bibliophile Apellicon, who pur-chased the library of Aristotle around 100 B.C. at a very high price, was also a native of the city."

What transpires from all this is that the very privileged place occupied by **Teos** vis-a-vis the other *Ionian* cities is to be attributed to its culture and political power.

If you have time, be sure to pay a visit to the small castle in **Sığacık** harbour. Climb up the few steps to the bastion and have a look at the view, and then go into one of the restaurants on the shore and enjoy the fish and the wine. If you feel like staying, there are several guest-houses around the harbour.

The countryside around **Teos** is quite rich in ancient remains. Twenty kilometres below **Teos** you will arrive at **Lebedos,** the least prosperous of all the early cities. According to *Strabo*:

> "...It was in **Lebedos** that the Artists of Dionysos, who were drawn from the whole of the Hellespont region, later took up permanent residence and it was here that they held an annual festival with games in honour of Dionysos."

If you proceed a little further inland from **Lebedos** (Gümüldür) you will arrive at **Colophon** (Değirmendere). That means a journey of about 25 km. According to *Strabo:*

> "Colophon was once renowned for its navy and its cavalry. The latter was so superior to any other cavalry force that in any doubtful engagement the Colophonians would at once call upon their cavalry, whose intervention was always decisive. Hence arose the expression, 'to put a colophon on it' , meaning 'to settle the matter once and for all'."

Akurgal gives the following description of **Colophon:**

> "The Colophonians gained great wealth as a result of the fertility of their soil and their maritime skills. This urban wealh transformed a comfortable life-style into excessive luxury. As many as a thousand citizens would stroll through the agora wearing luxurious garments and drenched in perfume. According to the ancient writers, this luxurious life-style led to Colophon's weakness and decline."

There is another city at some 15-20 km distance from **Colophon.** This is the city of **Notion.** It was actually the new city of the *Colophonians* who had lost their old power and freedom. The **acropolis** offers a wonderful view over the surrounding countryside. For scholars, the temple, the city walls of the **Hellenistic** period, the acropolis, agora and theatre offer invaluable opportunities for research.

...Quite near the old city of **Notion,** only about 2 km away, one finds another famous site with a **Temple of Apollo**: the ancient city of **Claros.**

With its spiral columns, column capitals and sacred well, **Claros** reminds one somewhat of a submerged city. This was the site of an oracle in the **Hellenistic** and **Roman** periods. It was, indeed, a world dominated by oracles.

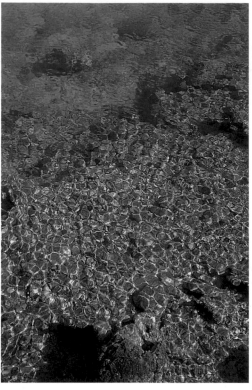

EPHESUS: CITY OF CULTURE, WEALTH AND EXUBERANCE

On the map, the road is shown bordered with green and yellow lines: meaning "scenic route".

A short journey along this yellow and green route from **Notion** will take you to **Pamucak** and **Ephesus**.

It confirms you in your hopes for nature and mankind. You never want to see another crowded city. Green and yellow routes are a real joy.

And then, quite suddenly, **Ephesus** appears in front of you, at the end of a tree-lined road.

It's time to gather your things together. Books, notes, and everything for a performance....

What performance?

No time to talk! The seats aren't numbered.

I have a large photograph in front of me. An aerial photograph. There are a number of names and signs on it but they in no way impair the value of the photograph itself. It is from the *Geo* magazine, March 1987 - a special number on Turkey. The three-page fold-out map is of **Ephesus**. The twenty-four thousand capacity **Ephesus** theatre looks out at me from the middle of the photograph like an oyster within its shell.

I find my place in the theatre. As in many a story, the shades of evening have not yet fallen. We are here to watch a performance by the *Moiseyev Dance Ensemble*.

The name **Ephesus** inevitably makes one think of *Artemis...*

With her elegant and noble stance, she has stood there smiling for thousands of years, surrounded by lions and griffons. In her breasts she bears the fertility of the soil and the fertility of mankind. Originating in

Central Anatolia, she has reigned since the time of the **Hittites,** the **Phrygians,** and the goddess **Kybele.**

George Thompson, in his book *"The Prehistoric Aegean",* declares that the Temple of Artemis at Ephesus existed there long before the arrival of the *Ionians.* If, as is generally supposed, the temple goes back as far as the *Hittites,* it must date from at least the 13th century B.C. According to *Thompson,* no other Greek temple has had such a long and uninterrupted history. At the same time he expresses his indebtedness to *Picard,* who has given a detailed account of the temple from the time of the Hittites up to the period of wealth and prosperity following its dedication to **Diana of the Ephesians.**

Artemis, in whose honour early summer festivals, dances and athletic competitions were held each year, is described by *Picard* in the following terms:

> *"She dominated the whole world. On the coming of spring it was Artemis who supervised the opening of the blossoms and the fertility of the soil. She ruled the elements and directed the winds and waters. She governed the life of the animals and protected all wild life. She was both a benefactress and the bearer of the souls of the dead. She was the healer of illnesses and the goddess of health. At the same time, she guided souls on their journey to the other world."*

It is impossible not to adore a goddess who thus symbolizes the harmony of nature. What objection could possibly be made to holding festivals in her honour in all the various branches of art, in all the beauty and exuberance of spring? A festival comprising poetry, drama, music and dance is the very epitome of the beauty of life, from whatever source it may spring. But all these must have some sort of foundation And that is why, in a polytheistic environment, the symbols created by human beings emerge in the form of gods and goddesses...

Statue of Artemis, symbol of beauty and fertility. Marble, 1st century A.D. Ephesus Museum.

As the lights dim, the *Moiseyev* dancers appear in brightly coloured costumes. *Moiseyev,* who was the first, over half a century ago, to found a dance company in his own name in the Soviet Union, exploits tradition-

al folk dances like a magician or a sorcerer. It is as if the **Ephesus** theatre were celebrating a festival of *Artemis. Moiseyev* utilizes to the full the whole potential of free human creativity. The dancers, gliding through the darkness of the night, manipulate the simple robes they are wearing with all the mystery of true sorcerers. All to the rhythm of a single drum...

The silversmith *Demetrius* made and sold small models of the **Temple of Artemis** at **Ephesus**. It was a very profitable trade, and it was not surprising that he should have been so strongly opposed to the mission of *St Paul*, who arrived in **Ephesus** to further the spread of Christianity. *Demetrius* collected thousands of people in the **Ephesus** theatre and shouted *"Great is Artemis of the Ephesians! Great is Artemis of the Ephesians!"* The crowd was finally dispersed by the authorities, but that was not the end of the affair. *St Paul* went on to **Macedonia,** and was later put to death. Meanwhile, *St John,* to whom *Christ* had entrusted his mother just before he died, arrived in **Ephesus**. Death and disorder continued uninterrupted in the city. That was why they chose **Selçuk** for the site of the **Church of St John.**

St John and the *Virgin Mary* are still revered at **Ephesus**, the one in the **Church of St John** in **Selçuk,** in which he is buried, the other in the **House of the Virgin** on **Bülbül Mt**. There are myths and legends in every age. The present-day legend of space is a modern example...

It is not only the marvellous architectural remains that attract the thou-

(above) Imaginary depiction of Ephesus in the 19th century. From La Borde "Voyage d l'Asie Mineure". (opposite page) From W.H.Bartlett, Ephesus in the 19th century.

(above) The large theatre at Ephesus.
(below) Meander motif inspired by the river of the same name. Temple of Hadrian.
(opposite page) Interior of one of the Ephesus houses on the slope, showing a harmonious fusion of art and life.

sands of visitors that visit **Ephesus** each year. Every building conceals a fascinating mystery.

And I am also fascinated by it. We may spend two fourths of our day chattering, but the other half is given over to our dreams. Either this dream or that! At least, at the end of the dream, you see monuments that have been standing here for thousands of years!

There has never been a community that could be described as an "empire of dreams". But empires, whether engaging in war or making or ensuring peace have dreams of their own... Perhaps this is the only-means by which a community can be preserved.

Let's do a little shopping. Let's go to the **Ephesus** market and the houses on the slope.

Actually I'm rather ashamed that in all those years I've never once gone out shopping in the **Ephesus** market.

Both sides of the road are flanked by meander motifs. In the centre, geometric designs contained in a circle; peacocks in each corner; the whole surrounded by floral motifs, and, immediately beside the floral motifs,

2

3

1,2,3. Nature, art, science and learning portrayed on the walls of one of the Ephesus houses on the slope.

spiral columns. This is the **Ephesus** market. Or rather a small road in the **Ephesus** market.

Just beside the market there is a flight of steps. This leads into a rather long road which curves to the right to bring us to the *houses on the slope*. These houses, all of which date back to the 2nd century A.D. or slightly later, once belonged to the shopkeepers in the market. Most of them have black and white floor mosaics, and a mosaic entrance leads one into a courtyard separated off by columns. There are frescoes in every room. The courtyard, which generally has a pool, provides the sitting space. The courtyard is well protected from the summer heat. Water is supplied to the slope through earthenware pipes and many of the houses have an underfloor hot air system to heat the rooms in winter. The kitchen is next to the bath. Some sections are decorated with vegetal motifs and figures of the gods, especially on the ceilings and vaults in the *eyvans*. Peacocks, geese and roosters are the favourite animals. There is a

continuous supply of water in the latrine and washplace. Some of the houses have two storeys. Every room contains statues of gods and goddesses.

I may be wrong but I think it's a story by *Oscar Wilde.* A hunter, at every return from the forest, tells of the mythical birds and creatures he has seen. He tells them the same story every day. One day, on his return from the forest, he remains absolutely silent. Nothing can make him describe what he had seen. They insist. *"Every time I come back from the forest I tell you what I have seen,"* he says, in a mixture of fear and suspicion. *"Well, yesterday I actually saw it!"*

Those who describe the **Ephesus** houses as *houses on the slope* have obviously never seen them. From the point of view of civil architecture and life-style they are pure myth.

These terrace houses, glimpsed through the monumental streets and monumental gates of **Ephesus,** remind one of *Oscar Wilde's* hunter. In such a case, neither seeing nor hearing is believing. And that for a period of some two thousand years.

1,2. Mosaics in the street in front of the Ephesus market.
3. The bees of the Aegean and the Mediterranean were transformed into a symbol. Piece of gold jewellery. Ephesus. 6th century B.C. Istanbul Archaeological Museum.

1,2,3. The Ephesus houses on the slope present a legendary example of domestic architecture.
4. Hawk, Terracotta. Ephesus. 6th century B.C. Istanbul Archaeological Museum.

The most striking thing is that these houses on the outskirts of this monumental city possess all the necessary household amenities. You probably know the Turkish villas on the **Haymana Plain.** I feel like asking you to come to **Ephesus** and take a look at the houses situated on this small insignificant slope.

Although I have promised not to make comparisons I know perfectly well I'm not going to keep my word. In any case, I haven't kept a single promise throughout the whole of this book!

I only want to congratulate the Austrians who carried out the excava-

tions here. This is a common effort based on the approach to culture as an international phenomenon.

There are so many things to amaze one here: the brothel, the expulsion of *St Paul* because he would have ruined the trade in the **Temple of Artemis**, the rabble-rousing silversmith *Demetrius*, the *houses on the slope.* One is also amazed by the tax immunity granted to teachers in higher educational institutions.

And those are not the only things that one may find amazing about the *Ephesians.* There is also their fickleness... First of all they support the *Seleucids* of **Syria**, then *Antiochus.* Then they support **Pergamon**, only to turn around and join the *Romans* against their former ally. And finally they join *Mithridates* of **Pontus** in his war against **Rome**. Their longest lasting friendship was probably that with the *Persians.* A whole fifty years!

The *Ephesians*, who regarded their city as the capital of **Ionia**, enjoyed the peak of their prosperity in the 6th century B.C. For the architects

Ephesus. The Curetes Street leading to the Library of Celsus seen from the houses on the slope.

who flocked into **Ephesus** from **Samos** and **Crete**, **Ephesus** was a continual source of employment. Such architects found their source of inspiration in **Assyria,** the **Hittite Empire** and **Egypt.**

On hearing the name **Ephesus** most of us immediately think of the theatre. Excavations have been continuing in **Ephesus** for over a century now, and although we should not, perhaps, judge on the basis of excavation and restoration alone, there can be no doubt that the **Library of Celsus** is something of which **Ephesus** can be truly proud. This was built at the beginning of the 2nd century A.D. by the Consul *Gaius Julius Aquila* in honour of his father *Celsus.* According to *Prof.Dr.Ekrem Akurgal,* he left an endowment of 25 thousand dinars for the purchase and care of the books.

The monumental character of the library resides in the architectural skill displayed. A certain amount of deception is required to give this narrow, two-storeyed building a monumental appearance. The deception consists of the optical illusion created by making the columns and capitals at the sides of the building smaller than than those in the centre. It is this stratagem, combined with the other architectural elements, such as

1

2

niches, statues, etc., that lends monumentality to the whole.

While strolling around the library I noticed a small opening where children were playing. This turned out to be one of two small doors in the interior walls opening into an inner chamber. This chamber was used to protect some twelve thousand scrolls from the effects of damp.

Let's turn to *Akurgal* for a more detailed description of the **Library of Celsus:**

> *"The library possesses a highly ornate facade which has been restored from the fragments yielded by the excavations. The facade was supported on four double columns with a niche behind each double column and a window and a door between them. On the first floor there are three doors with a window above each, while on the second storey there are three more windows on the same axis as those below. The reading room was thus illuminated by means of these doors and windows."*

The sarcophagus of *Celsus,* a magnificent piece of work adorned with garlands and rosettes, is to be found in a remote corner of the building.

It is impossible to draw a picture of **Ephesus** in one or two strokes.

This is an enchanted city... At every corner one finds a different civilization and a new mystery. War, treachery, folly, festivities, pomp and circumstance, destitution and scholarship all form part of this city's destiny.

But if you think that one day I'm going to open that *Pandora's box* and

3

1. The Curetes Street, named after the priests in the Temple of Artemis.
2. Entrance to the Temple of Hadrian on the Curetes Street.
3. Resting Warrior. Marble. Ephesus Museum.

147

(above) The Magnificent facade of the Library of Celsus.
(right) The street in front of the Library of Celsus, scene of festivities.

reveal the mystery you're quite mistaken.

The best thing is to find a place to stay in Selçuk and go backwards and forwards to **Ephesus** as often as you like.

The **Temple of Artemis** alone is enough to keep you fixed in **Ephesus**.

Let's see what the historian *Plinius* had to say about it in 79 B.C.

> *"The Temple of Artemis in Ephesus is a wonderful building of great magnificence. It took 220 years to build with the combined efforts of the whole of Asia. It was located in marshy ground so as to prevent damage by earthquakes, the marsh being covered with a layer of wool and charcoal, on which the temple itself was constructed. The structure is 425 feet long and 220 feet wide. The one hundred and twenty-seven columns were presented by various rulers. Each of these columns is 60 feet tall, and thirty-six are decorated with reliefs. One of the columns with reliefs was the work of the renowned sculpture Scopas."*

The **Temple of Artemis,** which soon took its place as one of the seven wonders of the world, was the first temple to be built on a monumental scale.

Let us not forget that the *Artemis* cult was an integral part of the Anatolian cultural tradition. *Artemis* belonged to the family of the moth-

The library built by the Consul Gaius Julius Aquila for his father Celsus at the beginning of the 2nd century A.D. contained 12,000 scrolls. The Consul Julius left 25,000 dinar for the purchase and conservation of the books.

er goddess *Kybele,* statues of whom, symbolising her as the goddess of fertility and dating date back to the 6th century B.C., were found in excavations at **Çatalhöyük** and **Hacılar**
This protectress of nature and animals, the symbol of plenty, the soil, rain and humanity appeared in the form of a number of different god-

House of the Virgin Mary. Interior.

THE VIRGIN MARY AT EPHESUS AND LOCAL LEGENDS

Christianity began to spread slowly throughout the region. It was one of the accepted traditions of the **Roman Empire** that Christians should also sacrifice to the cult of the Emperor. Should they refuse to comply they were proclaimed enemies of the state.

Four Christian youths who believed in the One God fled from the city for fear of their lives and took refuge in a cavern in **Mt Pion** near **Ephesus**. Here they remained in deep slumber for two hundred and fifty years.

The young men are known as *Eshab-ı kef,* or "companions of the cave". Their names were **Yemliha, Mislina, Mürselina, Mernuş, Tebernuş, Sazemuş** and **Kefeştatayuş.** There was also their dog *Kıtmır.*

In Western versions of the legend their names are given as **Maximilianos, Malchos, Marcianos, Ioannes, Denis, Serapion** and **Constantinos.** Their dog was called **Viricarius.**

The story has always been a very popular one in both the Christian and Islamic worlds. As a matter of fact, the legend of the **Seven Sleepers** is to be found even in the **Koran.**

The number "seven" has been regarded as a sacred number since the earliest times. The ancient *Egyptians, Sumerians, Iranians, Akkadians, Indians, Hittites, Greeks* and *Romans* regarded it sometimes as a lucky number, sometimes as an unlucky one. We find it in the *Seven Sages,* the *Seven Heavens* and the *seven-headed snake.*

The number seven still retains such qualities at the present day, particularly in folk songs.

Ephesus. Temple of Artemis. Seljuk.

The *Seven Sleepers* finally awoke and made their way into the town. On finding that their silver coins were no longer valid they realized that they had been sleeping for a great many years, for two hundred according to some people, for three hundred according to others. They also realized that there was now no one left who did not believe in the One God.

So they returned to their cave and fell once more into a deep slumber, this time for all eternity.

On learning of the event, the *Emperor Theodosius II* recognized in it a proof of bodily resurrection and initiated discussion on the subject. A church was founded on the spot where the *Seven Sleepers* had lain.

Ephesus, one of the most important centres of the Christian world, is a source of legend, of a world based on a fusion of dream and reality.

Before His death on the cross, *Christ* entrusted his mother *Mary* to the disciple *St John,* who was to devote the rest of his life to the protection and service of the *Virgin Mary.*

A few years after *Christ's* death, *St John* brought the *Virgin Mary* to **Ephesus,** and found a lodging for her near what is now the **Church of the Virgin Mary.** They later moved to the house on **Bülbül Dağı**.

This is now a very charming place of pilgrimage with a square, a cistern

and a restaurant, all set amidst trees.

But how was the house of the *Virgin Mary* discovered?

That is another product of the world of dreams and visions... A German by the name of *Catherine Emmerich* who had lived her whole life (1774-1824) in the one city and twelve years of her life confined to her bed, passed her time in journeys through the world of dreams.

She described in the most meticulous detail the place where the *Virgin Mary* had lived and was buried. And yet she had never in her life been to *Ephesus*. At first no one believed her, but subsequent researches undertaken by the Catholic Church confirmed her evidence and transformed her dreams into reality.

In 1892 the Archbishop of Izmir gave permission for religious ceremonies to be held there.

Controversy still persists in the Christian world on the question of the

1. *Seljuk hamam and the İsa Bey Mosque.*
2,3. *Entrance to the İsa Bey Mosque, an excellent example of Seljuk skill in traditional geometric decoration.*

The Church of St John and Seljuk Castle.

house of the *Virgin Mary,* but in 1961 the house was proclaimed a place of pilgrimage by *Pope John XXIII* and visits were made here to the site by *Pope Paul VI* in 1967 and *Pope John Paul II* in 1979.

It is a domed building constructed on a cruciform plan. The building itself would appear to date from the 6th or 7th centuries A.D. but experts have dated the foundations to the 1st century A.D.

It is not only for Christians that the house of the *Virgin Mary* is regarded as sacred. It has become a place of pilgrimage for Muslims.

*Vessel with clover-shaped mouth.
Bronze. 5th century B.C. Ephesus
Museum.*

Ephesus is an inexhaustible source for architects, researchers and travellers...

Don't be surprised if I tell you that the most extravagant example of **Seljuk** art is to be found here.

The **Seljuk** tradition was carried on in this city, then known as **Ayasuluğ**, by *Isa Bey* of the **Aydın Emirate**. During the *Emirate* period **Ephesus** was an important port much frequented by **Venetian** merchants and **Genoese** seamen.

Seljuk. Church of St John.

According to *Sabahattin Türkoğlu* in his book *"Efes'in Öyküsü:*

> *"Isa Bey gave great importance not only to public improvements and military matters, but also to art and scholarship. Aşık Pasha, in the introduction to a book dedicated to him, describes İsa Bey as 'both a scholar and a patron of scholars'."*

I don't know what it was about **Ephesus**, its climate or its character, but a distinguishing feature of its rulers was the importance they gave to art and learning.

That is why the **İsa Bey Mosque** is such a noble structure. The decoration and geometric design of the entrance door well substantiates any such claim.

Ephesus is not a place that can be fully appreciated at a cursory glance. Moreover, it isn't the sort of place that you can just "have a look at". Once you begin to walk along its main street there's no end to it. You will inevitably stop to examine the reliefs of the **Temple of Hadrian** or you will emerge as an art historian in pursuit of a beautiful young tourist!

But if you should go too far, you will be struck, not by the gods, but by the sun.

But whatever happens, **Ephesus** remains a great and fascinating city with its civilizations, its variety, and its interesting stories and events.

There is another city that completes this fascination. If you say "Oh no! Not another ancient city!" I can't blame you. But it's a town I'll just be passing through: **Selçuk.** If you don't like the idea I'll tell you the story of the seven youths reckoned enemies of the emperor who slept in a cave for two hundred years!

Ephesus is the living story of a monumental city and all the most valuable products of the city are collected together in the **Selçuk Museum.** It is in this museum that you can see *Artemis the Great,* as well as the

Artemis the Beautiful commissioned by a wealthy citizen some fifty years later.

But let us not ignore the small gold and silver figurines. Although small in size they are monumental in skill. The ivory frieze from one of the *houses on the slope* can hold its own with similar works in any other museum in the world in the skill and power of expression displayed by the craftsman.

This ivory relief depicts the war waged by the *Emperor Trajan* against the barbarians. The Emperor, his soldiers and horses are shown both before and in the heat of battle. It carries you right into the battle itself with all its fears, doubts and self-reliance.

Apart from this relief of the 1st century A.D. the museum contains theatre masks, a sun-dial, floor mosaics, a statuette of *Eros* riding a dolphin and, of course, the *God Bes,* which never fails to raise a smile on the spectator's face. All these are finds from the **Ephesus** houses. **Selçuk Museum** is a small but very rich museum. Moreover the peacock, doves and hens with little feet in the courtyard lend a particularly charming touch.

The guest-houses with their gardens and courtyards, the castle, and **İlyas Bey Mosque,** with its monumental entrance and the exuberant floral decoration that seems to mock the plainness of the wall, all make a visit to **Selçuk** an absolute must.

The other cities we have been talking about were located on the shore. They were all charactized by the presence of water, and blue and green colours. The learned citizens of the **Ionian** cities were well aware of the virtues of nature and the gods.

Now it's our own turn, and the turn of our own virtues!

Actually it's high time we were on our way. But first of all let us give the last word to *Stesicoras,* a writer of the 6th century B.C. who was struck blind for having libelled *Queen Helen* and who wrote the following verses

Seljuk. Stone carving from the Church of St John.

> *Forget war.*
> *This is an age for song.*
> *Take the Anatolian pipe*
> *Play the melodies*
> *Of the fair goddesses.*
> *The chattering swallows*
> *Are raising a clamour.*
> *Spring has come.*

KUŞADASI: A RIOT OF COLOUR AND COMMOTION

A woman with a large artificial rose in her hair. A tight white T-shirt. Wet shorts clinging to her body.

A man: Short and plump, with a vest with red lines on the edges and "Boss" in large letters on the front. Green, yellow, purple and red Bermuda shorts. Dark complexioned. Blue "tokyo" sandals. Trimmed moustache.

This is **Kuşadası.**

If you look up an encyclopedia you will get the following information about **Kuşadası:**

"The local inhabitants depend for their livelihood on tourism and agriculture. The southern shores of the Gulf of Kuşadası consist of sandy beaches. The first realization of the importance of tourism for the local economy was very soon followed by investments in a variety of fields and the construction of tourist accommodation in the form of hotels, motels, guest-houses and holiday villages, one of the latter being run by the French. This intense building activity has caused considerable damage to the natural and historical environment."

It was early evening when we arrived at **Kuşadası.** A building rather like **Galata Tower** rose up on my right. Probably a hotel. In another valley I could see a massive, pyramid-like building in process of construction.

A winding road leads down into **Kuşadası,** literally "**Bird Island**".. And then palms... Although visually, the palm is a tree of little significance, it is an indispensable feature of seaside towns. The streets are crowded. No one pays any attention to the traffic. The sound of music emerges from every shop, coffee-house and restaurant along the promenade and in the streets behind. All an invitation to the riot and revelry!..

I wonder if there really used to be birds on **Bird Island**? Perhaps some migratory birds. But there I go, yielding to temptation again. As if there

162

were any necessity for truth to conform to appearance.

We change our clothes and make our way by the side streets carefully avoiding cars and headlights.

I go into a grocer's on the slope to get cigarettes.

"Hello" says the assistant.

"Hello! , I reply, *"Two packets of Rothmans, please."*

"Hello, hello, hello!" he says. *"Anything else, mate?"*

"What do you do when a German comes?" I ask.

"Always hello, mate!" he answers.

Kuşadası is essentially an island of hills. Hills that suddenly begin on the other side of the coastal strip. Every street, every hill is a riot of colour and commotion. At the very bottom of a shop sign with "Restaurant, cafe, bar, pub" you'll find "Shish kebap".

The music emerging from every corner is mingled with the bleating of sheep. There are sheep tied to electric standards or door-knockers, sheep attached to the window grilles. Their voices are hoarse from

(above) Enjoying life on the Kuşadası embankment.
(below) The only beauty in Kuşadası that has managed to survive.

(above) Kuşadası. The marina and espanade with palm trees.
(below) Street alongside the Öküz Mehmet Paşa Caravanserai.

bleating incessantly thoughout the whole day. Even the swish and thump of the ghetto blasters in the passing cars can't drown out their pathetic bleating.

It's one thing buying meat from the butcher's, but it's quite another to see these sad creatures that remind you of the ram's heads of the ancient world. Anger mingled with an intuition of death.

Tomorrow it's Kurban Bayram. I shan't be able to go out. Perhaps the best thing would be to put my horse goggles on and set out for an ancient city. The most crowded part of **Kuşadası** is the pedestrian precinct beside the Caravanserai. And it's quite a gay sort of place. Everyone's drinking beer. There's an Ottoman pasha over there sitting on a stool, a great turban on his head! Epaulettes, medals. White beard and white moustache. He's chatting up a European bird in pidgin English. On the stool behind them there's someone playing a "saz".

We continue on our way, holding hands so as not to lose each other. This time we meet a Janissary. If it weren't that we usually try to find a place without music we would collapse into the nearest restaurant and have a meal. Fatigue is finally getting the better of us when the lights go out all over the city. The **Bird Islanders** are so used to it that generators immediately switch into operation in most of the shops.

When the lights come on again everyone cheers. And at last we are able to find a restaurant. I insist on drinking wine in spite of everything. Ice-cold wine, white cheese, shepherd's salad, melon and chips. It must be the effect of the wine but I am no longer disturbed by the crowd and torrents of music that flood past. But just then I hear the tinkling of a bell. I think of the sheep. *"Someone's tied a sheep up somewhere near here."* I think, and then I notice the little bell hung up in the ice-cream shop to announce the arrival of a customer. The area in front of the Post Office is probably the most colourful spot in town. There is a continual crowd of people from every nation in the world. It's a hunting ground for our tall, dark, curly-headed youth! The foreigners are only too pleased to find people taking an interest in them.

In holiday places the area in front of the shop-door has a very special importance; it's a conversation corner. It's the same in front of the counter inside. This particular shop was a jeweller's, I think. Foreigners were sitting there, some of them drinking tea, some of them *rakı!*

The **Kuşadası** shopkeepers are very friendly and good-tempered. They've really devoted themselves to tourism. They offer every possible service to the tourist. But the tinkling of bells reminds one of **Bodrum.** A coastal city that has lost itself in unbridled riot and revelry.

The two most beautiful palm trees in **Kuşadası** are those in front of the Caravanserai. These two palms form a striking contrast with the blank stone wall behind them. We sit under them drinking coffee and eating ice-cream. The sound of drums emerges from the main arched entrance. Western music in the background. They're probably presenting a special entertainment for the foreigners inside the Caravanserai.

Picking up our newspapers and magazines we begin to make our way up to our guest-house. There is a narrow flight of steps between the houses. The balcony of one house and the terrace of another open right on to this flight of steps. On the terrace in front of one of the houses an old man is sitting drinking *rakı.* With obvious relish he is cutting the meat off a large bone he is holding in his hand. He is probably preparing *kavurma* for the following day.

In **Kuşadası** the sound of riot and revelry steadily increases. It will stop at exactly five o'clock in the morning, then continue unabated throughout each of the following days, always stopping at exactly the same time....

We get up early. The sea is blue and calm. There are four ships in the bay: the *Ariadne, Samos, Renaissance* and *Pegasus.* Everything here is dominated by mythology and art.

Nightlife in Kuşadası.

We decide to have a swim and then get on our way. The beach in **Kuşadası** itself is the most suitable. They haven't started slaughtering the sheep yet. They're probably too tired to get up so early in the morning. There are some foreigners lying basking on the beach The sea urchins are visible on the floor of the sea. A couple of hours later a large group makes its way to the wooden landing-stage. Sunshades are opened up, tables and chairs are brought along. As soon as the music starts up and the clatter of backgammon begins we slip quietly away.

There's a place in **Kuşadası** my friends and I always go to. **Aşiyan.** Perhaps there's nothing very special about *Mehmet Aşiyan's* kilim and carpet shop, but every single one of the kilims he spreads out in front of

you seems to issue a challenge in the name of the Anatolian civilizations.

Each is a wonderful specimen of a tradition that dates back thousands of years. The stylized vegetal motifs, the hidden meaning, the technical excellence, the mastery of colour, are all characteristic of the sensitivity, exuberance and reserve of the local population.

Mehmet Aşiyan is marvellously skilled in telling the story that lies behind each of them. And he is also a connoisseur of culinary delights.

If I were to say that *Mehmet Aşiyan* is a real honour to **Kuşadası** I shouldn't be far wrong. And he is also a guide who has a detailed knowledge of the historical structure of Turkey, and here, in his shop, we meet friends from many different countries of the world.

Then we taste, one by one, the starters laid out in a quiet restaurant we know. After that we'll have fish baked in the oven.

Then back to the shop late at night to enjoy the knots and the dyes of the Anatolian kilims in a tradition of thousands of years.

The world of kilims is a festival in itself.

"Make the coffees 'orta', please."

(above) Mehmet Aşiyan, Kuşadası's
cultural ambassador.
(opposie page) A yörük kilim from
Mehmet Aşiyan's collection.

167

PRIENE, HIPPODAMOS AND ENDLESS NATURE: THE DİLEK PENINSULA

It is 20 kilometres from **Kuşadası** to **Söke**, and about the same distance from **Söke** to **Priene**. Both roads are quite good and very pleasant. The open square and coffee-houses at the entrance to **Priene** are quite unexpectedly quiet and attractive. That may, of course be just the way it appears to us after the spider's web of concrete buildings in **Kuşadası**, but I don't really think so. The small square, the trees, the stone walls, the terraced restaurant, the telephone box and, a little further on, the tea garden with pool under the fruit trees is perfectly suited to the entrance to an ancient city. There's a certain proportion in everything. In the rakı, wine, conversation, enthusiasm. Even in a certain craziness! Rural life is one thing, rural idiocy another. Getting merry is one thing, drinking like a fish another.

And it's quite another thing to cover beaches, forests and mountains with tasteless concrete buildings in the name of tourism.

Priene is an ancient **Ionian** city nestling against the mountain slope. A long, stone-paved road leads up to the **Temple of Athena**. Daughter of *Zeus,* the father of the gods, and patroness of the fine arts, *Athena* is described by *Hesiod* in the following terms:

> *And one day Zeus bore from his head*
> *The valiant, grey-eyed Athena*
> *The goddess that set the world at odds*
> *The indefatigable commander of armies*
> *The lover of battle and war-cries*
> *The highest of the highest.*

View over the Söke plain, once covered by the sea, from Priene, a city created by the ancient town-planner Hippodamos.

(above) Priene streets inersecting at right angles.
(below) Priene in the 19th century. La Borde,
"Voyage de l'Asie Mineure".
(opposite page) The Ionic columns of the Temple
of Athena rising up in defiance of Mt Mykale.

The fluted columns with their **Ionic** capitals are only just visible from the plain but each of them seems to be issuing a challenge to both man and nature. Whatever the field of activity in which they were engaged, the founders of the cities were skilled and well-informed individuals who, in the 4th century B.C., left a legacy to our own age. This skill and mastery did not, however, arise sometime in the 4th century B.C. The same skill and mastery was to be found in the 7th century B.C. and even earlier. *Prof. Dr. Ekrem Akurgal* describes the **Temple of Athena** as follows:

> *"The Temple of Athena in Priene was built by the architect Pytheos, who was also responsible for the Mausoleum of Halicarnassus, one of the Seven Wonders of the World and who presented in this building a classical example of Ionian architecture. We also learn from Vitruvius that Pytheos himself had published a book on architectural method."*

(It would be very interesting if our own architects were to reveal their architectural methods!)

Priene is now an inland city, but *Strabo* gives the following description of it in the 1st century B.C.:

> *"The soil was of a brittle, friable nature, and at the same time easily inflammable because of the large salt con-*

tent. It was probably because of this that the Meander [Menderes] continually changed its course and followed a winding path. At various times, silt was carried down to the lower ground by the river, while torrents washed part of the soil down into the sea. The accumulation of silt over a distance of 40 stadia converted Priene, formerly a port, into an inland city."

Research into the ancient world through its monuments and legends is a truly pleasurable activity, and it is also something of great interest to our own day and our own age. It is not for me to declare that they were good and we are bad, but there is one thing I cannot understand, and that is why we are so slow to learn from what has taken place on our own soil. It is because of our failure to do our homework that we have done so much harm to our country.

There was once someone in **Priene,** now known as **Güllü Bahçe,** or "rose garden" (and indeed it is set amidst flowers) by the name of *Hippodamos...* I wonder if you've heard of him? I certainly wouldn't if I

hadn't paid a visit to **Priene.** He is one of those that we tend to forget in the noise and bustle of modern life. He is said to have lived at the end of the 6th or the beginning of the 5th centuty B.C. His youth must have been spent at the time of the ravages wrought by the *Persians*. You are wondering what he did?

Hippodamos was the first town planner and the author of a book on town planning and administration.

Ord. Prof. Dr. Arif Müfit Mansel gives the following account of **Hippodamos** in his *Ege Tarihi* (History of the Aegean):

> *"The excavations conducted at Priene and Miletos and the soundings made at Alexandria and Antakya provide evidence that these cities were laid out according to the Hippodamos system with streets running parallel or perpendicular to each other to form square or rectangular blocks, and allowing the very skilful creation, where necessary by joining several blocks together, of public squares and public buildings. The best example of a city laid out in this orderly manner is offered by Priene."*

This grid system is known to have been employed in **Western Anatolia** prior to this date, but the Miletian expert who utilized the traditions of his own country to transform it into the *"Hippodamos System"* deserves to be treated with respect. The style became so popular and so widespread that it could be found all over the ancient world from **Macedonia** to **Alexandria**, and from **Italy** to **Rhodes.**

And there is something else we should remember. These cities do not consist merely of magnificent temples, theatres and monuments. Factors such as water, wind and temperature were also taken into account. The houses were five or six metres high and roofed with tiles. Almost all of them had courtyards. Finds include fragments of bedsteads, brasiers, oil-lamps and statues. And the bathrooms are certainly not to be ignored.

Alexander the Great, who undertook the rebuilding of the city, is said to have stayed in one of these houses during the siege of **Miletos**. This house was later repaired by the wealthy citizens of **Priene** and invested with a sacred significance.

The theatre at **Priene** is one of the most important theatres of the ancient world. Concerts and shows of various kinds were presented there, and appropriate measures were taken for speakers who went on a little too long. A water clock was permanently set up there, the pedestal of which is still standing today, but there was one learned citizen of **Priene** to whom I very much doubt if this time restriction was ever applied. Let's listen to **Strabo** for a moment:

> *"Bias, one of the Seven Sages of antiquity, was a native of Priene. In one place Hipponax remarks of someone that 'he will have to be more powerful in defence than Bias of Priene'."*

I have a feeling that when **Bias** ascended the rostrum the **Prienians** paid very little attention to their sandglasses!

The Senate House at Priene, open to an endless expanse of nature.

I experienced a strange sort of thrill on looking down to the plain from the **Temple of Athena**. In front of me there was an endless expanse of green, while behind me reared up the whole pomp and circumstance of past millennia. This is **Mt Mykale**, described by *Strabo* as being *"full of wild animals and covered with trees."* Today the mountain is saluted by

the five columns that have managed to survive, and we leave to nature the fate of the fragments that have been lying there for thousands of years.

On my right, **Doğanbey, Karine** and the **Dilek Peninsula.** This peninsula is now under conservation order. May the *Goddess Athena* bless whoever it was who took this decision.

The road that winds its way over the plain leads to another ancient city: **Miletos,** the birthplace of the town-planner *Hippodamos.*

Although the most ancient city of **Ionian** civilization, **Priene** never played a very influential role in political life, remaining for most of its history under the hegemony of **Athens, Pergamon** or **Rome.**

Hippodamos. so arranged the city that one could enjoy the cool breezes from the plain in the 4 m wide side streets.

It probably never occurred to them that this regular urban layout would be shared by so many other nations.

According to *Ekrem Akurgal:*

> *"The city faces south, with the main roads running east to west, and the side streets in the form of flights of steps cutting these at right angles north to south. The theatre, the stadium, the most important colonnaded buildings like the Sacred Stoa and the southern stoa of the Temple of Athena, as well as the living rooms in most of the houses, face south. In this way, the living and reception rooms received the sun throughout the winter, while in summer the sun was high above the houses and the rooms reasonably cool."*

Priene was undoubtedly a city of great magnificence, with its **Temple of Athena, Temple of Olympios,** agora, gymnasium, theatre, senate house and its bronze and marble statues. This was no doubt the reason for its being chosen as the seat of a bishop in the **Byzantine** period.

Of the statues, only the pedestals have survived.

The 190 m stadium and the theatre seating 5000, one of the finest examples of the early **Hellenistic** theatre, are now surrounded by pine trees.

The seats in the front of the theatre with the panther paws embrace the body so snugly you never want to get up - wonderful evidence of the skill of the marble mason.

The altar before which animals were sacrificed on holy days are placed exactly in the centre of these tiers of seats.

The early evening is the best time of day for a visit to **Priene**. In the set-

The 5000 capacity theatre at Priene was one of the most famous buildings of ancient times. Bias, one of the Seven Sages, gave his speeches in this threatre.

ting sun, the **Söke** plain in front makes you feel as if you were standing in the old port.

Another important feature of the city is its present-day aspect. With its square surrounded by pine, poplar and plane trees, the restaurant with its pool and fountain, the guest-house and tea-garden under the orange and tangarine trees, it offers rest and relaxation to the tired traveller.

Such features are enough, and more than enough, to persuade one to spend a few days in **Priene.**

Priene. Repairing carpets in Güllübahçe.

I hope that it will never be inundated by crowds of visitors, and that permission will never be given for the construction of new buildings. **Priene** is the most peaceful spot in the whole of the surrounding region. The people are very friendly. They keep all their troubles and anxieties to themselves. They show little inclination to back one another. Even if they wanted to preserve the environment the question as to who would profit most would very probably create silent storms in a glass of water.

If you go out on to the main road keeping **Priene** on your right, you will see a great expanse of level ground on your left. This is the famous **Söke** plain.

If you (I don't mean the driver, I mean the passengers in the other seats) look out towards the right you will see the **Temple of Athena** nestling against the slopes of **Mt Mykale** (Samsun Dağ) at a height of 100 m above sea-level.

The fluted columns with their **Ionic** capitals would appear to have stood for thousands of years in defiance of both man and nature.

I advise you to climb this road at 60 kmh. It is short, and with practically no traffic. The small villages of **At Burgazı, Tuz Burgazı, Doğanbey** and **Karine** all lie within 15 km.

The place-name *"burgaz"* is derived from a Greek word meaning *"small town"* or *"castle"*.

Immediately to the right of the **Yeni Doğanbey** and **Karine** road there is a very good road leading towards the mountains. This is the village of **Eski Doğanbey,** formerly known as **Domaçya.**

This is an abandoned village on the slopes of the *"National Park"* on the shores of **Dilek Peninsula.**

The village has undergone two emigrations. The first was when the **Greeks** abandoned the vineyards from which they had made their living and migrated to **Salonica** leaving the monastery, the hospital, the olive oil workshops and the one or two-storeyed houses just as they stood.

Priene (Güllübahçe). Statue of Aphrodite. Marble. Hellenistic Period, 3rd-2nd century B.C.. Istanbul Archaeological Museum.

The second emigration took place in 1983, when the inhabitants who had settled here after the departure of the Greeks decided to abandon the village with its narrow streets and poor communications for a site one or two kilometres lower down in the midst of vineyards, thus becoming inhabitants of **Yeni Doğanbey.**

And now the village is faced by new immigrants - the emigrants from the cities!

You know how it is.....

Eski Doğanbey (Domaçya Village), a popular refuge for writers, painters and scholars. The village, nestling against the slopes of the Dilek Peninsula National Park, is now under conservation.

In recent years a great flood has begun - of inhabitants of the villages to the cities and inhabitants of the cities to the villages and the shores. The whole thing is proceeding so rapidly that it's quite impossible to follow. It's coming to a point where we shall have to ask our friends their addresses as we pass them on the road!

Another inexplicable phenomenon is our combination of nomadic instincts with a deep-seated yearning for a settled existence, whether

179

Karine. A dead end forming, in a sense, the frontier post of the National Park. Here are to be found fishermen's huts made of reeds and fishermen's restaurants on wooden planks. Gray mullet and bream are bred in the fish-farms here.

our home is in a mountain village or a coastal city.... Whatever we could possibly need for our everyday existence we lug along to our new home.

As far as I can see, we Turks have never had much love for the sea or for sea-shores, and we've always been somewhat apprehensive of nature, with its flowers and green vegetation. For example, the **Bosphorus** was never really popular because of the supposed "dampness" while upland pastures remained confined to people who were used to the climate. I was amazed to hear the owner of a hotel one and a half or two kilometres from **Lake Iznik** tell me that in the whole of twelve years he had never once been down to the shore of the lake.

Now, "thank goodness", we are in an age of easy transport. As soon as we hear of something, we can get on a bus at midnight and be at that particular shore or that particular village the following morning. It's quite obvious that:

There is a village there, far away,
Whether we go there or not
It is still our village.

are sentiments now to be found only in books.

It is the **Aegean** and southern shores, which are the first to welcome the sun and the warm weather, that are experiencing the greatest flood of immigration....

Actually, the village of **Doğanbey** has nothing of the old magnificence of **Bodrum, Marmaris** or **Cunda Island.** Moreoever, it isn't on the shore. That's why writers, artists and scholars have chosen the place just to be able to be by themselves and to escape into the *"National Park"* against which it nestles or visit the inland towns in the vicinity. Just as I've chosen it for my own refuge!...

It is a real Utopia.

As in various other places in the mountains or on the shores, the sometimes taciturn, sometimes impetuous, sometimes garrulous, sometimes creative writer, artist or scholar, has chosen, in preparing a refuge for himself, to approach nature and the environment with full respect. He has begun to repair the narrow, cobbled streets and the abandoned houses. The planes, pines and olive trees that dominate the vegetation constitute an integral part of the natural environment.

Although the two hundred or so houses that have survived from the old village are in very poor condition (only some six or seven buildings are still standing) the abandoned village is now an object of the instinct of self-preservation, the most important feature of which is the desire of friends and family to be together. It has nothing to do with *"time share"* schemes or *"cooperatives"*.

There are no limits to dreams, and it is a very fine thing that craftsmen in wood, iron and stone should be sought out in **Istanbul, Bursa, Safranbolu** and **Denizli,** while at the same time local craftsmen should be encouraged to preserve the old features of the town.

But there is one danger. A rumour that has been spreading around since 1990 could, in a single night, transform the little village into a **Bodrum,** a **Marmaris**, a **Cunda** or a **Didyma**. We are like locusts. Once we pick up the scent we swarm around a spot without knowing why. We start off from a conviction that *"the intellectuals must know something!"* , and yet, for years, writers, artists and scholars have been doing everything they can to promulgate a knowledge of art and culture and no one has paid the slightest attention to them. But nowadays the term *"property"* immediately calls up the image of *"profit"* and no one is prepared to believe that you are just looking for somewhere to lay your head!

In face of this imminent danger, the *Izmir Commission for Ancient Monuments* has adopted a very imaginative approach to the conservation of the old village of **Domaçya** and its environs.

Let's be frank. The predominant notion at the present day is to gain pri-

As you sail round the tip of the Dilek Peninsula three islands appear in front of you: Tavşan Island, Su Island and Sandal Island. If you are lucky, you may catch a glimpse of wild horses roaming under the trees on Dilek Peninsula.

Open-air train museum at Çamlık on the road between Kuşadası and Söke.

vate profit through destruction. It seems to occur to no one to ask what sort of environment we are bequeathing to future generations, and yet for thousands of years almost every acre of Anatolian soil has played host to great civilizations. The city of **Priene**, situated quite near **Eski Doğanbey**, is one of these.

It is, therefore, essential that the whole region surrounding **Priene**, from **Güllü Bahçe**, the site of the ruins, and including **Dalyan, Zeytinlikler** and **Karine,** should be placed under strict supervision by the local authorities without bothering to await the issue of some official document.

It is the only hope for a sound environment and a healthy world in the future.

It is this hope that has resulted in the **Dilek Peninsula's** being placed under conservation.

The pine trees on the right hand side of the road leading from the village of **Eski Doğanbey** to **Karine** act as a shady awning over **Dalyan.**

Karine is a dead end, the edge of the *National Park,* but here you can find the wicker shelters of the the fishermen under the palm trees and, in summer, the fishermen's restaurants.

The sea at **Dalyan** is very shallow. You can't bathe here, but at least no one can interfere with the few surviving crested pelicans.

The sea is rich in fish - gray mullet, red mullet, dentex, sea bream, gilt head bream, sea bass and sole.

Dalyan supplies most of the restaurants along the coast as far as **Kuşadası** with fish, particularly gilt head bream and sea bass.

Dilek Peninsula, on the other hand, is practically virgin. The most striking proof of this, apart from the wild pigs, hares and stone martens that may suddenly appear on the road in front of you, are the herds of wild horses.

When I first heard people talk of wild horses I thought it was pure myth. Accounts given me by friends of what they had seen while walking along the mountain road through the forests sounded exactly like the old travellers' tales.

But when, while exploring the bays around the peninsula by boat, I saw three wild horses among the pine trees on the shore, I realised that it was no myth. They were of different colours - one was white, another chestnut and the third a bay.

The sea is dead calm. We can see the animals on the sea floor around **Tavşan Island, Su Island** and **Sandal Island.** Just then our notice is attracted by the movement of the horses under the pines. They're a long way away. It's too shallow for us too go any nearer the shore and in any case we don't want to startle them. We prefer to watch them through binoculars...

We decide to spend the night there and set about preparing our wierd meal. All the time we can hear the cries of the jackals from the shore.

To reach the **Dilek Peninsula**, or rather the *"National Park"*, you branch off to the right 28 km along the **Kuşadası-Söke** highway. It's a small road but it's sign-posted.

The road passes through **Davutlar**. The whole area is one great construction site. Thousands of summer houses. It's absolutely appalling.

One hates to think what would have happened to **Dilek Peninsula** had it not been placed under conservation.

As you pay the entrance fee at the gate of the park, you can see through the pines a number of small coves that join together to form large beaches. It's fairly crowded at weekends, but during the week all these little coves are free for you to choose. The sea is a variegated blue and green for as far as you can see.

Dilek Peninsula covers 11,012 hectares traversed by deep canyons. The highest point is **Dilek Tepesi** at 1237 m.

According to the good books it was formed by the action of the Meander River over a period of five hundred million years. It has a very rich vegetation cover containing examples of all the various types of vegetation characteristic of the **Aegean, Mediterranean, Black Sea** and **Marmara** shores: cluster pine, juniper, wild pear, myrtle, cornel, jasmine, chestnut, cypress, lime, plane, oak and larch, besides many varieties of heath and brushwood.

They also mention a type of *Mediterranean seal.*

Streams such as **Bal Deresi, Bülbül Deresi, Kavaklı Deresi, Karasu Deresi** and **Görünmez Dere** flow down to the shores. The **Şarlak Deresi** through **Doğanbey** is now dried up. Perhaps it will come to life again one day!

The **İçmeler, Aydınlık, Kavaklı** and **Karasu** beaches are open to the public.

Dilek Peninsula is a gift from nature to the people of our time. *"Come and* *see my loveliness and my unspoilt beauty,"* it seems to be saying.*"Then protect me for the sake of your own future."*

I don't expect anyone to pay any attention. If they had, a crackpot project like **Davutlar** would never have been allowed.

It may seem an over-harsh judgment, but we humans seem to have been created with a mission to destroy both our present and our future.....

If it hadn't been for the **Dilek Peninsula** I might have been able to put up with all the ugliness that normally confronts us.

But when I see such magnificent beauty I begin to ask myself if I am really a man for this age.

The answer is by no means a simple one.

The best thing is to go back to our own shores and our own cities. We'll spend the night in **Priene** and set out after breakfast.

There's another interesting feature about **Dilek Peninsula**: its proximity to the island of **Samos (Sisam)**.

"Karakol Point" on the **Dilek Peninsula** is only two miles from *"Katsouni Point"* on the island of **Samos**. Between them lies the island of **Boynak**.

According to *Strabo*, *"Cnidos and Smyrna and other places produce a very fine wine the effects of which are both pleasurable and of medicinal value. Samos cannot be reckoned very fortunate as far as wine is concerned, but in other ways they are very lucky."*

Samos is now famous for its *rakı*. It may not have been so successful with its wine but it has certainly succeeded with its *rakı*.

In 1993 I sailed to **Samos** with some friends in a boat called *"My Dream"!* The ancient city of **Pythagoreion** was dedicated to *Hera*, the most powerful of all the gods.

The district of **Vathy** nestling on the slope reminds one of the citadel of Antalya with its houses with red-tiled roofs, shuttered windows and narrow streets, its coffee-houses, in which wine is sold by the glass, the old women crocheting lace and the vine branches covering the roads.

Coffee-house in Vathy on the island of Samos two miles from Dilek Peninsula.

The use of the streets as sitting rooms is a distinguishing feature of the whole of the **Aegean** and **Mediterranean** region.

Below the city of **Samos** there is another city, immediately opposite **Dilek Peninsula**, in which **Pythagoras** was born in 580 B.C. and which was named **Pythagoreion** in memory of the renowned mathematician and philosopher.

While making your way from Kuşadası to Söke don't be surprised if you come across a landscape that reminds you of an Ottoman miniature.

It gives one a wonderful feeling to remember the famous thinker in the city from which he fled to Italy to escape the despotic rule of the tyrant of **Samos**.

Yes, a sea common to the **Aegean** and **Mediterranean** civilizations.

187

THE TEMPLE OF APOLLO AT DIDYMA AND THE OLIVE GROVE OF THE SCIENTIST THALES AT MILETOS

The oracular world of the Temple of Apollo may engage your intellect, but it is the decorative skill of the stone-masons that offers a feast to the eyes.

The ancient cities on the Aegean coast, although not exactly within visibility distance, are fairly close to one another. Would you think it an exaggeration if I were to say that it is perhaps the twelve colonies making up the **Ionian** cities that keep the Aegean alive?

And would you be angry if I were to add that these settlements, that constitute both a maritime and a land culture, give a considerable boost to our *"prestige"*.

There is no need to go into details. A glance at **Ephesus** and **Didyma**, without bothering about the ancient cities to the north and the south, will suffice.

I should imagine **Ephesus** is some 115 or 120 km from **Didyma (Didim).** It is 20 km from **Priene** to **Miletos**, and about the same distance from **Miletos** to **Didyma.**

What would you say if I told you that in that 120 km coastal strip there were four theatres capable of seating a total of forty-six thousand spectators?

These theatres, used for festivals, festivities, concerts, plays and judicial disputations, were all the products of an architecture that paid due respect to nature.

All this is not, of course, the only source of *"prestige"*, but it symbolizes it to a certain extent. When a festivity is in progress no one lies around in the meadow.

Let's look at the very sparse population in these cities, all so close to one another, in those days. No one would build a theatre to seat twenty thousand for a population of one thousand. The use of these buildings for the local inhabitants as well as spectators from the neighbouring

1. Columns in the Ionic order, the most simple and harmonious of all the styles of architecture so far attempted.
2. Engraving of Didyma in the 19th century, from Charles Texier, "Voyage de l'Asie Mineure".
3. The Temple of Apollo in the 19th century, from Charles Texier, "Voyage de l'Asie Mineure".
4, 5, 6, 7. The Temple of Apollo. Details of the decoration.

towns demanded a great deal of organization. There was the question of rain, water and wind.

But I don't want to make comparisons.

Meanwhile it would be a good idea to take a glance at *Heredotus.* Or even at *Homer.* In addition to combining the history of the 5th century B.C. with a number of legends and actual events he also quotes phenomena that reveal the social structure of the time. For example:

There may not be much connection between *Nitocris,* the queen of **Babylon,** and ourselves, but it's a good story:

> *"She had an open air tomb constructed on a platform placed over the busiest gate of the city and had an inscription carved on it. The inscription ran as follows: 'If any of the kings of Babylon that succeed me should find himself in financial difficulties, let him open this tomb and take as much of the treasure within as he needs. But beware, let him not open the tomb unless he is truly in difficulties, for in that case he will gain no benefit from it.*
>
> *"No one touched the tomb, until Dareios came to power years later. Dareios could see no point in leaving the gate unused and not profiting from a treasure that lay ready to hand. (No one could pass through the gate because it would have meant passing under the body.) So he opened the tomb. There was no treasure in it Only a corpse and a message: 'Had you not been so greedy for money and so shamelessly avaricious you would never opened up a place where the dead had taken refuge'."*

You can just imagine the humiliation *Dareios* must have felt in front of his people, and how eagerly the story of the incident would be related by one person to the next.

3

4

5

6

7

The Temple of Apollo dominates the sky.

I wanted to see **Didyma** first on our way through **Priene** to **Miletos** and **Didyma**. My aim was to see the monumental **Temple of Apollo** before proceeding to anything else.

Whatever book or magazine you happen to pick up or whatever post-card of **Didyma** you happen to see, you are sure to find a picture of the **Temple of Apollo** dominating the skyline.

Myriads of foreign tourists come to **Didyma** every year to see this temple with its one hundred and twenty-four columns.

There's no need to go into details of *Apollo's* nature and identity. A large part of mythology is devoted to either *Apollo* or *Dionysos. Apollo* repre-

The infinite meander motif and fluting are essential features of the Temple of Apollo.

sents a wholesome approach to nature, light, intelligence and aesthetic beauty; the noble beauty of power.

And when we look back at our books we shall find great fluted columns piercing the sky with a number of different floral motifs beside the simplified, stylized *Meander* motif which reminds most of us of the *Swastika,* the symbol of the *Nazis* and of *Hitler,* the great vandal. The simplicity of the motifs is the result of a long tradition. Books of art history mention this motif as representing the windings of the **Meander** River. Which may be true enough.... But the same motif is to be found among the **Hittites** as a symbol of life.

The decoration of the Temple of Apollo is inspired by nature.

If your dreams permit, and if you can escape from the metallic cacophony of car-horns and street vendors, you can make your way under the scorching sun into the mysterious atmosphere of the temple. **Didyma** was an **Ionian** sanctuary. The present-day structure was the third great temple of the **Hellenistic** world.

Its connection with *Apollo* ensured its careful conservation throughout the various epochs. The construction itself continued until well into the Roman period. On this temple alone the prosperity of the whole of the present-day population could be based. If only it were!.....

I take another look at the photographs. There are people sitting on the steps on all four sides of the temple - old, young, ugly and attractive.

In another photograph we find the head of a *Medusa*, with slightly raised eyebrows and a disgruntled, sulky expression. The lips are half open... The hair is curly. There's a knot under the chin...

As we entered **Didyma** we could see the temple in the distance. Then we passed quickly by and began looking for a restaurant. It was mid-day, we were hungry and we wanted something to eat. We went right to the end of the road. We were still wondering where the actual village of **Didyma** was when we found ourselves out on the seashore.

Or should I say "the beaches"? Right in the middle of rows of villas and hotels with as many stars as a *Metaxa* brandy bottle.

If I am not mistaken, this beach, shown on the map by a blue line and the legend "**Didyma Beach**" is known to the local inhabitants as "**Altın Kum**" (Golden Sand). And there was a real *"Gold Rush"* going on! The thousands of bathers reminded one of the old days at **Florya**.

We left not a single road or street unexplored. We landed up in a building site. They were building new villas. To find a restaurant needed considerable courage and persistence. All we came across were *Apollo* hotels or indoor restaurants in a noisy street.

But we refused to give up! What we were looking for was a table with a clean table-cloth in the shade of a tree. We ended up by taking refuge in the temple sanctuary. We settled down in a *"self-service"* directly opposite the temple itself. There was a street in between, and right on the other side of the street (there was no pavement) the temple began. It was surrounded by wire fencing, and how they decided on the limits of the temple I really don't know. The wire fencing skirted the fallen columns and the ancient stones.

Now and again visitors would get down from the tourist buses and

(left) Ionic column (detail).
(above) Two passages, on the right and the left of the Temple, open on to the space at the rear.

form long queues in front of the food. To tell you the truth, my dreams collapsed like a punctured balloon. I bent my head and gave all my attention to the fried peppers, aubergine, puré, cheese, shepherd's salad and *"hors d'œuvres"*.

I thought of *Heredotus* and *Queen Nitocris* of **Babylon.** We were all just as obsessed with the treasure as *Darius* had been and ready to loot it at any moment. The present-day pillage of **Didyma** is a perfect example of pure, shameless greed.

This time I had recourse to *Ezra Erhat.* She was describing **Didim.** Not **Didim**, **Didyma.**

> *"The Temple of Apollo at Didyma on the territory of Miletos, the largest city of Ionia, was known as the 'Didymeion'. The early writers offer no basis for the name, which means twin temples or twins. but some have suggested that it refers to a twin-peaked mountain or the two twins so loved by Apollo. But Didyma is not a Greek word, and must, like most Anatolian place-names, have belonged to a language of the pre-Greek period. Any attempts to link it to Greek are quite futile. Didyma was no doubt a place of worship long before the Greeks arrived in Anatolia."*

Some may not be convinced by the views put forward by *Azra Erhat,* who is, unfortunately, no longer with us. So this time let us appeal to *Strabo:*

> *"The area surrounding the sancturary is large enough to house the inhabitants of a city. Inside and outside this area is an exquisite sacred grove, while in other sacred parts of this area can be found the oracular cell and various cult objects. The temple was adorned with votive offerings consisting of ancient works of art."*

I am visiting the temple for the last time.

I climb the steps and make my way between the columns. There are passages on each side. As soon as you enter one of these passages you can feel the coolness. There is a short slope down with a narrow canal at the bottom of the walls running along each side. It must have been to prevent the rainwater from flooding out on to the road.

And now here's a little story:

One of the **Didyma** oracles was a woman who would sit here holding a staff in her hand. Before prophecying she would fast for three days in the temple. One day *Croesus, King of Lydia,* sent to three oracles, **Didyma, Delphi** and a third whose name we do not know, to ask what he was doing at that particular moment. Only **Delphi** was able to give the correct answer, but the king felt no resentment towards **Didyma** and even sent gifts to try to console them.

On leaving the temple I noticed the head of the *Medusa*, whose sulky frown can be seen on all the books and picture postcards. It lay on the shore like a fallen rock.

The area that *Strabo* described as large enough to house the inhabitants of a whole city must have been the area now covered by the ruins. It is

The frowning, resentful face of the Medusa has become the symbol of present-day Didyma.

now surrounded by a main road that owes its present-day function to the guest-houses and restaurants that line it.

In other words, the **Temple of Apollo** and its environs are now enclosed in a wire cage. So it's time for us to go if we don't want to get too depressed at the sight.

It is 20 or 22 kilometres from **Didyma** to **Miletos**.

Now **Miletos** appears as a cool oasis in the midst of all the heat. At least there is no building going on in the vicinity, and, what's more, there are

197

Storks on the red-tiled dome of the İlyas Bey Mosque.

The most important of these were Naucratis in Egypt, Cyzikos on the south shore of the Sea of Marmara and Sinop, Amisos and Olbia on the Black Sea."

The mere plan of the city of **Miletos** is in itself sufficient to give some idea of its ancient magnificence.

A **Hellenistic** theatre capable of seating an audience of only 5,300 was transformed in the **Roman** period into a theatre for 15,000.

Miletos, with its theatre, stadium, agora, public baths, harbours, statues,

ceremonial ways, temples and houses, possessed a geometrical layout that displayed a skill and mastery that always took the natural environment into consideration. For this skill and mastery we are indebted, on behalf of future generations, to the great town-planner *Hippodamos*.

On leaving the theatre, if you are not too tired, you should make your way across the fields to a small domed structure you will see a little way off under the trees.

The very plain and simple architecture is surmounted by a red-tiled dome . It is as if the craftsman that shaped the marble was issuing a challenge to his age.

Niche in the İlyas Bey Mosque.

The **Ilyas Bey Mosque** displays all the elegance and refinement characteristic of the beginning of the 15th century. It is as clear and limpid as a poem by *Yunus Emre.* Geometric interlaces are placed on the entrance door like knots in the plain marble.

The pointed, slightly rounded arches, seemed to have been placed in the centre of a block of granite. All four sides of **Ilyas Bey Mosque** are encircled with decoration. The rays of the sunset in the courtyard, the storks and their young in the nest on the roof, all transport you back to the 15th century.

I know how difficult it is to make the transition from the strength of the ancient world to the skills of another age. But there are no limits to skill and art.

It was here that the writer *Aristeides* of **Miletos** wrote the stories that were to form the basis of the **Satyricon** and *Boccaccio's* **Decameron.** So much was to be found together on **Miletan** soil.

Only man remains indifferent to the dilapidated nature of these buildings.

The best thing is to end the day with the good humour of a traveller...

BAFA LAKE.
THE SUMMER RESORT
OF
THE GREAT CITIES:
BODRUM.
BLUE LIBERATION

After **Dilek Peninsula** the geography of the **Aegean** meets freedom, a freedom that comprises the whole of the **Mediterranean.**

What does this freedom consist of?

Gods, ancient cities, seamen, untouched trees, unnamed bays and voices unknown to man.

Such a definition obviously cannot be applied to every settlement.

We Turks, who:

Arriving at the gallop from far-off Asia
Pushed out into the Mediterranean like a horse's head,

by taking the number of children to the square metre as the criterion of our virility, transformed the shores into a market-place. Thank goodness there are some places we didn't reach. And for an obvious reason. No roads.

We pack twenty-five or thirty people into small boats and launch out into the deep waters for a picnic (!), but we are soon in trouble. For nature has its own laws.

Ardent picnickers who, because of the lack of roads, are forced to make their way here in small boats, are confronted, if they stay too late, by the hostility of the sea. Some god, whether it is **Zeus** or **Poseidon,** I wouldn't know, suddenly raises the winds.

Moreover, the rulers of the sea will present those that make the mistake of saying, *"Let's stay a little longer, the sea's so lovely!"* with a treacherous ground swell.

LYDİA
İZMİR
AEGEAN
EPHESOS
HOUSE OF THE VIRGIN MARY
KUŞADASI
NYSSA
AYDIN
SAMOS (SİSAM)
HİERAPOLİS
DENİZLİ
PRİENE
MYUS
MİLETOS
ALİNDA
ALABANDA
APHRODİSİAS
BAFA GÖLÜ
HERAKLEİA
LABRANDA
DİDYMA
CARİA
KALE
İASSOS
MYLASA
MİLAS
LEROS
BARGLİA
MUĞLA
KALİMNOS
HALİKARNASSOS
BODRUM
KERAMOS
KOS
MARMARİS
KAUNOS
DATÇA
KNİDOS
GÖÇEK
SİMİ
TELMESSOS
FETHİYE
RODOS
MEDITERRANEAN

After that you are as sick as a dog.

The trip is transformed into a disaster!

It is very fortunate that there are difficulties and a price to be paid in any attempt to improve communications. For example, the rocks are so steep that no road could ever be built over them. Only a mountaineer can get across.

There are seas that make it impossible for you to approach the shore or cast anchor. You either ground the boat or strike the rocks.

All you can do is to edge your boat gently towards them.

Of course, it needs a great deal of effort to capture beauty. And you won't get far with an effort that isn't backed up with skill and experience. And when, after all these difficulties, you finally capture that beauty, you will feel all the greater esteem for it.

That is why those who have been using these same seas and these same shores for thousands of years approach nature with deep respect.

A careful examination of the shores of the **Aegean** and the **Mediterranean** beyond this point will reveal two main features. One of these is the difference between the seas and the soil.

The other is the establishment of ancient civilization and cities mainly on the shores.

Let me explain what I mean. They founded a great many cities, but not just any type of city. Each one of them was adorned with monumental buildings.

It would be useful to see what *Vitruvius* has to say on the matter.

> *"The most important thing is the choice of a healthy site. This should be at a certain height and there should be no marshes in the vicinity. The poi-*

Lake Bafa in the 19th century. From La Borde, "Voyage de l'Asie Mineure".

sonous breath of swamp creatures mixed with the mists brought from the marshes by the morning winds blowing towards the city at sunrise render the site insalubrious. Nor could a site on the shore facing either south or north be regarded as a healthy one, as in summer the southern skies begin to warm up as soon as the sun rises and by noon have reached a scorching heat, while on the western front it begins to heat up after the sun has risen, becomes quite hot in the middle of the day and reaches a blistering heat in the evening."

So many of the cities we have founded or enlarged on these shores are blisteringly hot! When the wind blows it carries away everything before it.

We are not, however, concerned with factors like cold and heat, or winds or diseases. All we are worried about is building something just anywhere at all.

You may smile, but I'm going to have to give you another quotation from *Vitruvius*, this time on the skills required for the foundation of a city.

"When our forefathers were about to found a city or a military garrison they would sacrifice several of the cattle grazing on the proposed site and examine their entrails. If the entrails of the first sacrifices turned out to be dark in colour or in any way abnormal they would make further sacrifices to find out whether this arose from disease or from what they had eaten. They would never venture upon the construction of defence establishments without making certain by means of a number of such experiments of the existence of water and nourishment that would produce strong and healthy entrails. But if they continued to encounter abnormal

The most pleasant part of the journey from Söke to Milas is along the shores of Lake Bafa with its pines and olive groves. Lake Bafa was formerly an inlet of the sea named after Mt Latmos near which the city of Heracleia was founded. The outlet to the sea was blocked by the silt washed down by the Meander and the inlet transformed into a lake.

entrails they would conclude that the water and nourishment offered by the region were incompatible with human health and would abandon the site and go off in search of another."

So far so good.... But Lake Bafa awaits us.

If you are coming by Söke, 25 km after that town you will come across a quite unusual phenomenon, one that we have already mentioned. This is **Lake Bafa,** or, according to its new, meaningless name, **Lake Çamiçi.** The lake is only about 22 km from **Didyma.**

Bafa is the largest lake in the **Aegean** region. It is 65 km long but, you may be surprised to hear, only 10 m above sea-level. It is 25 m deep, but the depth varies according to the level of the water in the **Büyük Menderes (Meander)** river.

Lake Bafa was formerly an arm of the sea known as the **Gulf of Latmos.** **Mt Latmos** was regarded as sacred by the Christians and was a centre of habitation from the 10th to the 13th centuries. It was during this period that a number of frescoes were made in local caves and monasteries.

The silt carried down by the **Meander** cut off the passage to the sea and the salt water gulf was converted into a lake.

Bafa owes its popularity to the olive groves surrounding it and the presence of migratory birds.

It would be no exaggeration to say that **Lake Bafa** escaped death by a hair's breadth. Every beautiful thing is threatened by pests. But in this case these are not the migratory birds like the *crested pelicans, cormorants, herons, sea eagles, reed hens, ducks* and *cormorants* that come here every year to nest and roost, but by two-legged human beings.

Thank goodness, all the efforts of this species of animal to have the region opened up for building have so far proved abortive. Now **Lake Bafa** is under a conservation order (except, of course, for its name).

There are no buildings here apart from the fishermen's restaurants and camp sites.

The loveliest part of the journey from **Söke** to **Milas** is the section along the shores of **Lake Bafa.**

Another important feature is the wealth of historical remains. The ancient city of **Heracleia,** founded to the east of the ancient **Gulf of Latmos,** is remarkable, besides the city defence walls and the interesting towers constructed by *Lysimachos* in 287 B.C., for the famous grid system introduced by the town-planner *Hippodamos.*

Nor did the **Gulf of Latmos** escape the attention of the geographer *Strabon:*

> "*The gulf contains a small town by the name of Heracleia with a small harbour. The town was formerly known by the name of the mountain on the skirts of which the upper part of the city is located.*
>
> "*The journey from Miletos to Heracleia along the turns and twists of the coastline is a little over a hundred stadia. On the other hand, the direct route from Miletos to Pyrrha is only thirty stadia. Thus the journey by land along the shore is very much longer.*"

In another section of the work *Strabo* gives the following description of the city:

> "*Heracleia is a city with very fine harbours as well as several other valuable features, such the colonies it has founded, among which Chersonesos and Callatis can be counted. In ancient times it was an independent city, but was later ruled for a time by tyrants, after which it regained its independence. Later it came under Roman hegemony and the rule of kings. The inhabitants accepted the position of a colony of the Romans, with whom they shared part of the territory and its cities.*"

A member city of the **Delian Confederacy**, Heracleia continued to change and develop throughout the **Pergamese, Hellenistic, Roman** and **Byzantine** periods.

Today it still retains its mystery, with its **Ionic Temple of Athena** dating from the **Hellenistic** period, its agora, the **Early Christian** and **Byzantine**

(right) Bodrum from the Castle.
(below) One of the camels frequently to
be encountered on the Bodrum roads.

monuments on the islands and all its stories and legends.

Its *grey mullet, sea bass* and *eels* all form part of the legend, but the most important thing of all is to observe, like some investigative traveller, all the changes in the lake from the sunrise until sunset. It is, in the full meaning of the word, a source of dreams and visions for anyone who attempts to discover the mystery that lies concealed behind the beautifully carved stones.

Heracleia is the only city on **Lake Bafa** itself, but one should not ignore places in the vicinity like **Myos**, only 15 km from **Miletos,** and **Assessos** between **Miletos** and **Didyma**, while everywhere there are traces of the ***Ionians,*** the ***Romans*** and the ***Byzantines.***

But if you've set your heart on **Bodrum** and you're heading hell for leather towards that city, there's nothing more to say. No one can hold you back. For, after all, **Bodrum** is the summer resort of the cities.

In other words, a great multitude of solitudes.

Come and stroll through its streets shoulder to shoulder with its thronging crowds.

*A motor-vessel,
an essential feature of
the Aegean and the
Mediterranean.*

Floor mosaics being dscovered during excavations conducted by the British towards the end of last century in the Hacı Kaptan Meydanı. From C.T.Newton, 1862. "A History of Discoveries of Halicarnassus, Cnidos and Branchidæ.

Sleep by day and go crazy by night.

But I still intend to tell you something about **Bodrum,** for within the **Bodrum** of today you can still find something of the **Bodrum** of the past.

Any mention of a coastal settlement at a point where the waters of the **Aegean** and the **Mediteranean** meet will inevitably call to mind the cities of **Bodrum** and **Marmara**. Both harbours form starting-points or ports of call on the *Blue Voyage*.

For myself, I have never had any great liking for either of the two. Nor for **Kuşadası**. The only attractive aspects of the two cities are their descriptions by the *Fisherman of Halicarnassus* and *Eyüboğlu*. **Bodrum, Marmaris** and **Kuşadası** in the heat of the summer remind me of the touts in the intercity bus terminals.

For *the Fisherman of Halicarnassus*, **Bodrum** meant a *"Blue Exile"*. As far as I can see the "blue" has completely disappeared, blotted out by the crowds. **Bodrum** has been drowned by its own popularity!

If you take my advice, you'll re-read the *"Blue Exile"* by *the Fisherman of Halicarnassus.*

Then you will be able to compare for yourself the virgin beauty of nature and of passion.

But I must confess that there is one thing that attracts me at any mention of **Bodrum,** namely **Bodrum Museum.**

That isn't because of my interest in the history of art or any crazy notions connected with it. It's because there is always something new in

Bodrum street and houses.

the **Bodrum Museum** and always something of absorbing interest. It is housed in a castle with four towers built on rocks; a castle that every seaman who arrived here stormed and captured and stamped with his coat of arms.

All you have to do is to have your photograph taken sitting with your back against the castle keep and all the civilian buildings of **Bodrum** as a backdrop. This great heap of stone is enough for the sunset and enough and more than enough for a souvenir.

For us, who will tolerate no criticism of our history or our forefathers

(above) Bodrum Castle from the shore.
From C.T.Newton, 1862. "A History of
Discoveries of Halicarnassus, Cnidos
and Branchidæ.
(right) Bodrum Castle from the marina.

(above) Street in Bodrum.
(left) Peacock in Bodrum Museum.

but are too lazy to take any real interest in them or to carry out any genuine research into the matter, that much history should suffice!

But actually, in any visit to **Bodrum Castle**, that much history does not really suffice. You feel yourself surrounded by something living, something breathing, something stirring around you.

The most concrete proof of this lies in the children. My little daughter is well accustomed to trips of this kind. But she sometimes gets bored climbing up hills and mountains. But in **Bodrum Castle** she is always pointing things out to me. That is quite significant, isn't it?

(opposite page) Bodrum Castle from the shore.
(above) Bodrum in the 19th century from Bodrum Castle. C.T.Newton, 1862.
"A History of Discoveries of Halicarnassus, Cnidos and Branchidæ.

The *"museum"* in **Bodrum Castle** is an integral part of life itself. The doves alight on your head or your hands and the peacock spreads the beauty of its tail against the whole mythology of the **Aegean** and the **Mediterranean.**

The ivy in a coastal city that pursues the light of day, the white, pink, purple begonias (or bougainvilia?...)

You are perfectly justified in asking *"What on earth have any of these to do with the museum?"*

You're perfectly right. Nothing at all!

And now it's my turn to ask a question. *"Those people who for thousands of years set up families and created works of art, what sort of environment did they live in? Did they drink their wine with chickpeas and beans?"*

The museum is not a tomb in which dead bodies are laid out... Nor,

obvously, are pigeons and peacocks the only things to be seen. Every object is displayed along with an account of its history, evolution and mode of employment, as well as examples of its present-day use.

Most of us are interested in amphorae. They display such beauty of form. But the form they display was determined by the goods to be carried, ease of carrying and the style typical of the region from which they came. A pitcher from **Rhodes** is quite different from a pitcher from **Cnidos.**

(above right) Bodrum from the shore. (above) Meander motif inspired by the Meander River and a coat-of-arms relief in Bodrum Museum.

A sea captain would judge his task successfully accomplished if the pitchers in these tiny boats were brought safely, through winds and storms, to the harbour in **Bodrum.**

In the walls of this museum history is made attractive, without any pedantry or drudgery. Here you will find charts showing how much you could buy today with the coins of that time. A little further on you will come across an extraordinary exhibit, which took ten years to set up, in the form of a **Fatimid** vessel, some 20 metres in length, that sank in **Serçe** harbour in 1025 A.D. with a three ton cargo of glass. You can also follow the event by video.

Nothing is neglected in the manner of display. In other words, an event that took place thousands of years ago is brought to life, step by step, before your eyes. After a visit to this wreck, preserved at a special temperature, you are brought back to real life by the begonias (or bougainvilias) that still surround the building in spite of all the environmental pollution.

There is one thing we must never forget. This castle, once used as a dungeon, is the symbol and pride of **Bodrum**, and behind it there is a name, as firm as any castle: *Oğuz Alpözen.*

Underwater archaeologist and Director of the Museum, *Alpözen* contin-ues the tradition of enthusiasm, eccentricity and creativity initiated by the *Fisherman of Halicarnassus*.

I have seen *Oğuz* diving. I have seen him supervising the repair of the finds. I have seen him re-educating the young people of the neighbour-hood. I have heard him describe the objects he has found and exhibited as if presenting them in some ancient theatre or at a *Dionysiac* festival.

As a nation, we have very short memories. We remember the specula-tors and profiteers but we immediately forget those who for thousands of years have served the community by working away with bougainvil-ia, doves, sunken wrecks, stones and castles.

But I am sure that the names of *Alpözen* and his colleagues will be remembered for a very long time. Each of them served their apprentice-ship in the salt waters of the **Aegean** and the **Mediterranean** before mak-ing the acquaintance of the deeper seas.

And there's another feast to be enjoyed in the **Bodrum Museum.** The skill displayed by a museum renewing itself.

The skeleton of a *Carian Princess* who is thought to have lived in the 4th century B.C., discovered in the excavations of the foundations at the

(top) View of the castle. From C.T.Newton, 1862. "A History of Discoveries of Halicarnassus, Cnidos and Branchidæ.
(above) Coat-of-arms in the castle wall.

221

Church in Bodrum Castle. From C.T.Newton, 1862. "A History of Discoveries of Halicarnassus, Cnidos and Branchidæ.

entrance to the **Bodrum Museum,** is exhibited with all its jewellery and replicas of its garments.

The method of display, the presentation, the music, the choice of replicas and the combination of simplicity and detail are all quite fascinating. One has to see to believe how it is possible to create a whole world using a skeleton and one or two pieces of jewellery.

Still wearing sandals on your feet, beads around your arms and neck and torn off shorts, in other words, whatever you happen to be wearing at the time; filled with all the intoxication of the **Mediterranean** and whatever energy you may have left over from the night before, just try visiting this musem.

(top) *Details from Bodrum Museum.*
(above) *The English Tower, which has been given a very colourful function.*

Believe me, you will feel really relaxed. And you'll also feel you're really alive, for you will find exhibited here the civilizations that for thousands of years spread their sails in the **Aegean** and the **Mediterranean.**

In the *"Blue Guide to Turkey"*, published in 1989 in London and New York, Bernard McDonagh praises those in charge of the museum for the extraordinarily skilful way in which they have exploited the castle's magnificent situation, as well as for their success in representing most effectively the Hell**enistic, Roman, Byzantine, Medieval** and **Turkish** periods of the city. He describes the museum as one of the most romantic and imaginative in **Turkey.** He also refers to the collection, within the castle itself, of the various trees and plants typical of the vegetation of the **Bodr**um region and to the lovely perfume of roses that greets the visitor on a stroll through the castle grounds.

I can't help giving an example on my own account. If you should ever pay a visit to the castle on the island of **Cos,** which was built by the

(left) The Serçe Limanı wreck, exhibited in Bodrum Museum. These are the remains of an 11th century boat thought to have been under Fatimid command and to have sunk in a storm off the shores of Syria in 1025 A.D. The vessel was found at a depth of 16 m.
(right) One of the Bodrum Museum underwater archaeologists diving for amphorae.

Knights of St John at about the same time as the castle of **Bodrum**, you will see the extraordinary difference between the two.

The difference? Simply the ability to inspire museology with the breath of life.

And it is no easy thing to keep a living museology alive in a coastal town.

The reason? The mere fact of its being a coasal town! The fact that holiday visitors prefer sun and sea to wandering around a museum.

It is very encouraging that, in spite of everything, there are always queues waiting to get into the museum. And if not every year, perhaps, but certainly every two or three years, you will be able to see quite amazing examples of the **Aegean** and **Mediterranean** civilizations. You will be sure to find that yet another salon full of visual interest has been added to the salons you visited on previous occasions.

Amphorae carefully stored in Bodrum Museum.

Now we come to the *"dungeon"*. At the entrance you will see a notice: *"Is your heart strong enough for a visit to the dungeon? Please do not bring children!"*

This note is a vital warning.

On another day, in a part of the castle full of stones and weeds, you will find yourself confronted with a ship that sank 3,300 years ago off **Kaş-Uluburun Point** - a merchant ship that set out from **Egypt** and made its way past **Cyprus** and along the shores of **Anatolia.**

> *"As captain of this ship, I feel great pride in having been entrusted with the treasure of the Great Pharaoh, now safely stored in the ship's hold. The treasure consists of exqusite gold and silver bracelets, necklaces and rings, the work of Canaanite and Egyptian jewellers, rare ebony boxes from tropical Africa, even rarer amber beads from northern lands and tusks of elephants and hippopotami hunted on the shores of my own country.*
>
> *"Shall I drink a toast from this great golden goblet?"*
>
> *"After setting out from Egypt and leaving the shores of Syria behind us,*

THE HALICARNASSUS OF HEREDOTUS

Bodrum is represented by two symbols, one of them being Herodotus, the father of history, who lived from 490 to 425 B.C.

This great historian was a native of Bodrum...

The second symbol belongs to our own age: the Fisherman of Halicarnassus, Cevat Şakir Kabaağaçlı.

Herodotus begins the first page of his history as follows:

"This is a work dedicated to the public by Herodotus of Halicarnassus. My sole aim is to ensure that what man has performed should not fall into oblivion, and that the works created by both Greeks and Barbarians should not remain anonymous.

I shall also attempt to explain why they engaged in wars one with the other.

"The Persian chroniclers say that it was the Phoenicians who began the war when they came from the sea known as Erythreia and landed on our shores (the Mediterranean)."

History is undoubtedly a chronicle of conflicts. But under the conflicts lie concealed a myriad different aims and objectives. Expansion, power, food, culture, riches and the elation of victory are only a few of these.

Oğuz Alpözen begins the history section of his book on Bodrum as follows:

"Bodrum was founded on the site of Halicarnassus, one of the most famous cities of the ancient world. The finds preserved in the Museum indicate that Bodrum and its environs have a history of some 5000 years, and the existence of objects belonging to various civilizations show that the region was invaded and occupied by a number of different peoples. Most of these invaders arrived in this region via the islands. In ancient times the name Caria was given to the region, which comprised the land now covered by the whole province of Muğla and part of the province of Aydın. In ancient times, as at the present day, Anatolia was divided into different regions. According to the ancient writers, Caria extended from the Meander in the west to the Dalaman on the east. The region was inhabited by the Carians and the Lelegians.

"In the Iliad, the Carians are referred to as an indigenous Anatolian people who were said to have joined the Trojans in their struggle against the Greeks..."

The Carians founded Bodrum in the 11th century B.C.

According to Herodotus, in the 7th century B.C. the city was one of the six cities making up the Hexapolis League.

In 468 B.C. the city joined the Delian Confederacy, but was later stormed and sacked in turn by the Lydians, Persians and Alexander the Great.

Under King Mausolus, Bodrum became the capital of the surrounding region, and in the 3rd century B.C. the city was used as a base by the Lagos dynasty in Egypt.

The city came under the hegemony of Rome in 192 B.C., of Rhodes in 189 B.C. and of Pontus in 88 B.C. It later came nder the control of the Byzantines.

In the second half of the 13th century Bodrum became part of the Menteşe Emirate, and in 1415 was captured by the Knights of St John. Finally, in 1522, Bodrum was annexed to the

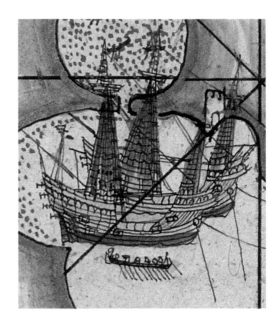

Ottoman Empire by Süleyman the Magnificent.

The Castle, which covers an area of 180 x 185 m, was built by the Knights of St John. It contains the English, French, Italian, German and Spanish towers, and 249 coats-of-arms can be seen on the walls.

In his book, Oğuz Alpözen quotes a Latin inscription engraved above the 6th gate which may be translated as follows: "Lord, protect us while we are sleeping and while we are awake. If you do not protect us, no one can do so."

This inscription again proves that Herodotus was right.

The world has never been free of conflict, but it would appear from this inscription that the Knights entrusted everything to God, while they woke or slept.

I would understand it if they had said "strengthen us while awake"...

It isn't war exactly, but in my opinion "fear" is the worst thing of all.

The castle is an inexhaustible source for all who see it...

One of the most important of these sources is the theatre dating from the Mausolos period which, though it may seem small today, is thought to have held 13,000 spectators. A host of stories will be yielded by the investigations and excavations now being conducted by Professor Ümit Serdaroğlu: accounts of the Dionysiac festivities and stories of the actors and gladiators.

The theatre and the castle that hold both shores have one common enemy at the present day: the supposedly "traditional" Bodrum houses...

Until quite recently a village of fishermen and sponge-divers and now proclaimed a "first-class holiday resort", how, I wonder, will our city of Bodrum be described by the historians of the future.

God knows!...

It took the archaeologist *Cemal Pulak* and a team of researchers under the direction of *George F. Bass.* ten years to raise once more to the light of day the wreck of the ship the tutelary goddess had failed to protect. Twenty thousand dives were carried out during this ten year period.

The first dives carried out by the Director of the **Underwater Archaeological Museum,** *Oğuz Alpözen* and his friends, brought news of a past civilization to the modern world.

The tutelary goddess has just embarked on a new adventure, and is taking witnesses with her. The most important witness is the only gold ring in the world belonging to the *Egyptian Queen Nefertiti.* Then there is the gold necklace with a figure of the goddess. **Syrian-Palestinian-Mycenaean** swords. The elephant and hippopotamus tusks, copper, ingots of tin, cymbals and amphorae mentioned in the story...

Oğuz Alpözen, Director of the Bodrum Museum, who invested Bodrum Castle with the character of a true museum.

And it is we who can peer through to the mystery concealed in each. It is we who bathe in the same sea.

In one sense, **Bodrum** owes its fame to the *Fisherman of Halicarnassus. Cevat Şakir* became acquainted with **Bodrum** during his years of exile there on account of an article he had contributed to the periodical *Resimli Hayat* (Illustrated Weekly). For *Cevat Şakir* this exile was a *"Mavi Sürgün", a "Blue Exile".*

Exiled to **Bodrum** for a term of three years, he stayed there nearly twenty-five. Here is a passage about **Bodrum** from his book *"Mavi Sürgün"* first published in 1961, which tells the story of this strange exile:

> *"One talks about the air and water of a country. And yet surely the sounds of the country, its voices, its noises and its smells are just as important as the air and water. Two of the distinguishing features of a city are the noise of the trams, buses and cars, and the smell of burnt petrol and rubber. Here nature rejoices, like a schoolchild at the beginning of the summer holidays, at being free from the annoyance caused by the stones and concrete of the city, the noise of the buses, the smell of petrol. Here the fragrance of the orange and lemon blossoms mingles with the twittering of the birds and the cooing of the doves. The sea breezes carry this lovely fragrance of the orange blossoms and the blossoms of other citrous fruits out to the open sea. If these weren't life restoring we shouldn't send patients from the city into the woods and mountains, into the lap of mother nature, for her to cure her child.*

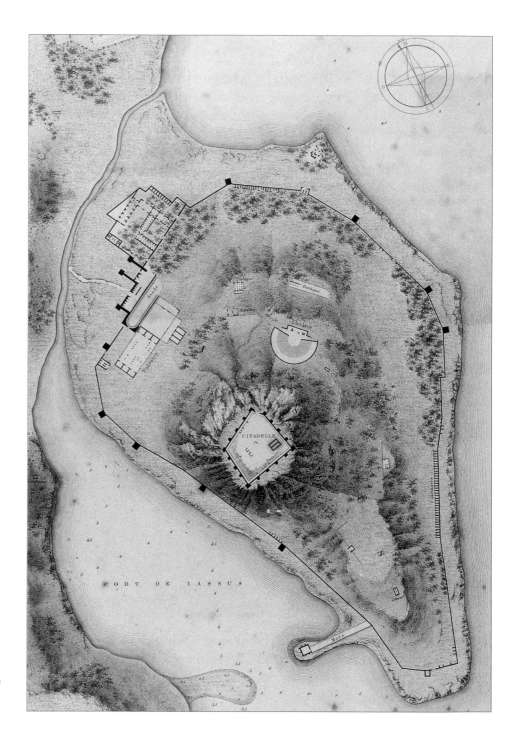

Plan of the city and defence walls of Iasos. From Charles Texier, "Voyage de l'Asie Mineure".
(opposite page, below) Iasos theatre.

bays into which Mandalya is divided. The above-mentioned bay lies squeezed between Tekeağaç Point and the city of Myndos at the extreme end of the Bodrum Peninsula.

"According to legend, the city of Iasos was founded by peoples arriving from Argos during the Mycenaean period. On their arrival, they

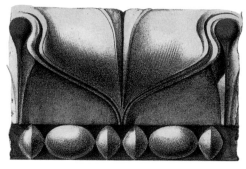

Decorations employed in the Mausoleum. From C.T.Newton, 1862. "A History of Discoveries of Halicarnassus, Cnidos and Branchidæ.

site in 1856-1857, sent the statues and reliefs discovered in the course of these excavations to the **British Museum** in **England.** Plaster casts of these can now be seen in **Bodrum.** How nice of them! We should be really grateful!

Vitruvius, writing in the 1st century B.C., makes the following observations on the monument and its architect ***Pytheos:***

> *"In Halicarnassus there are brick walls belonging to Mausolus, the mightiest of kings, covered with highly polished plaster that glistens like glass and which, although everywhere adorned with Procones-sian marble, is still, even today, in a quite extraordinarily sound condition. It is obvious that it was not poverty that led the king to employ brick as a material, for the ruler of Caria enjoyed a vast revenue.*
>
> *"As for his skill and creativity as builder, these can be seen below.*

Although born in Melassa, he soon realized the importance of Halicarnassus as a natural stronghold, with excellent port facilities that made it a suitable site for a commercial centre, and decided to make his home there. The site presents the appearance of the cavea of a theatre, the lower row being occupied by the forum beside the harbour. A great road was built leading towards the centre of the semicircular slope at a point opposite the central aisle of the theatre, and it was here that the Mausoleum was constructed which, because of its extraordinary features,

Horseman relief on the frieze of the
Mausoleum. From C.T.Newton, 1862.
"A History of Discoveries of
Halicarnassus, Cnidos and Branchidæ.

has come to be regarded as one of the Seven Wonders of the World. In the
middle of the summit of a hill stands a temple of Mars containing a won-
derful statue, said to be the work of the celebrated sculptor Leochares,
though by others it is attributed to Timotheus. The temple of Venus and
Mercury is located beside the Salmacis spring to the right of the hill."

In addition to the observations on the building itself, **Vitruvius** relates
such a fascinating story regarding the queen who succeeded to the
throne after **Mausolus'** death that I really can't help quoting it here:

"Artemisia became queen on the death of Mausolus. The Rhodians,
regarding it as an indignity that the Carian states should be ruled by a
woman, equipped a fleet and set out to conquer the kingdom. On receiv-
ing news of this, Artemisia gave orders that the crew and oarsmen of the
fleet should conceal themselves in the harbour, that the citizens remain-
ing should appear on the defence walls and offer to surrender the city. As
soon as the Rhodians left their ships and entered the city Artemisia led
her ships from the lesser to the greater harbour through a canal which
had been opened between them. The soldiers then disembarked and led the
empty ships of the Rhodians out to sea. Left stranded without any means
of retreat, the Rhodians were surrounded and destroyed in the above-
mentioned forum.

"Thereupon Artemisia put her own seamen and oarsmen on the Rhodian

ships and set sail for the island of Rhodes. Seeing their own ships approaching adorned with laurel wreaths, the citizens of Rhodes imagined that the ships were returning in triumph and freely admitted their enemies to the city. After thus conquering the city and executing the leading citizens, Artemisia had a trophy erected there consisting of two statues , one of herself and the other representing the city of Rhodes."

That should be a lesson to us all. Never underestimate women!

As for **Bodrum,** men and women now live in perfect freedom and perfect equality in the crowds that form and reform every day.

There are three islands in the **Aegean** not far from **Bodrum: Cos, Pserimos** and **Kalimnos.**

The island of **Cos** is about 90 minutes journey by boat, if your boat can do 18 knots. With its harbour, its castle, its new houses and restaurants,

(above) Castle on the Island of Cos, constructed at around the same date as Bodrum Castle.
(right) Street in Cos.

it is a typical **Mediterranean** island.

The most pleasant part of the island is the district around the castle. This is occupied by restaurants, *meyhanes* and bars which, like **Bodrum**, are filled with a hectic night-life.

This castle, too, was built by the **Knights of St John**, at about the same time as **Bodrum Castle**. As I mentioned above, a comparison of the two castles will make you realize even more clearly the true importance of the **Bodrum Underwater Archaeological Museum.**

There is a small square beside the castle where the famous tree of

Hippocrates once stood. There is also the mosque built by *Hasan Pasha of Algiers.* A lovely little square.

I don't want to go into too great detail concerning **Cos, Pserimos** and **Kalimnos.** After all, the book is supposed to be about the Anatolian shores. But I'd like to say just a few words about the islands since they lie so close and share the same sea.

The same sea and the same *hors-d'œuvres...*

There's a famous *meyhane* on **Cos. Aegean** friends of mine recommended it. **Turkish** and **Greek** friends.

It's called *Arap Restoran.* One of the four restaurants in the square. All of them are **Turkish**: *Arap, Ali, Şerif* and *Cin...*

The *Arap Restoran* has stood in this little square for half a century. The friendly relations that the founders of the political structure have been

unable to establish are to be found firmly established in this little restaurant. The plane tree in the courtyard must be about three hundred years old. The *Rezina* wine and the *hors-d-œuvres* are beyond praise.

They put white cheese and mint into the shepherd's salad with coarsely chopped onions. The fried cheese is known as *sağanaki*. The mixture of aubergines, squash and fried peppers is called *"yoğurtlu sala-ta"*. They haven't given a new name to strained yoghurt, it has the same name on both shores of the **Mediterranean.** But here they have a stuffed squash they call *andros* that is simply out of this world!

In all this eating and drinking affair there is a common taste,

The "Arab Meyhanesi" in Cos, famous for its 'mezes'.

a common palate. This arises spontaneously from the market-places and the fruit and vegetables.

The ruins of the ancient city of **Asclepieon** are to be found about 4 km from the centre.

Pserimos is located 8.5 miles from the island of **Cos**, but it sn't as attractive as **Cos** itself.

Kalimnos is a quiet, peaceful sort of island with its own typical style of domestic architecture, but the noise of the motorbikes is absolutely unbearable. Otherwise it is given up to sponge-divers and fishers.

Here new, ugly building construction reaches a pinnacle of achievement.

The women of **Kalimnos** occupy a very special place in the world of mythology. They used to hold poetry competitions with the men. Here is a poem written by one of these women poets:

> *"Are we so weak as to bow to petty advantages?*
> *Let our cries rise to the heavens.*
> *Our old way of life is dead.*

I don't know whether *Sappho* took part in these competitions but she differs from her poetic colleague in refusing to indulge in sadness:

> *"Mourning is not for us.*
> *It isn't right*
> *That mourning should enter*
> *The soul of poetry.*

Sappho, who was born on the island of **Lesbos (Midilli),** is said to have recited this poem to her daughter as she was dying. This is mentioned in a note by *Talat Halman,* the translator of the poem.

When it came to the men's turn in the competition things became rather hectic!.. *Archilous* was obviously thinking of other things when he wrote:

Bust of Sappho, who enchanted the generations following hers with her poems. Roman copy of a Hellenistic original. Izmir.
Istanbul Archaeological Museum.

> *"He is twice the age of his apprentices,*
> *His wife has the face of an old witch,*
> *But he's still a master of the craft!"*

A GATE OPENING ON TO INFINITY: THE MEDITERRANEAN AND THE BLUE VOYAGE

The first Blue Voyage (1986) began with the pomp and circumstance of blue waters and grey rocks embracing the blue.

My first *"Blue Voyage"* trip was in 1986, when I set out with a few very close friends on the *Durukos*, a boat that my friend D.Duru had had specially built for yacht tourism.

The notes I made during this trip were published in ten consecutive issues of the *Güneş* newspaper beginning 21 August 1986 under the title *"The Blue Civilization"*.

This was the story of an excursion through the deep waters between Antalya and Marmaris and the various city states along the coast.

It was then, perhaps rather late in life, that I acquired the taste, which was later to become a passion, for sea-trips of this kind.

The very next year I set out on a fifteen days' trip. An account of this was published in *Güneş* between 11 and 14 September 1987 under the title *"Blue Holiday"*.

And in the meantime I have made several short journeys by sea and land.

I prepared a series of articles for the *Cumhuriyet* newspaper entitled "Ancient Travels in the Aegean". This was published between 25 and 28 July 1990.

And then... It looks as if it will go on for ever!

My aim in writing about each of these trips has always been to share these wonderful experiences with others. And I'm afraid I've lost count of them all.

So if I tend to repeat myself the fault is entirely mine. You must ascribe the habit to the sheer excitement and enthusiasm these blue seas have aroused in me.

Only two of of the articles composed from my notes and impressions, the ones originally published under the titles *"Blue Civilization"* and *"On the coasts of Caria"*, are repeated verbatim here, and I feel that the eight years that have passed since I wrote them have lent them a certain documentary value.

Or am I just taking an easy way out?

Who knows!... But I simply can't help including these notes in the present work. I'm a natural chatterbox!

At the moment I am on the salt waters of the **Aegean** and the **Mediterranean.** I never wash my face. As soon as I wake up I just dive into the sea.

What day is it?

I haven't the faintest interest in day, date or time of day!

I am in a boat called *"My Dream"* moored to the rocks in a mysterious harbour below **Küçük Kargı Bay** a little way south of **Göcek Island.**

My Dream is a 20 metre schooner built in **Bodrum.**

It belongs to my schoolfriend *Üstün Karabol*. The captain is *Haydar*. Our seaman the poet *Uğur*.

When *Üstün* was young he used to row to and fro between the two shores of the Bosphorus.

The dream of his childhood and youth was finally to come true. He was

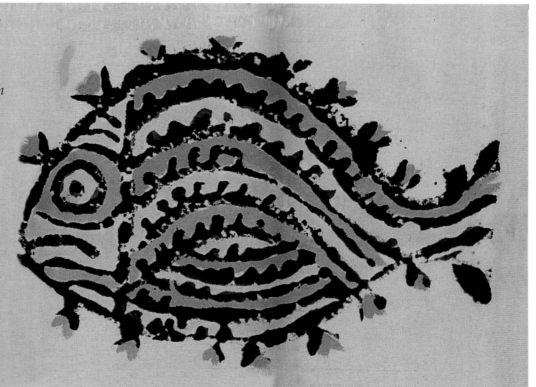

THE BLUE VOYAGE

The blue voyage is a tree
The sea its branches
The blue voyage is a garden
The sea its roses

The blue voyage is a child
The sea its cradle
The sea its teeth
The sea its eyes

The blue voyage is a dream
that has never been
dreamed
The blue voyage is a book
that has never been
written
The blue voyage is a tale
that has never been
told.

Bedri Rahmi Eyüboğlu, 1974

to become the owner of *My Dream,* a name he himself would never have dreamed of giving.

Now we are listening to a choir of cicadas as we sip the water of life from our glasses.

But let's keep a hold on ourselves!... Let's preserve the documentary nature of our book. It is 1994. July. Sunday. In other words, 3 July 1994...

As I am an educated, literary man (!) *Üstün* prepares me a campari cocktail and his wife *Seher* brings it to me as I sit writing up my notes on the **Aegean** and **Mediterranean.**

My God!

How could one avoid writing in such a state of bliss!

It's such sheer happiness to wander around in the *Blue Civilization,* to bathe in its waters and to throw away all one's cares and anxieties.

There's only the dawn of the day and the red of the sunset; that's all.

Now I understand why the inhabitants of the **Aegean** and the **Mediterranean** are so carefree, relaxed and light-hearted.

So those that are to accompany me on the trip shouldn't expect a careful chronological arrangement of cities... And let them not expect a description of the series of new and old cities! I couldn't care less for geographical order...

On the contrary, I just flow like a river. You can never tell where I go down and where I come up.

I have cast the chains of everyday life into the depths of the sea.

Welcome to *"Blue Civilization"!*

Even if it's for only a short time, I leave the wounds of my body to waters washed in salt and sun.

There is an inexhaustible phosphorescence in the depths of the sea.

Tiny fish leap with joy on the surface.

Forgive me! I've caught the disease of the city.

I'm like a spoilt child, you've given me the sky and the sea and the whole of the day...

The choir of cicadas pay no attention. Perhaps because they look upon me as a guest.

But in that case they're wrong. I'm one of them. As soon as I pop my head out of the water their song rings in my ears.

Welcome to *"Blue Civilization".*

THE BLUE VOYAGE...

I feel like a raw recruit going off to the front. I have a shopping list in front of me in three languages: Şarap ve biralar - Vins et Bieres - Wine and Beer. Sebze ve meyveler - Fruits et légumes - Fruits and vegetables. Kasap - Boucherie - Butcher. A *Blue Civilization* list with exactly 133 items.

If anyone should say "prepare for food shortages" I would immediately distribute these scholarly lists of food shortages to the general public! A comprehensive list of how much you should buy, from jam to toilet paper, green peppers to cracked wheat and fly-killers...

It's obvious we aren't a sea-going nation. How *Piri Reis, Barbaros Hayreddin Pasha* and *Turgut Reis* ever became sailors I really don't understand. And, what's more, in boats no bigger than nutshells...

There is still a month and a half to go before we set out on the *Blue Voyage*. I go to see my boyhood friend *Üstün* in his office in Beyoğlu. *Ali* brings along a *"list of necessities"* from people who have been on previous trips. It is really quite a useful list. *Azra Erhat,* one of the first to take part in a Blue Voyage writes in her book that *"the various stages of preparation for the Blue Voyage take me about a year."* And she's quite right. It isn't the sort of trip where you just pack a few things in your bag and set off. Besides food and drink you've got to think of possible illnesses: sunstroke, insect bites, sea-sickness etc. etc.... *Üstün* is a chemist so I can rely on him. Meanwhile there are telephone calls and faxes to be made. It's practically impossible to telephone anywhere from **Cağaloğlu** or **Beyazıt.** You just can't get a connection. You try for half an hour for a connection and when you get it the number turns out to be engaged. It's really maddening! That's why I go to *Üstün's* office rather than try to phone from the newspaper.

A good boat and a good captain are the most essential things on a Blue Voyage. And next comes the ability to get on with your companions.

Casual acquaintance in the street is one thing, friendship in houses quite another. In a boat, black clouds will gather overhead at the slightest friction. And then come the thunder showers!... If you take the plunge as soon as you feel angry, the sea is golden. If you wait, rain and storms! And if the whole point of going on this trip is to get away from the racket and rows of the city, then you're done for!...

Think of it! You're getting away from all the pushing and shoving in the city, the political inanities, the empty declarations, the children who never grow up, the people who have forgotten how

1. *Antalya harbour, where I first learned to swim, has been classified a conservation area and converted into a marina.*
2,3,4. *You can stroll like a sleep-walker by the houses and streets of Kaleiçi in Antalya. If you do this at night, you will feel the fragrance of jasmine and orange blossoms in your nostrils.*
5. *Theatre in Termessus, the city that Alexander the Great besieged but failed to capture.*
6. *Flowers in Kaleiçi.*

of Antalya is situated and which, together with **Lycia** and **Caria**, formed the southern and south-western civilizations, has a somewhat older history of habitation. There is also the fact that the freedom-loving Solymians, who ruled the region from the 2nd millenium B.C. right up to the Byzantine era, founded the city of Termessus on the highest peak of **Güllük Dağ** in the province of **Antalya**. **Termessus** is no ordinary city. Rumour has it that it was founded by old pirates as a place where they could spend their last declining years. They chose an inaccessible spot on precipitous rocks for their city so as to avoid being disturbed by the younger pirates. But let us not forget that this is only a rumour.

The inhabitants of **Termessus** were as passionately fond of freedom as their ancestors the Solymians. So much so that they frustrated even *Alexander the Great*, who laid siege to **Termessus** but failed to capture it. The citizens offered a heroic resistence. Furious at his failure to take the city he burned everything he could find in the vicinity. The ancient city now lives its own legend, with its theatre, cisterns, agora, gymnasium, temple, school buildings and royal road…

When we arrive at the yacht harbour in Antalya, whose name derives from that of Attalos II, King of Bergama, the Blue Voyage boat *Durukos III* is waiting for us. Our captain is the thirty-three year old *Ertan Tınaztepe,* with his mates *Yıldıray* and *Hüseyin. Yıldıray* has known the sea since he was nine.

The appearance of the *Durukos III* got full marks from the fresh Blue Voyagers, and not the slightest flaw was to be found in the beauty and attractiveness of the yacht harbour.

1,2,3. *Antalya. Street life in Kaleiçi.*
4. *The Forty Steps I used to climb with my brother Metin as we entered the little house of my schooldays with its pool and courtyard.*

We were to set out on our trip the next morning. We had a whole day in front of us. I was very eager to see **Antalya**, particularly **Kaleiçi**, where I had spent my childhood. We went together around **Kaleiçi**, now a conservation area. The little house with the pool where I lived during my schooldays stands directly opposite the **Kırk Merdivenler** (Forty Steps) leading up to **Kaleiçi**. The ground floor is now a grocer's shop. The whole building is in a sorry state of neglect and dilapidation.

Kaleiçi gives us a great big welcome with its little side streets, houses with bay windows, wide doors, and various remains from the Roman period. Like the welcome from the *Fisherman of Halicarnassus*. The enchanting beauty of the palms, the banana trees, the red and white oleanders and, above all, the bougainvillea that has become the symbol of the **Mediterranean**, hold up a delicate curtain against the chaos of the city.

"Take a blind man to Pamphylia, or even further west to Lycia, and he'll immediately know from the smell of the air exactly where he is. The acrid

4

perfume of lavender, the pungent fragrance of wild mint and thyme, will tell him he is in Pamphylia. The Pamphylian air is different from the air anywhere else. It also carries the fragrance of jasmine, honey-suckle, myrtle, and lemon and orange blossoms."

I felt what the *Fisherman of Halicarnassus* calls the perfume of Pamphylia in my nostrils as I walked through **Kaleiçi**. The white jasmine blossoms hung down from the stone walls. I walked, not towards the street, but towards the fragrance. The small green fruits on the tangerine and orange trees vied with the jasmine. But the contest of nature in no way resembles that of man. It is a silent and meaningful contest, without any noise or bombast...

I inevitably look at **Kaleiçi** with a different eye from that of my childhood. With its narrow streets, its stone or wooden houses, it is simply cut out to be a tourist city. It is the inevitable first or last step to be taken in the Blue Voyage.

As darkness falls we return to the yacht harbour. We have been invited by our **Antalya** friends *Ahmet* and *Semiramis Uluç*. We open the door into the blue with girida fish, soup and wine laid out on a long table on the embankment, immediately opposite the boats.

1. *The Yivli Minaret, a Seljuk monument.*
2. *From the Blue Voyage.*
3. *Kaleiçi. Streets running down to the harbour.*
4. *Antalya Museum.*

THE SMOKED FISH OF
MATRIARCHAL LYCIA

The yacht harbour of the coastal city of **Antalya** lay absolutely silent. In spite of the early hour the sun was already scorching. We had breakfast on board. The blue voyagers woke up fresh and lively from their first night's sleep on the boat as it lay moored to the land. Vegetables, fruit and drink, as well as piles of ice had been loaded onto the *Durkos III* the previous day. Now we lacked nothing. In fact, we had much too much.

It is a completely different feeling from rushing down to the sea from the great cities and spreading yourself out on the beach. Especially if you think of all the blue days in front of you.

I've also managed to seduce my **Antalya** friends *Ahmet* and *Semiramis Uluç*. They're going to follow us in their 9.5 metre boat the *Belâ*, bringing their daughter *Lâra* along with them.

We abandon the idea of going in separate boats. The *Belâ* will follow us under its captain, *Attila*. We decide to renew the years' old pleasure of conversation with *Ahmet, Semiramis* and *Lâra*.

Our first stop is **Kemer.**

We make our way along by the **Beydağ Mts.** The whole range always has one particular layer of colour. If it happens to be purple or grey in one place then it will be purple or grey right along the coast.

I have been in love with the **Beydağ Mts** for as long as I can remember. It is as if they had girded on the same love of freeedom as the old **Termessians.** They look capable of creating new gods at any moment.

We make our first stop in **Kemer** bay. The residents from the French holiday village are bathing topless. As soon as the *Durukos III* casts anchor

(right) Beydağları from the Antalya harbour.

everyone on the boat, children and grown-ups, abandon themselves to the mysterious blue of the **Mediterranean.** From the shore, the orange and tangerine groves follow the mountains as they stretch up into the sky.

We weigh anchor. We pass by **Karaburun** and **İnceburun. Bavul Limanı** lies just behind **İnceburun.** I don't know why it is called **Bavul Limanı** (Luggage Harbour). Perhaps the seamen prepared for their voyages there!

After we turn **Aser Point, Tekirova Bay** comes into view. There are plenty of cooks on board. *Üstun, Alı, Ahmet, Oktay* and myself are keen on *meze.* But just as we are wondering what we should make for lunch our nostrils are greeted with the smell of green beans. Pilaff with raisins, piles of salad and a melon. *Captain Ertan* had rolled up his sleeves and disappeared into the galley. We open bottles of chilled wine on the broad stern of the boat. Beans, pilaff and wine may not go too well together but we are prepared to enjoy ourselves. At a bright, shining table in the middle of the blue only people who have no appreciation for the good things of life could possibly fail to enjoy themselves.

I gaze fixedly at the sea and, from afar, at the yellow vegetation and the oleanders. The pine trees wink at me from the slopes. I have no idea why they called the place **Tekirova.** Ancient cities should be called by their own names. It is history and nature that gives a city its identity. And what is the point of names that have no connection with the sea. It's as if we were bent on proving that we are not a sea-going nation.

The city that was known in ancient times as **Phaselis** is situated on the **Pamphylian** border. It was a member of the **Lycian League.**

It isn't an easy city to penetrate. I tend to be rather cautious and circumspect. I look around for roads into it from the shore. Actually **Phaselis** is a very flat city.

Nida, Lâra, Üstün, Seher, Ülkü, Zeynep, Belâ and myself get into the ship's boat and make our way to the shore. *Ayşegül,* our "cabin boy", insists on coming with us. We let her join us to stop her sulking. The rest of the group are in the bosom of the sea.

Don't, as soon as you set out on the Blue Voyage, immediately start off asking what the point is in wandering around ruins.

The idea of the Blue Voyage is not simply to enjoy the pleasures of the beach. It also includes visiting and investigating the surrounding area and getting to know the shores, both their past and their present.

Our world is not confined to the twentieth century. And besides, the **Mediterranean** has a very special quality of its own. The **Mediterranean** is a civilization that combines both nature and history. Moreover, it is a story that contains so much that is still unknown. Scratch the soil, and you will find a thousand and one facts about its seas and its legends.

We make our way into the forest by red oleander bushes and heaps of garbage on the shore.

Most of the visitors arriving by land in automobiles and caravans are

I don't know if the sea has ever driven men mad, but the dark depths of indigo certainly intoxicate.
(above) Porto Geneviz harbour.
(below) Antalya marina.

1. *The citizens of Phaselis, one of the cities of the Lycian League, would sacrifice smoked fish at their religious ceremonies. Phaselis was a matriarchal community.*
2. *Remains of the city of Phaselis.*
3. *Phaselis. The public baths.*

foreigners. I have difficulty in finding the way. We walk along, treading on the dry pine needles and guided by my memory of the place from my last visit to it years ago. As usual, old **Herodotus** is our guide. *Athenos* made some notes on **Phaselis,** based on **Herodotus.** Here is a quote from him…

Lakios arrived in **Phaselis** at the head of a group of colonists. They met a shepherd on the shore. They asked him how much he wanted for the land. *"Do you want barley bread or smoked fish?"* they asked him. *"Smoked fish",* replied the shepherd. From that day on the inabitants have sacrificed smoked fish to Kylabros.

I don't know how one can sacrifice smoked fish, but "poisson fumé"

and wine certainly go very well together in the **Mediterranean**!

Whether you call it faith, or a ceremony reflecting the joy of living, man, in every age, has combined the pleasures of the palate with the reality of the world around him. That's why legends combining faith and pleasure suit us so well.

In our stroll around **Phaselis** we are accompanied by the smell of the pines and the chirping of the cicadas.

On suddenly arriving at an arched gate and entering a wide street I expected to find myself immediately surrounded by a bustling throng of Phaselians in their long white garments. Suddenly there emerged in front of me a tall, slim, perhaps rather non-plussed, absolutely naked individual. Who knows, perhaps he expected that I should be expecting him!

I have no intention of giving you a detailed account of this city. Suffice it to say that after 200 B.C. it was a member of the **Lycian League**, origi-

261

(opposite page) The Durukos and the Belâ lying asleep.
(left) Phaselis.

nally founded in 690 B.C., though it was excluded from time to time because of charges of fraud.

I have no love for dryasdust history, but who could possibly fail to take an interest in **Phaselis** on hearing how this people, whose secrets are slowly being unearthed through archaeological excavations, exported cedars from the slopes of Tahtalı Dağ to a great many distant countries, and imported roses, dates, attar of roses and lilies from Egypt for sale to

(above) Phaselis. The main street under the pines.
(opposite page) Sazak harbour.

the other colonists. There must be some reason behind this bringing and selling of roses and lilies all the way from Egypt two thousand five hundred years ago. It would seem to hint at something more than just trade for trade's sake.

To digress again for a moment. I hope fathers won't be angry or take offence, but in **Lycia** children took their mother's name, not their father's. It was a matriarchal community. If you have any objection you'd better settle the matter with **Herodotus!**

It wasn't only the men of **Phaselis** that had something to complain about. The **Athenian** merchants were also fed up. *"No one can beat the Phaselians in borrowing money. They take it, and that's it! They'll do anything to avoid paying it back."*

We were all very much impressed by the magnificent street that divides the city in two. There are steps on each side of it. It's obvious that they liked a street where you could sit down, get your breath back and have a good gossip. On the right hand side of the street as you go down to the harbour there is a small theatre that would delight even the most puritanical. The performance has just finished, and the spectators are strolling down towards the harbour chattering vivaciously away. Or at least that's how I imagined it!

The arches of an aqueduct emerge from amidst the pines and cedars. The harbour shines like **Venetian** glass. There are two harbours, very close together.

The bees of **Phaselis**, where Alexander the Great stayed for some time, are a terror to us all. And that's no exaggeration. According to one legend, the citizens had to abandon the city because of an invasion of bees. They are the one **Lycian** race that has never become extinct. Just as you are making your way through the bushes a wasp will buzz past as if to say, "What right have you to be here amongst these ruins?"

The boat is waiting on the shore to take us back to the yacht. We set off. We intend to spend the night at **Porto Ceneviz.**

The sea here is enough to send anyone completely crazy. It was here that I made the acquaintance of indigo, after years as a painter... There are two yachts in the harbour. Just as we are preparing to cast anchor in the indigo waters of **Porto Ceneviz**, Ahmet announces that *"there is a bet-*

1

2

3

1. *Roses, dates, attar of roses and lilies arrived from Egypt at Phaselis Harbour to be sold in the neighbouring cities.*
2. *Phaselis goats sheltering from the sun.*
3. *Sazak Harbour or Yalancı Bay.*

ter bay behind Porto Ceneviz." That's the whole pleasure of this sort of trip! We set off again, leaving a wake of foam behind us.

I am absolutely amazed at the sight of the rocks and the fishes. Here and there between the rocks the greyish-white turns to indigo or light green. This is the bay *Captain Ertan* calls **Sazak Harbour.** According to the captain of the *Belâ* it's called **"Yalancı Koy"** (Liar's Bay). *"Who's the liar?"*, I ask *Attila. "The Genoese,"* comes the reply.

The darkness of night falls first on the water and then on the rocks. Over the steep rocks a single pine tree rises up straight and tall.

Tonight I'm on the side of the **Lycian League.** For the beauty ordained by nature my god is the grey cliffs, the indigo sea and the noble pine.

The smell of shish kebap and bay leaves is coming from the fire lit in the bow of the vessel. The chirping of the cicadas mingles with the crackling of the bay leaves.

On hearing shouts of joy from one of our friends we turn and look out to sea. The moon is rising full and red from between the black rocks.

WELCOME TO ZEUS

I'm drinking my morning coffee in **Sazak Harbour** (or **Yalancı Bay** if you prefer). Yesterday I decided to wake up early this morning but I seem to have completely lost track of both day and time of day. *Yıldıray* has already prepared breakfast - white cheese, olives with thyme, Manyas cheese, butter, strawberry and cherry jam, honey, milk, kaşar cheese and eggs.

The early risers dive into the salt water of the **Mediterranean** as soon as they wake up. The boozers are still half asleep! It's as if they had incurred the wrath of Jove. They lean on the rails gazing blankly into the sea. Then feet first into the water…

The blue voyagers suddenly gather at the stern. Bargaining is going on for a six kilo bream the fishermen have just caught. For myself, I'm thinking of **Olympos.** We have decided to climb **Olympos**, the abode of *Zeus*, the place made famous by the winged horse of *Bellerephon*. *Seher, Üstün, Ali, Nida* and myself prepare to set out for **Olympos**, or **Çıralı** or **Yanartaş**, as it is also known. *"Our rag and bone merhcants are off again!"*, says *Oktay.*

We set off for the shore in the *Belâ*'s Zodiac. *Üstün* has two bottles of water in his hand. The foreign bathing belles in their bikinis are returning home from the foothills of legend.

There's a strange thing about the **Mediterranean.** Its blue waters reflect the fate of man. The brushwood covering the honeycombed rocks and the exuberant, neverending chirping of the cicadas may seem rather monotonous, but the depths of the sea open themselves up to the power of nature and the creations of mankind. On the one hand there are the loves and adventures and the preposterous commands of *Zeus,* and, on the other, the submerged cities in the bosom of the sea.

*(above) Frescoes in the apse of the small temple on Mt Olympos (Çıralı).
(opposite page) Zeus, the Father of the Gods, to whom appeal was made in every field in the polytheistic civilizations of the Aegean and the Mediterranean. Demirci, Çine, Aydın. Marble. Hellenistic period, 2nd-1st century B.C. Istanbul Archaeological Museum.*

IN THE SHADOW OF MYRA. DEMRE AND SANTA CLAUS

We are having breakfast in **Gökkaya Bay** where we have just spent the night. *Captain Ertan* gives us the good news. There's not a drop of water left in our five-ton tank. People come out of the sea and go straight into the showers... Some are taking five or six showers a day. The only solution is to sail right past **Kekova Bay** and make straight for **Kaş.**

Kaş is the nearest point where we can get water. It's a three and a half hour's sail. Then as long, perhaps longer, in taking on the water. We had planned a tour of **Demre** and the **Lycian** rock tombs. *Ahmet's Belâ* provided a solution to the problem. The *Durukos III* would go on to **Kaş** while we went into **Demre Bay.**

While *Durukos* set off for **Kaş** we ourselves set out for **Demre.** We arranged to meet in **Kalkan.**

The bay doesn't stretch as far as **Demre** so we had to make our way to **Demre** from the sandy beach at the mouth of the **Kokarçay.** Moreover, the water was too shallow for the *Belâ,* which has quite a deep draught, so we had to have a small motor-boat come and pick us up. Taxis were waiting on the shore to take us first to the **Lycian** rock tombs and then the ruins of the city and ancient theatre in front of it. The water problem meant that all the "blue voyagers" were forced to become "rag and bone merchants". They could choose between sitting in the restaurant by the shore or visiting the church, the theatre and the rock tombs. They all chose the latter. And everybody, quite naturally, was interested in **Santa Claus!**

In actual fact, no one was breaking any rules or regulations. One of the most important principles of the Blue Voyage is that everyone shares a common interest in both man and nature.

The sacred fabric of Demre extends from the Lycian tombs of the 4th century B.C. to St Nicholas.

274

Formerly known as Myra, the settlement had a long history comprising the Lycian League, the Hellenistic period, and the Roman, Byzantine and Ottoman worlds.

Demre, known in ancient times as **Myra,** boasts a very long history reaching far back through the ages: the **Lycian League,** the **Hellenistic Age**, **Rome**, **Christendom** right up to the Middle Ages, the **Emirates**, the **Ottomans**…

It's really strange… Men have regularly treated the cities belonging to the civilizations preceding them as if they were their own property. At **Demre** the **Romans** built their magnificent theatre right in front of the **Lycian** rock tombs, although there was no real need for it, and at the same time converted the area occupied by the **Lycian** tombs into their own necropolis. And why not?

A whole family can be
seen depicted on a relief
on the tomb of a **Lycian** nobleman: men, women and children seem to
be watching an ancient play from one of the boxes in the theatre. Two
civilizations one within the other. No one asks whether you are
Byzantine or **Ottoman.**
The theatre is no ordinary building. The imposing stairway leading to
the upper floors is covered with a vaulted roof. There are shops beside
it. Everywhere there is evidence of vitality and enterprise. Now the theatre is surrounded by greenhouses growing summer vegetables for the

19th century view of Myra, the theatre and the Lycian tombs. From Charles Texier, "Voyage de l'Asie Mineure".

Myra. Roman theatre.

big cities. No one bothers about the past.

What is the importance of the rock reliefs, the huge stone building that was used first as a theatre and then as an arena, when compared with the price of tomatoes, aubergines and peppers?

On our way back from our climb up to have a close look at the rock tombs and reliefs we lost our way and found ourselves in a labyrinth of row upon row of greenhouses. That was when we realized the their real importance.

A name the whole world knows: **St.Nicholas**, or **Santa Claus**.

The symbol of the 20th century.

Patron saint of seamen and children.

We no longer believe in **Zeus** and his pantheon of gods. And what about **Santa Claus? St.Nicholas** was born in the city of **Patara**, not far from **Kalkan**. He later settled in **Demre** and after the spread of Christianity in

the region became a part of legend. The church and chapel which is said to contain his tomb have become the cynosure of the Western world. The tomb stands in a niche.

We certainly cannot claim to have fully exploited the touristic potential of the most famous and honoured personality in the **Lycian, Roman** and **Christian** world.

(above) Joy and sorrow have existed together in all theatrical periods. This truth is symbolized in a relief belonging to the theatre near the Myra rock-tombs. (opposite page) Myra. Entrance to the Roman theatre.

The church and tomb of **St.Nicholas**, otherwise known as **Santa Claus**, could have made **Demre** world famous…

The ability to seize opportunities like this is a matter of culture …

"Daddy," asks Ayşegül on hearing the name of the place we were about to visit, *"Was it Santa Claus that brought me the Barbie doll?"*

It's a sad thing if we can't even exploit a myth that's become an inetgral part of every child's world…

Yes… The climate at **Demre** is very suitable for greenhouses. That's why it's famous for its fruit and vegetables.

We went back the way we came. There's a restaurant on the beach

where the **Kokaıçay** empties into the
sea. We had our lunch there. A little
later a gypsy passed by with a sweet
little bear. To the sound of the tambourine and under the influence of
the scorching sun the little bear hopped up and down showing us how
"mothers-in-law wash in the hamam"!…
It now occurred to us that it was about time we got into the motor-boat
that had brought us there and went back to the *Belâ*. If we stayed any
longer we'd be caught in the darkness, and all the tumult and ruthless-
ness of life on the shore!…

A native of Patara, St
Nicholas later settled in
Demre where he embarked
upon the promulgation of
the Christian faith and
became a legendary figure.
The floor mosaics at the
entrance of the Church of St
Nicholas display a skill on
a par with the legend.

1, 2. Church of St Nicholas. Views of the interior and exterior.
3. Column capital in the Church of St Nicholas.
4, 5. Floor mosaics in the Church of St Nicholas.

We went back to the boat...
When I opened my note-book in the cabin in the *Belâ* I come across another note:
"The blue disaster continues. The third day of days of nightmare. The characters in the group make me absolutely ill As soon as I get back to Istanbul I'm going to spend a week resting in a clinic. And I'm sick and fed up having to contend with some animal or other every day. Yesterday it was wasps. Today it's flies... And on top of it all, bilge water in the cooker Both men and women suffering from bowel infections! On the rear deck rows of bodies like a leper colony! Drunken discussions on reli-

(above) Sarcophagus in the side aisle of the Church of St Nicholas.
(below) Stones in the garden of the Church of St Nicholas.

gion and the history of art. They've finished five tons of water and they still stink like goats! A dreadful consumption of compensan, dramamine and coffee. That's the blue voyage in a nutshell!"

I look up to find all my friends in the door of the cabin roaring with laughter.

I go out…

The loveliest bays in the whole **Mediterranean** point the way forwards. It isn't only the infinity of blue and indigo that draws us on towards the unknown; it is the emergence of civilizations in front of us in the form of white breakers.

We go from one unknown to the other. A little way in front of us fish

(left) Church of St Nicholas. Interior.
(above) Church of St Nicholas. Stone carving.

pass by in shoals, leaping in the water. We can't help turning around them. The island of **Kekova** begins on our left.

Imagine a corridor, a very long corridor… Mountains and maquis on both sides. Fill this long corridor with the water of the **Mediterranean.** Let there be moss and rocks at the bottom. Go along and sit in the bow of the boat. Have one eye on the mountains and one eye on the sea. If you can, find a sentence for the beauties that emerge in front of you. This is **Kekova**; you can ignore the rest…

KEKOVA
AN EARTHLY PARADISE

Now I know why seamen can't live on land. At **Kekova** one constantly hears the call of the sea. You have only to stretch out your hand for the sea to approach you. You shiver. Not because of the coolness of the **Mediterranean**, but perhaps because you had forgotten the colour of the water. Or perhaps, in this age of ours, because we feel a yearning for friendship. It's so near, and yet so far! You see the relationships of everything, and of nothing at all. Just when you think you know it all, you find yourselves surrounded by unknowns.

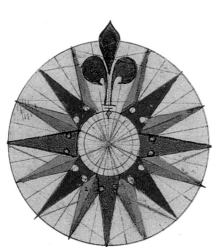

"The place called Kekova is well known as a paradise on earth. Here man and nature go hand in hand, to reach the ultimate in beauty. Kekova is, in every respect, an unsolvable mystery. Its real name, unknown in the past, is still unknown today. Kekova is actually the name of an island - a long island known as Kale, or "the castle", right opposite a village cheek by jowl with the ancient site."

That's how *Azra Erhat* describes **Kekova Island** and **Kale.**

If you reach **Kale (Simena)** without having had your fill of the sea you may be tempted to greet what I write with an "I'm absolutely fed up with these romantics. They're always carrying on about something or other." In that case you can go off and eat fish by the shore to the sound of arabesque music. But if I were you I wouldn't miss the little houses, the old Ottoman castle and the **Lycian** tombs on the slopes. The single **Lycian** tomb in the water on the shore carries you off into the unknown, just like the deep waters of **Kekova.**

The reality that meets you in **Kekova** is that of solitude and moonlight, and in the **Mediterranean** that of the cicada. That's all we know. And, as

(above) Sea and stones at Kekova.
(opposite page) Kekova from Kale. 1994.

290

Kekova from Kale, 1994.
Kale streets, 1994.

we keep repeating, all we don't know!...

There is no way of reaching the settlement of **Kale** (I wouldn't call it a city) by land, so our blue voyagers, after gazing on it for ages from the sea, finally decided to land all together on the shore. How could

they resist such a magnificent prospect?

When I came here years ago there was no colour or activity in **Kale** outside the stone houses and the **Lycian** tomb in the sea.

This time, there was a row of restaurants on the shore, some with every language (except Arabic), some that were content with their own. But our warmest welcome came from the women and children that as soon as we cast anchor came rushing towards us in their rowing-boats with baskets of *yazmas* and crochet work.

In **Kale,** don't expect to find a monumental street like the one in **Phaselis**, or an alley or even a path. Make straight for the house that has caught your eye. That's what I did, like a sheep that strays from the flock. From the rock I had climbed on to in my passion for taking photographs I jumped on to the flight of small stone steps in front of me. I soon came to two stone houses and an alley between them. But the alley was completely blocked by a cow. I just didn't have the strength to search for another road. I pushed the black cow as hard as I could and managed to slip past. The cow couldn't care less!

A little way above, on a little terrace, a woman was giving a boy an English lesson. Whichever way I looked I was absolutely amazed at the view. On the slope to my right stretched a long row of **Lycian** tombs

Kaleköy, Simena-Kekova.
Kekova. Girl selling yazmas.
The "Blue Voyagers" in Kale.

with lion heads; in front of me the stone walls of the castle, and behind me a wonderful view of **Kekova Island** in the sea's embrace.

I could hear *Semiramis* calling from somewhere above. She was pointing out the way up to the castle. As I ascended the slope I realized that it wasn't the castle but the infinite expanse of the sea behind it that was the real attraction. Behind the castle there was another sea.

Man can't do without myth. Though sometimes a fairy-tale will do. But here there isn't even a hint of one.

> *"Even the oldest inhabitants can't tell you when it was that people first*
> *settled here. Kekova is an enigma, and will most probably remain one."*

Azra Erhat is right. We ought to have made up our own myth.

When I got up to the towers of the castle I found several foreigners there. An old woman was crocheting away while at the same time trying to sell the *yazmas* in her basket. I was more interested in the wells

Üçağız rock-tombs.

liked to have toured around under the light blue, glass-green water.
The *Belâ* hugged the shore. We all seemed to be searching for jewels in
the shallow water. We could see square recesses in the walls of the little
rooms. They may have been made to hold the beams supporting the
wooden roof.

Towards the bottom end of **Kekova Bay** we could see the dockyard used
by the **Ottomans.** Now yachts are moored there. This is the only place
where you can stop.

299

Our voyage continued along the rear shore of **Kekova.** This shore is completely deserted. Our "blue voyagers" soon got bored. *"How far is it to Denizatı?"* they kept on asking us. *"Is it just past this point?"* Ah! If I only knew… Would I ever have come here? I would have declared myself a **Lycian** and settled down in **Kale!**

As a matter of fact I soon began to be plagued by a few doubts myself. It was beginning to get dark. The sea was rising. There was no clue to be had from the seaward shore of **Kekova.**

"Let's ask by wireless," we suggested. This time *Captain Atilla* wasn't too keen.

"I'm at the helm," he said. And *Ali* and *Üstün* had cast their fishing-lines in the hope of having a catch.

I had my eye on the bays. No one was saying anything. I had a feeling they didn't know whether to express hope or alarm. We would certainly get to *Denizatı,* but we might get grounded on the rocks in the darkness.

Hope turned to pessimism as we reached the end of **Kekova Island.**

*In the peace and tranquillity of Üçağız.
An Üçağız fisherman.
Kekova Island.*

3

301

"This must be it!" I heard myself saying. But there was no sign of the *Durukos* in the place we were heading for. It was impossible to miss its 20 metre mast. But there was nothing there. We wound our way a little further into the bay. *"Who was it said this was Denizatı Bay?"* came the voice of one of our female blue voyagers. I didn't say anything, but I had my doubts. We had to make for the bottom jaw of **"Sea-Horse" (Denizatı) Bay.** But it was the steep, high rocks that prevented us from seeing the mast of the boat behind them. At our third turn the *Durukos* sudenly appeared waiting for us like a bride at the altar.

Kekova Island. The dockyard.

The shores rang with shouts of *"Hurrah for Durukos! There's nothing like her!"* The *Belâ* is suddenly abandoned as they clamber on to the *Durukos* like a band of pirates.

We take our places at the beautifully prepared table, on a calm, indigo sea. The drinkers get down to business. Now I realize why there are so many wine pitchers at the bottom of the sea. The **Mediterranean** has been literally consecrated with wine. The sailors call us to the feast.

We are completely shut off from the open sea. No pirate ship could possibly find us here in the darkness! And the **Lycians** are our friends.

I have a conversation with *Semiramis, Zeynep* and *Üstün* about the submerged city: the little trough-shaped houses, the dockyard restaurants with wooden roofs, and the gossip in the light of the torches...

And of course the theatre for three hundred had its share of the midnight chatter.

Our dream world opens its sails to contemporary myths.

303

KAŞ AND UNDERWATER CIVILIZATION

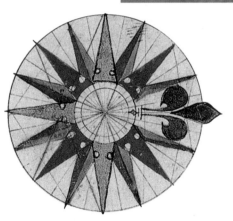

A Kaş kilim with stylized motifs drawn from a thousand flowers being washed in the salt water of the Mediterranean.

We have become used to the indigo of the **Mediterranean**, and its occasional glass-green… We have begun to take it all for granted. But there is one thing that remains rather strange. The fact that the bays and ancient cities bear not the faintest resemblance one to the other.

I was thinking this over as I sat at breakfast in **Denizatı Bay**. Just try and find any resemblance between **Sazak** and **Denizatı**! The mountains are the same mountains. The sea is the same sea, the **Mediterranean**. What resemblance is there between the city of **Phaselis** and **Simena (Kale)** and **Uçağız**?

No answer…

Add myth to the individual identity of each city and its natural environment. And lose yourself in dreams as you spend the night in a boat on the water..

I think it's in a story by *Oscar Wilde*. A hunter comes back from the forest every day with stories of birds of quite incredible beauty and all sorts of strange and frightening creatures. One evening the talkative hunter comes back and just sits there without saying a word. After a great deal of pressure he finally replies. *"This time I actually saw them!"* That's how it is with the **Mediterranean**…

Truth or fiction? You'd better see for yourself and decide.

Late at night *Captain Ertan* told us of a submerged city with sarcophagi in the sea. He is an old sponge-diver so he knows what he is talking about when it comes to the underwater world. We decide to go and see it.

We pass **Gönül Island** and the strait of **Akar** and then turn right. There

is a very interesting site in the bay known as **Sıçak İskelesi.** Massive defence walls, gates and **Lycian** tombs are visible from quite a distance. The sea was rather rough so the *Durukos* couldn't go too near the shore. *Üstün* put on his goggles and dived into the sea. *Seher* and I got into a rowing-boat and made our way to the shore.

We could see the remains of the harbour down below in the water. There are also two **Lycian** tombs. At the same time, ruins stretch all the way up the slopes. The **Lycian** tombs, weathered to a reddish-brown, are scattered around amidst the olive trees like ruins from a bombardment. Human interest in archaeology must go back a very long way.

Probably a rather casual and summary sort of interest!…
Some of these tombs, hewn from a single block of stone, lie upside down on the ground. In other cases the bottom has disappeared and only the top remains. Some are untouched. And here is a tomb that the looters were careful not to damage too much, opening a hole just big enough for a child to get through!…
Tomb robbing is not a phenomenon confined to our own age. Mankind has been pillaging and looting them for thousands of years.
There are one or two villages in the bay but we are prevented from visiting them by time and the waves. We are forced to return to the boat with our curiosity unsatisfied.
I rummage through the books I brought with me. An unexcavated site. A little known city. The name, **Aperlae**. **Lycian, Hellenistic** and **Roman** periods. City coinage of the 5th century. Judging by the defence walls surrounding it, its inhabited area, its harbour and tombs, it would appear to have been quite a large town. Landing-stages had been built

1. As we make our way down the winding road to Kaş (Antiphellos) we suddenly find a magnificent landscape spread out before us.
2. Kaş harbour
3. Kaş. Under the plane tree.

where ships could be moored every 15 metres. The ruins we saw underground must have been the remains of these landing-stages.

So we leave behind us another city full of unknowns. It will have to wait for another spring. As it is, if the sea gets any rougher we'll be marooned here. We just stand looking at each other without being able to go ashore.

We are going to spend the night in a bay not far from **Kaş**, but we have some business to do in **Kaş** itself. We'll be taking on some vegetables, a few drinks and cigarettes. And we'll also take a stroll round the city. Most of us have already seen it...

A cool sea breeze fans our cheeks. Most of us are sitting in the stern of the boat... Those who prefer to live cheek by jowl with the **Mediterranean** are sitting in the bows. We are washed now and then by spray from the foaming blue waves. As we approach **Uluburun** we catch sight of the famous boat *Virazon*.

Three thousand four hundred years ago, a Bronze Age merchant ship, unable to hold out against the waves of the **Mediterranean,** went down at this very spot. Actually, those parts of the sea that were to be feared thousands of years ago are still those that are feared today. That's why *Captain Ertan* announced that *"we should get into a bay before it gets any later"*.

3

1. Kaş harbour.
2. A tomb in Aperlae.
3. Famous Lycian tomb in a Kaş street.

The specially-equipped *Virazon* under *George Bass* has recovered the most amazing finds in the source of its underwater explorations - gold goblets and jewellery, amphorae with lovely perfumes and flower seeds, **Egyptian** necklaces and all sorts of glass-ware found lying at the bottom of the grey rocks. And their dates were such as to astound the whole of the scholarly world.

It isn't we who insist that blue is the colour of civilization. It's this single wreck and the **Mediterranean.** The finds we are presented with comprise the whole life and skill of mankind.

As we approach **Kaş** we see new buildings ripping a gash in the natural environment. One of them must be government house.

This city on the **Teke** peninsula was known in ancient times as **Antiphellos.**

Meis Island, directly opposite the grey and green, looks across to the lovely little **Kaş** theatre. This theatre, along with the remains of the old city and the **Lycian** tombs can be seen from the upper part of the city.

1. The submerged city of Aperlae
2,3. Kaş and detail of tomb.

1

The new town is inextricably intertwined with the old. The best example is the street in which the **Lycian** tomb is located. This is lined on both sides by old houses and is used as a market for the kilims and carpets of the **Kaş** region.

To get the most magnificent view of **Kaş** you have to go up to the main road. And those who arrive by this road rather late in the evening, and especially those who arrive at sunset, are absolutely done for! They immediately stop on one of the bends. It's just the place for a *"God Almighty!"* You can't help feeling the moisture of wine on your lips. The little bay in the peninsula to the right is filled with a phosphorescent light. In no time at all you find yourself in a restaurant by the shore. It's nothing to do with us! The wine was your idea!

I wonder what the people who used to discuss whether **Kaş** was capable of development would say if they saw it now! Let's just hope it never becomes a sort of **Bodrum** the *Fisherman of Halicarnassus* would hate!...

As soon as *Ali, Ahmet* and I had seen to our *"daily bread"* we made straight straight for the *Durukos.* The debate on what we were going to

2

3

eat, which occupies us day and night, now flared up in all its intensity. What shall we cook?…

In response, *Ali, Üstün* and *Ahmet* rattled off a list of all the dishes they knew from fish soup to baked macaroni. From the opposite camp came testing suggestions for baked beans with *pastırma* and baked shrimps. There were also special requests for raspberry tarts for afternoon tea.

We weigh anchor with the intention of crossing the calm sea and spending the night in **Ufakdere Bay** opposite **Kaş.** While others are downing gins and tonic with tangarine segments *Ali, Üstün* and *Ahmet* are displaying their skills. At the helm, *Captain Ertan* smiles from afar at our idle cooks. Let us give them their due. If they actually went into the galley they would offer their clients the most extraordinary sauces!

As soon as we anchored in **Ufakdere Bay** everyone dived into the water. Some struggle with the waves in an attempt at surf-riding. The coolness of the water has done wonders. The lovely smell from the galley has everyone guessing. *Captain Ertan* insists on preparing baked rissoles with peppers and tomatoes. And all sorts of *meze* to go with it…Our

1

2

midnight conversations again centred on the **Lycians**. Some of us make fun of the whole thing. But no one says they're fed up with this intellectual sort of conversation. Some of us discuss the question of the identity of the **Lycians** who were buried together with their jewellery and most treasured possessions. "I wonder if there were Lycian profiteers?" I wouldn't know, but the cicadas finally fall silent and mark the coming of night.... I drop off to sleep gazing at the stars…

1. *Small theatre on the Kaş road.*
2. *Bay on the Kaş shore with one single individual!*
3. *Kalkan houses.*
4. *The My Dream in a bay opposite Kalkan.*

> *"Keep a good lookout right and left,*
> *Let's not get ourselves into trouble.*
> *Let's spend some nights together,*
> *But see to it your people don't find out!"*

While I was dozing and dreaming we've anchored in **Kalkan** harbour. The sound of drum and zurna fuses with the strident voice of a singer in one of the restaurants by the shore. A convoy of minibuses escort a new bride. I go into a shower and wash off the whole accretion of arabesque, drum-and-zurna and motor horns.

When I come to myself, I see some of the blue voyagers returning from a stroll round **Kalkan**.

XANTHOS, OR HOLOCAUST

Anatolia has created a language of its own. A language that emerged quite spontaneously, to be consolidated through long experience. When you arrive somewhere the villagers will say, *"Göç gide gide düzelir"*. This is normally said for Turcomans or migrants but actually it suits all travellers.

Our own journey was now going well. It's as if our blue-landlubbers with the seaman's spirit had been cruising around on the seas for a thousand years. None of us now looked down on the boat, the bays or the waves. Nobody mentioned wide streets, blocks of flats, cinemas, television or crazy videos, even just to annoy. Now, as soon as we come ashore, they are all off exploring every hole and corner of the town. Just like sailors who, wherever they may happen to cast anchor, come back to their cabins with presents they have bought for their girl-friends at home

Actually, this habit helps us to see the unknown in nature and the old cities. It proves that the seas, to which we are quite unaccustomed, consist of more than just water. It reminds us, even if only for a very short time, of the virtue of being able to take a good look at nature and mankind.

Mumbling away to myself in this fashion I step ashore at **Kalkan,** where we are now moored. The side streets evidence a very real concern with the conservation of the old houses and the old urban fabric. The little shops and guest-houses are arranged in perfect harmony with their environment. But there are also signs of the emergence of the concrete disease, like a rotten tooth. An extraordinary type of architecture that

Kalkan. Houses and flowers.

belongs neither to sea or land. I ask myself what this get-rich-quick jerry-building is doing in the **Mediterranean**. The inhabitants of **Kalkan** are saying the same thing. Most of them are refugees from the great cities who have chosen to make their home in the heart of nature. They

1,2. On the shores of Kalkan.
3,4. Sidyma (Dodurga). Stone
carvings of cow and rabbit.

are afraid that **Kalkan**, too, may be destroyed in front of their very eyes. And yet the region is surrounded by ancient cities: **Xanthos, Patara, Sidyma, Letoum**… Each of them a city with an architecture, a way of life and myths that have survived to our own times, while **Kalkan** is under pressure from both past and present…

This time our journey will continue by land. I examine the maps of the coast and my plans of the old cities. I find **Xanthos**, the old **Lycian** capital, **Patara** and **Letoum**.

Xanthos lies about 8 km inland. **Letoum** is 4 km from **Xanthos**. **Patara**, which lies 1 km from the sea, is 11 km from **Xanthos**. Actually all those cities are between sixteen and twenty-two kilometres from **Kalkan**. *Ahmet* hires a minibus while I search for volunteers for a trip to the cities of stone and earth.

This time we have too many customers. The old rag and bone merchants are joined by the children. We are always worried that *Ayşegül* and *Ceren* will get sunstroke or get tired or get thorns in their feet, but everywhere we see little kids you could carry on your back, kids that belong to the foreign tourists from all over the world. When they grow up they come back as archaeologists or art historians. Some conduct excavations, others write books on **Anatolian** culture…

Lycia is an amazing civilization. Whichever coastal city you go to you will be confronted with interesting scenes from the depths of history combined with the blue of the sea.

The history of **Xanthos** is not the sort to be simply bitten off and swallowed. It's a question of the noble inhabitants of a great city who wrote their own tragedy in the cause of freedom. It's the story of a nation who preferred suicide to life without honour.

3

4

Xanthos, founded 2700 years ago by the **Lycians**, found itself confronted in 42 B.C. by a hostile **Roman** army led by *Brutus,* the man to whom *Caesar* addressed his famous *"Et tu, Brute!"*

Brutus had asked the **Xanthians** for soldiers and money but had received an unfavourable reply from the capital of the **Lycian League**. According to *Appian,* **Brutus** sacrificed the whole of the surrounding region to his wrath. Cities and fields alike were deluged in the flames. Everything was burned or destroyed. But the **Xanthians** stood firm. The city refused to surrender…

Brutus entered the city just as the sun was setting. The *Xanthians*, old and young, men, women and children had chosen suicide. Some cast themselves on to flaming pyres, some threw themselves from precipices along with their wives and children… *Brutus* was furious. He promised a reward to anyone who brought in a *Xanthian* alive!…

The territory belonging to the city whose inhabitants had surrendered themselves to such a holocaust now belonged to the **Romans**. The **Xanthian** collaborators did *Vespasian's* work for him. After all, it isn't only heroes who have monuments erected in their honour. Traitors and double-dealers are also rewarded. A triumphal arch was erected in honour of *Vespasian*. A shameful act, perhaps, but that's life!…

The **Esen Çayı** flows quite peacefully through country that has known **Lycian, Roman** and early **Byzantine** rule, just as if nothing had happened. Whereas, in actual fact, **Romans** used the magnificent theatre for gladiatorial combats and fights between men and lions.

First a theatre, then a battle-ground. That's the lot of mankind. Life can't always be a bed of roses! A little blue, and then a little blood-red!...

As one wanders around amidst these ruins one can't help thinking of the ancient *Xanthians*, once the wealthiest of all the inhabitants of the province of **Lycia**.

A youth with a straw hat saunters up to me and asks me if I want to visit the ruins. We stroll together around **Xanthos**, which covers quite a substantial area. We start off with the **Lycian** house-tombs. Our guide is called *Ömer*. He's the son of the keeper in the local museum. He is wearing a shalvar and a straw hat. I've seen dozens of these shalvars in tourist shops. I ask him why he's wearing them. *"It's an advertisement. A friend of mine makes them. The tourists see me wearing them and go off and buy a pair."*

He's a real smart boy, *Ömer*. While we stroll around **Xanthos** he takes the opportunity of chatting to all the French tourists we meet. He embroiders everything he says. He tells us why. *"If I told the tourists plain and simple they'd say 'He doesn't know anything'. So I fluff it out a bit."*

He has learned French all by himself. He can get by in English too. Now he's set his sights on Spanish. It seems that whatever nationality most of the visitors to **Xanthos** are, that's the language he's interested in. After finishing lycée he entered the University Entrance Examinations for French. He's waiting for the result.

"The Lycians and the Romans built their tombs according to the way they lived." *Ömer* explains. *"The Lycians made house portraits on their tombs, the*

(opposite page) Wrestlers and musicians, ceremonial scene. Limestone, last quarter of 6th century B.C. Found in the vicinity of Xanthos. Istanbul Archaeological Museum.
(left) After the Xanthians, who preferred mass suicide to life without honour, the territory was occupied by the Romans and Byzantines.

*/right) Remains of the city of
Letoum.
(below) From Xanthos.*

Romans made pictures of their ships." "Not portraits," I correct
him, *"Portals. If you were studying archaeology as well as French
they would never pass you!"*
"What do you expect?" he replies with a smile, *"Who could
think in this heat."* We are all delighted to find there's someone like that in **Xanthos.** This city has been pillaged for centuries. Now there's someone to look after it. Ömer is there!…
Another thing I noticed during our trip was the emergence of
a new generation comprising anything from driver to sales-
man. Some are dark-complexioned, long-haired type play-
boys with a gold chain round their necks like their Italian
counterparts. Others know every detail of every old ruin
around them and are eager to guide you around with their
smattering of a foreign language. I fancy that the natives of
this city and shore were aware of the profit potential long
before the *Ministry of Culture and Tourism.* I have noticed the
same thing in **Olympos, Kaş, Kalkan** and **Xanthos.** Don't be
surprised if a new race of smart guys emerges in the
Mediterranean amidst all this talk of native and foreign!…
And here's another story about **Xanthos,** now known as **Kınık.** I suppose you've heard of Charles Fellows.
It's not a question of the Black Sea remark. "If he doesn't know me I
don't know him." He knew us Turks very well. And he knew the little
importance we give to the culture on which history is built.

The British researcher Sir Charles Fellows arrived in **Xanthos** in 1840. Let *Azra Erhat* tell us the rest of the story:

> *"Using quite incredible methods, Fellows removed the huge sarcophagi from the soil, cut out reliefs from the rock tombs as if he were slicing butter, somehow or other managed to load tons upon tons of carved marble on to a warship, and finally succeeded in safely depositing them in the British Museum. Let me give you the list: the Nereid monument, the Pajava sarcophagus, the Harpy Tomb built by the Lycians in 470 B.C.... All these are now in the British Museum."*

Let's make do with what is left! In any case there's plenty of it!... There's the theatre, the agora and the palace, and dozens of houses, monuments, rock tombs, sarcophagi!... While we were wandering around all this wealth of material *Zeynep, Semiramis* and *Emine* got lost.

I found them among the houses with the floor mosaics looking on to the **Esen Çay** behind the theatre. The place where the **Lycian, Roman** and **Byzantine** inhabitants once lived. They, too, knew the meaning of holocaust. The houses in which the **Lycians** went to a mass death shows that for mankind tragedy is a way of life.

"What on earth made the Xanthians commit mass suicide?" I asked *Ömer*. He hesitated for a minute. *"What else could they do?"* he replies, turning to look at me. *"They couldn't surrender, could they!"*

From this great and honourable city we make our way by minibus to **Letoum**. They make you buy a ticket to get into **Letoum** but there were no tickets to get into the capital, **Xanthos.** Perhaps the Ministry ignores **Xanthos**, regarding suicide as being incompatible with the rules of Islam!... It's difficult to make out the reasoning behind it.

Letoum has all the appearance of a submerged city. The stones and columns of the temple are covered with water. *"In winter the whole of the old city is flooded"* the villagers tell us.

Letoum was dedicated to the goddess **Leto.** It has three temples, to *Leto, Apollo* and *Artemis. Leto* was one of the wives of *Zeus. Apollo* and *Artemis* were their children.

Apollo, the god of light, nature, reason and strength, was the favourite god of the **Lycian League**. *Leto's* pedigree can be traced back to the **Anatolian** goddess *Kybele*.

But if I go on tracing everyone's pedigree and their relationship to one another I shall get everything myself in a complete muddle. The best thing is just to ignore family relationships. Otherwise I will be joining the caravan myself!...

In its theatre and its fluted columns this little city of **Letoum** offers magnificent examples of a superb architecture.

Leaving the city of the gods we make our way to **Patara**, located at about one kilometre from the endless sandy beach that runs along the shore. There are two important personalities connected with **Patara**: *Apollo,* and *Santa Claus.*

The theatre is covered in sand-drifts. If excavations were carried out here who knows what might be unearthed. Then there's also the harbour, the lighthouse, the agora, the baths and the triumphal arch…

Leaving the ramshackle restaurant with its smell of *kebaps* beside the legendary shore, we go back to **Kalkan**.

The talk of the day is *Ahmet's* captain, *Atilla*. The night before he had gone out fishing with the *Belâ*. He had shut off the wireless so we couldn't find out what was happening. All we knew was that he had taken beer and a large bottle of rakı and gone off fishing. *Ahmet* was furious. We were all pretty excited too.

Just as things were working to a climax the *Belâ* hove in sight. *Ahmet* was sitting waiting, apparently quite relaxed, but as tense as a tiger. We were also anxiously waiting to see how *Captain Atilla* was going to explain his fishing escapade! What's more, he had gotten permission

from *Captain Ertan* and taken *Hüseyin,* a crew member of the *Durukos,* along with him. All the blue voyagers were gathered in the stern. They didn't want to miss anything of the confrontation.

They cast anchor and moored the *Belâ* to the *Durukos.* Not a sound. *Atilla* being very dark-complexioned his face was giving nothing away. He just seemed a bit sullen. But no sooner had he said *"Ati..."* than *Attila* and *Hüseyin* brought out an enormous *laos* and struck a pose. Cameras started clicking amid cheers and applause.*Attila* complains about the shark that attacked the fish on the line.

Ahmet's face relaxes into a smile. *"Come and have a rakı",* he says to *Atilla...* And we begin the night at **Kalkan.**

1. *Patara. The theatre. From Charles Texier, "Description de l'Asie Mineure".*
2. *View from the Patara theatre.*
3. *Triumphal arch at the entrance to Patara.*

1

2

3

A MYSTERIOUS ISLAND: GEMİLER AND KAUNOS IN THE LABYRINTH

In the Blue Voyage, one of the most important things is the choice of a place to spend the night. The captains are intent on finding a calm, quiet bay, while the passengers expect a beautiful prospect that begins with the sea and ends in the sky, or rather never ends at all. Their greatest ambition is to spend an endless night spent drinking in the open air.

Is drink so essential?... Not at all. Drink is to be used as a seasoning, something to lend savour, not as a means of intoxication. *Dionysos*, the god of wine, exerts no pressure on anyone. It's enough if we share the beauty and the blessings of nature. The only people *Dionysos* can't stand are those who don't find a vital pleasure in beauty. Those whose places in life are "vacant" even when they are alive.

"There's colour in nature. There's music. There's pleasure. There's the exuberance that fills the festivities. Without it, would the flowers bloom? Would people fall in love in the spring?"

European type cafés have opened up on the shore at **Kalkan**. *Zeynep* never misses such places. She makes a tour of them for the fun of the thing. Of course she exaggerates everything. We go along to the café for *Irish Coffee* and *tartelette aux framboises*.

We are approached by a bearded, foreign-looking waiter. An argument springs up between *Üstün* and *Ali* on whether Irish coffee is made with brandy or whisky. The waiter can give no answer to this vital question. We order something to eat and drink. The same question crops up. No word from the waiter. And no sign of the order. The waiter's back again.

Sunset at Gemiler Island.

324

The question is repeated. Finally the waiter replies. *"I only drop in here in the evenings. I wouldn't know."* Now the proprietor appears with the news that it is made with whisky. A little later the Turkish waiter with the beard and the gold chain round his neck appears with the order. While serving the coffee he knocks against my shoulder. *"Sorry!"* he says, turning to me. We all look at each other. It's all we can do to get back to the *Durukos* without collapsing.

We're going to spend the night at **Yeşilköy Limanı**, a place just

Gemiler Island. A witness to the natural and historical fabric that still conceals its secret at the present day.

beyond **Kalkan**. This will be in the nature of a farewell evening for *Ahmet*, *Semiramis* and *Lâra*, who will be going back to **Antalya** from **Kalkan**, while we ourselves will be setting out early the next morning for **Fethiye**.

This time Ahmet's doing the cooking. The *laos* caught by our fishermen is to be prepared for the feast. *Captain Ertan* has cut it into slices and is now busy frying them. *Ahmet* boils the other fish, picks out the bones, arranges them on a dish and covers them with a Béchamel sauce. Then he adds a few tomatoes and a lot of grated cheese and puts it in the oven.

Wine and rakı, in moderation. Towards midnight I fall into a doze. The blue voyagers make their way to the prow, taking their drinks along with them.

After a short nap I wake up to the sound of people calling me. A bewitching new moon is rising over the **Mediterranean**. I open my eyes to a cool breeze from the sea. I feel angry with myself for falling asleep on such a night.

We are chatting away with *Ahmet* at the table in the stern of the *Durukos*. "*Look after number one,*" Ahmet is saying, "*Forget anything else!*" All the chaos and confusion of the city, all the meaningless conflicts and frustrations of everyday life are comprised In this one sentence. The enjoyment of life is something very difficult to capture. But the **Mediterranean** and this endless expanse of nature put it back on the agenda. They open up a heart grown old in the face of so many difficulties and disappointments...

There are seven stormy capes ahead of us. Some of us are sleeping in the cabins, some on deck. I awake with a shiver, in the cool spray from a rising sea. One by one

A view from Gemiler Island.

we pass by **Zeytin Point, Kılıç Point, Yassı Point, Kalkamak Point, İnkaklık Point, Sancak Point** and **Kötü Point.** It was only later that I learned from my friends how difficult it had been to round these seven capes without being tossed about too much.

In the **Mediterranean,** every stretch of sea between two pieces of land is quite different. Perhaps I keep repeating myself.

I'm not a good angel that likes everything he sees. But I've taken up sailing rather late, and I am only now discovering the joy of travel that *Eyüboğlu* and the *Fisherman of Halicarnassus* discovered thirty years ago. One thing that hasn't changed is the beauty of it all, and the more or less untouched virginity of this sea.

We cast anchor at **Gemiler** or **Gemiler Island.** The island is very close to the mainland. It's a perfect place to moor. Lines of yachts, most of them under a foreign flag, lie along the shore of **Gemiler Island.** I open *Ezra Erhat's* book:

> *"After making your way through the bushes on to the island, at one point you will find the remains of a lovely mosaic, and at another, on the*

GEMİLER. 1994.

Sometimes you don't want to see a place you think you have seen before. You think the water is the same, the air is the same. Yet even a slab of marble can change in the course of time. It gets darker. It gets covered with moss... And, what's even more important, you yourself may change. The thing you look at may rermain the same but the way you look at it is different.

If our planned itinerary allows it there are two places I always want to anchor at: the one is Gemiler Island, the other Kekova...

Gemiler Island was one of the places we stopped at during our trip on Üstün's boat in August 1994. What attracts me to the place, quite apart from the beauty of the sea, is the closely-guarded secret of Gemiler Island.

Ölü Deniz lies right beside Gemiler Island, but believe me, in spite of its remarkable beauty, I am not particularly attracted to it. The reason is obvious. During the holidays it's like a fairground. Moreover, nothing about it has been left untouched.

A single gate gives access to the ancient remains on Gemiler Island. There is a certain amount of supervision over entry and exit, but this very important settlement has neither guide nor guardian.

The remains of the old shops on the shore where the boat is moored are still standing. No one has touched them.

My friend Seher Karabol and I climb on to the island. It's lucky that there is still an hour to sunset. I want the island and the magnificence of the landscape to enter every square of the photograph. The sea of Zeus would appear to be sleeping its beauty sleep behind the arches of the chapel. Everything is full of life and vitality. As we make our way along the paths I keep on turning to look back. Gemiler Island is like a gift presented to us on a silver tray. Now I understand why in both polytheistic and monotheistic times places of worship are so often built on the tops of hills. The aim is to use nature to influence man.

The mosaics that have survived pillage and looting are fading in places. The child's tomb hollowed out of the rock fills one with melancholy.

We walk right to the end of the island, sometimes going along the road with the arches, sometimes going off to examine a stone that has attracted our attention.

On arriving at the western end of the island we see Baba Dağı with Ölü Deniz nestling on its slopes. In the old days there were no water skiers or people being hoisted up from the waves by coloured parachutes. Tourism has arrived fully equipped.

As we turn towards the west I follow the light step by step. As darkness falls, I pursue the sunset towards Karacaören. Gemiler Island still guards its secret.

summit of a steep hill, the ruins of a church. No information about the island can be found in any of the usual sources. Gemiler Island would appear to have escaped the notice of the archaeologists."

Captain Ertan has got used to my antiquarianizing. *"Are you going to go ashore and have a look?"* he asks. *Ali* had been there before. He mentions the mosaics on the island. He also mentions a covered road running right down to the sea made especially for the wife of the king.

As soon as myth comes into play no one can hold me back. But I wait for the sun to decline a little. Strolling around in the noon heat is pretty

(opposite page) Gemiler Island. The covered sacred way known as the "Royal Road".
(below) sunset on Gemiler Island.

329

Parachuting at Ölü Deniz and the Ölü Deniz beach.

well unbearable. Besides, the posters have made me interested in **Ölü Deniz,** now quite a legend.

I go ashore at **Gemiler Island** and hire a motor-boat. Yachts are not allowed to moor at **Ölü Deniz**, a precaution taken against possible pollution. *"It's a wise decision,"* says *Captain Ertan. "But it would be better if they made it compulsory for every boat to have a bilge tank. Pollution is reduced at* **Ölü Deniz***, but it's just transferred to all the other lovely bays and harbours."*

We make our way through the long strait in which we are moored. Then we turn sharp left. An endless stretch of sandy beach and forest. Two bays, one within the other. Believe it or not, **Ölü Deniz** is exactly like **Ataköy** or **Florya** on a Sunday. Families with children, beach mats and the smell of kebaps. And let's not forget the cases of soft drinks and nylon bags. Perhaps we happened to arrive on the most crowded day. **Ölü Deniz** (Dead Sea) would appear to have been transformed into a sea swarming with life.

After trying to make up our minds where we should bathe we set off back to **Gemiler Island**. And that was the end of the legend.

A handful of tiny pebbles and the thick grains of the transparent, many-coloured sand from **Ölü Deniz** beach is standing in front of me now in a glass on my desk...

As the heat and glare of the day recedes *Seher, Üstün, Ali* and I set out for **Gemiler Island** in the *Durukos* cutter.

On a large rock on the shore there is the picture of a drinking-glass in small red pebbles. On the left 1965 and 1976. Below, the word *"Hürriyet"*. This inscription by the first blue voyagers is mentioned in *Azra Erhat's* notes: It records the fact that*"From 1964 until now, the Eyüboğlus have always made the blue voyage in the "Hürriyet" motor-boat."* I get a queer feeling. The water of the **Mediterranean** illuminates this tall, handsome young rock in the spring of its youth.

We moor the boat and step out on to the shore. The climb is rather difficult. There are ruins scattered everywhere amid the olive trees. We each break off a fairly thick branch. Partly as a support, partly as a precaution against any snakes that may emerge from under the stones. As we approach the ridge, **Gemiler Island** appears even more imposing, surrounded by the sea. In any case, we are hungry for any kind of beauty.

We skirt the ridge. *Ali* shows us the mosaics on the ground. *"When I saw them a year ago,"* he remarks, *"they covered quite a large area."* There is a vaulted chamber at the place where the mosaics are to be found. This time, instead of walking from one end of **Gemiler Island** to the other, we decided to go down to the shore and continue the journey in a rowing-boat. The thought of walking the whole way was a bit daunting. As we passed the *Durukos, Captain Ertan* offered us tea. We drank it in the boat and then rowed on to find the covered road leading down to the sea.

The pleasure given by a view of the **Mediterranean** from a hill-top is as unique as that of swimming in salt water. After making your way along, looking down through the olive trees to the sea and the boats, you finally, caught in the skein of the unknown, get a view of the whole wonderful vista.

This time we clamber up **Gemiler Island** by another route. And soon we are all shouting with joy. We see a narrow street. In the corner of the house there is a place for an oil-lamp. And a dried up, very old ivy. And then a flight of steps...

"We don't want you to hurt your feet. And we want to protect your head from the Mediterranean sun. We'll make you a road so that you can walk very comfortably down to the sea in your fine white garments." That was how the architect and his foreman persuaded the wife of the king to allow them to build her a road down to the sea…

The Blue Voyage. *Sabahattin Eyüboğlu* couldn't have found a better name. It isn't as easy as you think to find your way around the colours. Neither yellow nor white nor black nor indigo is actually a single colour. Every colour has a thousand shades. For example, take autumn, the driest season in nature. We say that the leaves have turned yellow, but actually every tree, every shrub meets autumn in its own peculiar way. Bay leaves change from dark green to brown, the leaves of the water lily from yellow to red, the magnolia leaves grow white in some places and display a thousand and one colours in a single leaf. But blue is a journey into the infinite. *Eyuboğlu* approached blue as he approached his translations from European languages.

And in setting out into the **Mediterranean** he captured the infinite significance of every sentence, even every word of the poem.

The Blue Voyage offers you the choice of an infinite beauty. Choose what you will. Swimming in the foaming sea, floating on the calm water. Thrilled by the sight of your shadow on the indigo you choose whatever beauty you desire.

The **Mediterranean** I saw as a I climbed up **Gemiler Island** was quite different from the **Mediterrean** I had swum in or sat beside. That's why the voyage in the blue is immortal. And a voyage in the blue of the **Mediterranean** is civilization…

A Byzantine symbol on Gemiler Island.

The narrow street we saw in **Gemiler Island** was just beyond the long stepped street. The street with arched openings on each side had collapsed here and there. The underside of every arch had been painted with a crimson band.

At the bottom of a wall I saw a cross painted the same colour. *Ali, Üstün, Seher* and I decided to follow this road even if it might get dark. The road said to have been built for the wife of the king was transformed from a contemporary legend into a sacred story.

The flight of steps over the slopes was roofed by a vault, like a tunnel. It was obviously made to ensure a confortable, enjoyable walk. The vaulted roof had been cut here and there, at quite long intervals, to form window openings, like the openings left between the stairs in old houses to let in light. As we mounted higher I could see the sea through these openings. It was impossible not to be impressed by the beauty of the view. It must have been a quite unique sort of pleasure to make one's way down to the shore along this road in hot or rainy weather without perspiring or getting wet.

Come, let's peep through the doors of our contemporary myth. There is nothing extraordinary in anything we are going to say…

Festivities are being held on the peaks in **Gemiler Island.** Feasts to celebrate the New Year. The inhabitants of the island leave their houses and light the small lamps in the street. The women are wearing flowing

Gemiler Island. Side streets in which sacred ceremonies were performed and through which the inhabitants would stroll in their white garments.

white garments. Possibly just in case it gets chilly they have brought with them the shawls they wove in their houses. They make their way to the covered way by the light of the moon. It's the smartest road in the city.

The road stretching from one end of the island to the other is filled with gossip and small talk. They speak about the olive groves, the perfumes brought from **Egypt.** They accuse the new seamen on the shore of profiteering, complaining that in their desire to get rich quick they sell the incense and flower seeds they bring from **Egypt** at exorbitant prices, that they are not at all like the old merchants and that morality has degenerated!...

We soon learn that the story we dreamed up on behalf of the inhabitants of the islands is not mere fancy. We are like hunters stalking their prey. Suddenly, there emerges in front of us a small building with stone roof and a small dome. It also has ventilation slits. Right in the middle of a road that opens up in four directions...

I stop immediately under the dome and look at the opposite shores. Not

Gemiler Island. Remains of the church.

a ripple on the surface of the sea. The small green trees on the mountains stand lonely and deserted. I remember the road to **Mt.Olympus**. We had christened that road, built thousands of years ago, the "sacred way". I've decided to call this the "sacred passage". Suddenly I hear *Üstün* calling me. A large building; columns with a single spiral and pink carved marble slabs. The arms of the console with the spiral motif and the mosaics spread out on the ground like a carpet bear the distinguishing features of the early **Byzantine** period. Now we have solved the mystery of the long road. This is the site of the great church of the **Gemiler Island** where the New Year celebrations were held.

The mosaic floor of the church is covered with earth. The 4-5 m^2 section now visible has just been cleared. And 70-75 m^2 of mosaic has been removed and carried away. It is obvious that this pillage took place quite recently. Pink marble slabs with coarse motifs look as if they are laid ready to be taken away. We immediately look around. There's no one in sight. And yet this pillage must have been carried out within a matter of one or two hours. We pick up other sections of mosaic that have been dug out ready and hide them behind the bushes. It's obvious that **Gemiler Island** is being systematically looted.

On the way back we see more of these mosaics between other houses. We cover them with earth as best we can. There's nothing else we can do. It isn't like the pillage at **Xanthos**. This is being done at the present day in front of our very eyes!

An unpleasant day on the Blue Voyage. As I look out at the silhouettes of the yachts in the blue of the dusk I can't help glancing suspiciously around me.

It is imperative that **Gemiler Island** should be placed under conservation as quickly as possible. I can't understand how an island so near **Ölü Deniz** should have been overlooked in this way. Yachts are not allowed to moor at **Ölü Deniz** for fear of pollution and the shore is turned into a "beach" so that kebap smells can spread all over the countryside. And yet a two or three thousand years old site immediately beside it is left abandoned to its fate. When things come to this stage it's time to make a real fuss.

Conservation isn't just a matter of "trespassers will be prosecuted". The ruins on **Gemiler Island** in the middle of the **Mediterranean** form one organic whole with houses, streets, temples and mosaics. Excavations should be undertaken without delay. At the moment it is buried in its own silence. The easiest solution is to forbid anyone to bathe there or land on the island. Areas of sea or land fenced off by prohibitions can make no contribution to culture.

The important thing is to conserve and keep alive... I wonder if we can do it?

At first this island of blue civilization in the middle of the **Mediterranean** was a source of real joy for us. But our blue was later shrouded in melancholy. Here there remain vestiges of who knows how many past civilizations! Who knows what myths and identities are preserved in the tombs carved out of the rocks, in the sacred way, the streets, houses, mosaics and small, one-doored stone houses?

But the one thing we saw that we really drew pleasure from was not any attempt to recreate history. It was the research into a past that mankind has long forgotten. For the civilizations of the past are, in a sense, our own dreams. The dreams are ours. The reality is ours. The only thing that remains from past communities and powerful states is the living culture of the people. In that lies the essential beauty of the Blue Voyage.

Floor mosaics on Gemiler Island.

We start off on the road down. Now and again losing our way. Where did we leave our boat? The slope is so steep we can't see the shore. *Seher* and *Üstün* are coming along behind. *Ali* and I are in front. *Durukos III* has weighed anchor. They shout to us where to find the boat. I ask *Üstün* why they were late. They tell us that a youth we saw at a distance on the island had started following us. *Üstün* and *Seher* are looking for

1

2

1. The city of Telmessos in the 19th century.
2. Telmessos in the 19th century.
3. Rock tombs in 19th century Telmessos.
From Charles Texier, "Description de l'Asie Mineure".

3

Lycian and **Carian** civilizations is marked by a change in the type of tree. But whatever the vegetation on land, even a short voyage by boat is enough to prove that the **Mediterranean** is a way of life all of its own and that the **Mediterranean** is also a civilization all of its own. No exaggeration…

We enter the gulf of **Fethiye**. It was known in ancient times as **Telmessos**… The imposing rock tombs with their Ionic capitals appear in the distance. From the sea, **Fethiye** is not very attractive. The reason for that lies in the new buildings in front of the rock tombs that appear like great heaps of concrete on the slopes of the straits. And when you consider that this is an earthquake area the sight of these buildings scarring the countryside - however few there may be - appall both the eye and the heart. But we are the only ones to be afraid. Those who live by the seashore on rocks always liable to tremble aren't afraid at all!…

While the *Durukos* was taking on water we went for a short stroll along the shore. Then we set off on a trip to **Tersane Island** directly opposite **Fethiye**.

All the blue voyagers are at sea. The wire fish basket *Ahmet* brought from **Antalya** stands like a statue on the deck. *Üstün* puts some bread

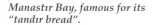

Manastır Bay, famous for its "tandır bread".

THE GULF OF FETHIYE, OR THE ARCHIPELAGO, 1994.

Many of the cities that have given their name to a gulf have lost all their attraction through shoddy, uncontrolled building construction. Fethiye is one of these. Yet the slopes behind the town are adorned with a number of rock-tombs, among them the 4th century B.C. Ionic rock-tomb of Amyntas.

There is an interesting anecdote about Telmessos, a city famous for its scholars and the fruit it produced. More accurately, it is an anecdote handed from one teller to another about an interpreter of dreams from Telmessos. İlhan Akşit relates the story in his book on the Blue Voyage.

"Philip, the father of Alexander the Great, summoned the soothsayer Aristander from Telmessos to interpret a dream. Aristander told him of the birth of Alexander and the fate that awaited him. When Alexander grew up he never allowed this soothsayer from Fethiye to leave his side and formed a close friendship with him. The soothsayer from Fethiye even accompanied Alexander on his Eastern campaign. It was thanks to Aristander that Fethiye surrendered to Alexander without resistance, thus avoiding pillage and destruction. The commander Nearchos captured Telmessos castle by means of a stratagem.

"When the fleet arrived at Fethiye harbour, Nearchos, its commander, asked the citizens of Telmessos to allow his musicians to enter the city and, on receiving their consent, he sent them in with their shields and lances concealed amongst their instruments, and so captured the castle."

Did the citizens of Telmessos lose their city for the sake of a bit of entertainment, or were they the victim of the soothsayer's treachery?

Telmessos came under the hegemony not only of Alexander the Great but also of Pergamon, Rome, Rhodes and Byzantium.

Perhaps the best parts of Fethiye today are the markets where you can find all sorts of food and fish.

Other fine features are the things created by nature rather those created by man.

An important feature of Göcek, which has now been transformed into a yacht harbour, is its connection with the airport at Dalaman. Tourists from home and abroad make their way to Göcek by roads winding through the forests. And then?

And then a cruise in the archipelago...

To lose yourself in the silence of the bay and its cool waters that suddenly transform you after all the noise and exhaustion!... And it's no dream! If you take a stroll around Göcek, the marina of Fethiye, and then sail out to sea you can throw away whatever perfume you normally use and allow your body to be swathed in the fragrance of the salt water as if in a silk fabric.

Where is the first place to go in this gulf?

If you want a real shock after the noise and bustle of the town it's a little difficult to choose. There are so many beauties lying hidden between the Dockyard and Domuz Island on the one side and Manastır Bay, Bedri Rahmi Bay and Boyuz Bükü on the other.

Perhaps the best thing, considering the time of arrival of the night plane, is to leave Göcek immediately and anchor at Doruklu Koyu, the nearest bay. If I were you, I would bathe at night. I would feel the water of Doruklu Bay on my skin, for a really beautiful sleep.

The next day, immediately after breakfast, I would hide myself in one of the inlets among the pine trees of Boynuz Bükü. If you have only three or four hours to spend, you're done for! It's so difficult to leave one beauty to run in pursuit of another!... But let me tell you something. The bay named after the painter, writer and poet Bedri Rahmi is just a little way beyond Boynuz Bükü. You can see the fish he carved on the rock. If you look up towards the pine forests you will see the rock-tombs.

You must definitely see Merdivenli Iskelesi and Çamlı Bay. But be sure to spend a night in Manastır Bay before ending the trip.

If you enter Manastır Bay one mile south-west of Boz Point at sunset you can moor your boat to a rock beside the landing-stage or the thick trunk of a pine. If you want to be near the restaurants you'll have to go right into the bay. And there's something else you must do. Jump into a rowing-boat or a cutter, make your way to the shore and order some of the *tandır ekmeği* (bread baked in an earth oven) made from village flour for your next morning's breakfast. Don't worry if the vendors seem a bit slack and unenthusiastic.

When the cicadas fall silent and you can hear the tinkling of the bells of the goats in the forest, give yourself up to the sea in all its myriad aspects. Then get into the boat or cutter and go ashore. Before picking up your *tandır ekmeği* you should visit the little (possibly Byzantine) stone building beside the wooden landing-stage. And don't forget to take a look at the foundations in the water, because the submerged foundations of the stone building will recall a whole civilization.

What you ought to omit after all this I really don't know, but I certainly wouldn't miss the small island in Manastır Bay at sunrise or at sunset. It may remind you of a cicada caught in a pine, but I'd watch it without even drawing breath...

And, as a matter of fact, that's exactly what I did.

Water, trees and clouds... Do colours undergo change through the power of enchantment? I wouldn't know.

I imagine by this time you have become a bit subdued. You must have decided that chatterboxes like ourselves were making much too much of our ordinary, everyday affairs.

If you don't feel like it you can go on sleeping. The ceremony of sunrise in Manastır Bay requires no assistance... For thousands of years it has been awakening the Aegean and the Mediterranean from their sleep...

As I have already said, a cruise in these seas depends very much on the time at your disposal. But I certainly wouldn't advise you to return to your sacred duties without sailing around the islands and finding out new havens.

343

(right) Göcek behind broom bushes.
(opposite page) Manastır Bay and Byzantine remains.

and some tomatoes into it and lowers it into the sea. *"Why don't you put a small bottle of rakı in too,"* says *Oktay,* *"and give the poor creatures a good time!"*

We go out of one bay and into another. As we pass **Domuz Island, Manastır Bay** and the waters in which *Cleopatra* once swam, the shades of night begin to fall over the forest. *Ali* wants to demonstrate his skill as a chef. He adds all sorts of spices to the meat for the grilled *köftes* while we supply him with rakı. We may have no connection with the ancient **Romans**, but on seeing how the food and drink is consumed everyone begins to question the other's pedigree. Perhaps your great-great-grandfather called in at **Rome** on his way to Europe!…And everybody was singing away in a cordial glow, *"Let every day be like this one!"*

Next day it's the turn of the capes of **Kızılkuyruk** and **Kurtoğlu**. A strange feeling comes over us all. Is it because of the way our few days are slipping by? Is it because of the calm seas at one point and rough waves at another, or here and there the melancholy colour of the water? I feel that the source of all melancholy and rapture in the **Mediterranean** lies in the **Lycian** sailors, those skilled mariners who brought drinks, fabrics, seeds, jewellery and dried foods from **North Africa** to **Anatolia**.

I think of the tempests of joy we have tried to raise in a short trip in a mere span of water. I seek consolation in the thought that *"The Blue Voyage is a journey of rediscovery of the beauty that lies deep within you that you were unable to find and draw forth."*

After making our way round **Akça Point, Kara Point, Dişbilmez Point** and **Şeytan Point** we enter **Köyceğiz** harbour…

Ekincik is located directly opposite **Köyceğiz** harbour. We send a wireless message calling a motor-boat from the *Ekincilik Cooperative* all the

motor-boats are attached to. This time our voyage will be over the fresh waters where **Dalyan** opens out to the sea. We leave the *Durukos III* moored at **Ekincik Harbour** and set off for **Dalyan**. It is very shallow here. We are all amazed as we make our way over the shallow water and disappear among the reeds.

We seem to be in a fairy-tale world for grown-ups. There's no knowing where these reed canals begin or end. A motor boat will suddenly shoot out from behind a bed of reeds. The canals are completely hidden by them. It's by no means a short journey. We travel for ages in a maze and labyrinth of reeds. And just as we are going along through this world of make-believe like a spoiled child on skates the rock tombs of **Lycia** and **Caria** suddenly rise up before us.

Could you blame me if I say, *"Now the doors of myth are opening onto an unknown world!"*

I wouldn't be at all offended if you were to reply, *"Not content with describing every single stone and every single piece of ground on the Mediterranean shores, you are now beginning to create new myths!"* I would only say, *"Every age has its own myths."* Enough!

(following page) The dawn that for thousands of years has awakened the Mediterranean from its sleep creeps silently into Manastır Bay. 05.00

Manastır Bay.
1. 05.07
2. 05.12
3. 05.17
4. 05.22

We land. In front of us rises up the most magnificent of all the **Lycian** rock tombs. I can't see the purpose of the two openings large enough for a man to pass through beside the burial chamber itself, as if hewing the tomb out of this enormous rock wasn't enough. It is dated to the 4th century B.C. And just beneath it there is a village cemetery of the 20th century. *Seher, Üstün, Nida, Yusuf, Ali* and I, together with other blue voyagers who join the antiquarian convoy, set out in a motor-boat for the ruins of **Kaunos**. We enter the harbour through gates that open to let us pass and close immediately behind us so to prevent the fish escaping from the weir. We reach the **Kaunos** ruins after a walk of some 10-15 minutes.

Kaunos, with its theatre, basilica, baths, nymphaeum and agora, is a city dating from the **Hellenistic** and **Roman** periods. And let us not forget the **Lycian** and **Carian** leagues... And there's another thing we shouldn't forget: there were more than fifty theatres between **Kaunos** and **Pamphylia**, in other words, the city of **Antalya**. You ask me what I mean by that? Nothing! But without having to ask someone who knows, and without looking at a secondary school atlas, I can tell you offhand that these fifty theatres are all located in one section of the country between **Antalya** and **Muğla**.

According to this, the **Lycians** would appear to have been devoted to culture and art!... How is that? Isn't it the case that those godless, polytheistic **Lycians** only knew how to drink?

That's what I learned from the **Mediterranean**!

We return to the *Durukos* by the way we came. And now we're heading for **Marmaris.** We are getting ready, to the sound of the indigo sea heard through the little windows of the cabin. We are enjoying our last coffees and last drinks. This is the end of the first voyage. The second part will have to be left to another summer. Everybody wants to do it with *Captain Ertan* and the *Durukos*.

3

4

I followed the ceremony of sunrise in Manastır Bay holding my breath like a cicada hanging from a pine. It was as if I was being offered a Dionysiac poem and rapture.

1. 05.27
2. 05.30

It isn't easy to bid the **Mediterranean** farewell. Some set out with a fleeting sort of affection, but as the distance grows you find how that brief love takes firm root in your heart.

Some conceal their enthusiasm behind a veil of silence. Days and nights later, while recounting the love of the cicadas that has long matured in the depths of your heart, your own love will suddenly give itself away.

The **Mediterranean** is full of myths and gods and mysteries. We too make our way over the deep blue of a love that mankind has preserved for thousands of years. You may believe it or not, but just bathe once in the water of the **Mediterranean** and you will realize that life is not composed simply of our own personal existence...

The **Lycians** have the last word. They realized this truth, and are calling

(opposite page) Köyceğiz-Dalyan. Rock-tombs of the 4th century B.C.

KAUNOS AND CARETTA-CARETTAS. 1994.

In some corners of nature, cities are founded by men and in others by animals. Men's cities are predictable: you will find a castle, defence walls, houses, a theatre, a market, water conduits, temples and tombs. The cities built by the other animals are also predictable, but in most cases it needs a good deal of research and investigation, or perhaps just pure chance, to find out where and how. If it hadn't been for the rash of buildings constructed here and there in the name of tourism, we would never have thought of scratching out the worlds of the turtles. The whole problem is the matter of "disturbing" the Caretta-Carettas. The expanse of sand around the delta through which Lake Köyceğiz empties into the Aegean is known as İztuzu, and this broad expanse of sand is the homeland and birthplace of these lovable creatures. Can this over 4 kilometres of sand serve both as a bathing-beach and a quiet nest? Our little monster friends find it convenient to lay their eggs in July! Apparently they leave their eggs there after nine o'clock at night. We take the precaution of not allowing the Dalyan motor-boats to work

after that hour, but during the summer the beach is packed at all hours of the day. We are amused to see the Caretta-Carettas roaming around under our feet while children are rushing here and there and adults playing ball. We can also take them home and look after them, but the poor animals don't respond too happily!... And just think of the fate that awaits the baby turtle that two months later begins to worm its way out of the egg! The sympathetic approach of the local inhabitants has prevented the Caretta-Carettas from being deprived of the homeland they have possessed for perhaps thousands of years. After all, they take as much pleasure as we do from the seas and shores of the Aegean and the Mediterranean.

And, what's more, they are as distinctive a feature of the İztuzu beach as the gray mullet, sea bass, bream and crabs.

The city of Kaunos has such a marvellous location!...

Man is sometimes amazed as the monumentality of nature, sometimes at the choice, skill and strength of civilizations. Köyceğiz, Dalyan, İztuzu and the Lycian tombs that rise up

from the reed beds are the joint products of man and nature. And here we find a labyrinth winding its way through the reed beds. No other example of the kind can be found anywhere else on the Aegean or Mediterranean shores...

The citizens of Kaunos founded a city on a hill with rock-tombs looking down on the labyrinth and a dockyard and harbour which, according to Strabo, was sometimes closed.

Each citizen the hero of a novel!...

"The inhabitants of Kaunos," writes Herodotus, "are, in my opinion, indigenous to the region, though some say they came from Crete. Whether it was Carian that influenced the language of the Kaunians or the language of the Kaunians that influenced Carian is a point of controversy that has not yet been solved. But as far as traditions are concerned, those of Kaunos are quite different from those of Caria or any of the other regions. They used to arrange drinking parties, but in doing so took they paid strict attention to men, women and children, as well as relations of age and friendship."

In other words, they knew how to enjoy life...

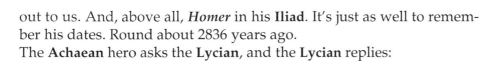

out to us. And, above all, *Homer* in his **Iliad**. It's just as well to remember his dates. Round about 2836 years ago.

The **Achaean** hero asks the **Lycian**, and the **Lycian** replies:

> *"The race of man is like the leaves of the tree.*
> *You look one way, and the wind blows them to the ground.*
> *You look the other, and spring returns.*
> *It gives birth to the new, makes green the forest.*
> *Thus one race departs, and another is born…"*

1,2. The ruins at Kaunos.
3. Köyceğiz-Dalyan. Sailing through the labyrinth.
4. The sandy beach where the caretta-carettas lay their eggs.
5. Small Dalyan crabs.
6. Kaunos flowers.

THE CARIAN SHORES FROM MARMARİS TO BODRUM

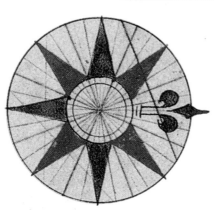

E scape... Everyday the desire grows stronger to free the heart from its shackles. It is not ourselves or our environment that we find unbearable. It is the noise and confusion of the great cities, the frustration, the ever-deepening debasement and degeneration. Sensitivity and refinement in human relations have come to be based solely on profit and self-seeking.

But is flight the only way out? Whatever the answer, every single one of the friends I have spoken to are preparing to slip the cable!...

I suddenly remembered an article of mine that appeared in the *Politika* newspaper of 30 October 1975 and set about finding it among my papers. The heading was, *"The Great Exodus"*.

I had noted that:*"The city is a place of suspicion and fear. It is full of noise and confusion."*

In another part of my article I wrote:

> *"The villagers were forced by the violent unrest that broke out at the beginning of the 17th century to abandon their land and their hearths and homes and set out to seek life on the frontiers of death. Some went to the cities, but, unable to settle there, they found refuge in remote spots on the mountain heights. Some escaped to precipitous rocks or impassible forests where they created new farms and formed new villages. This period is known as the 'Great Exodus'."*

Is **Istanbul** the city of the *"Great Exodus"*. I wouldn't know!...

There is something wrong somewhere. While parts of the great cities are moving to the shores and the mountain heights, people from mountain villages and coastal towns are flocking to the cities. In any case we founded the other. It is all a complete mess!...

But nine of us, with wives and families, set out one night from **Istanbul** to find a place of refuge. Two friends from **Antalya** were to join us in the boat at **Marmaris.**

We stuffed our cameras and maps and books about the region into our bags. And also some specially nice *mezes* !…

A bus journey by night is like waking up from a feverish illness drenched in sweat and fear. The rule is to wake you up in the middle of the night for a meal of soup, meat-balls, aubergine and peppers with yoghurt, and water-melon. And then a cascade of eau-de-cologne from the bus hostess! And just as you are getting off to sleep again a fifteen minute stop for tea. Back from the tea-break for another cascade of eau-de-cologne!

We just have to take things as they come. The only thing that matters is that we should ultimately find ourselves on the shore of a deep blue sea…

We cross from **Eskihisar** to **Topçular** in the car-ferry. But on getting off the boat there is such a difference in height between the deck and the landing-stage that our sump tank gets damaged. Result: telephone calls and another bus sent from **Istanbul.** That means at least a three hours' wait. Stranded in **Topçular** in the dead of night!…

Our flight grinds to a halt in complete dejection. A queue immediately

(above) Marmaris harbour.
(below) Chart of Marmaris harbour.
From Piri Reis, "Kitab-ı Bahriye".

357

1. Marmaris harbour
2, 3. Marmaris streets and Marmaris
spice-vendor.

1

forms in front of the single telephone booth on the landing-stage. *"We must tell the captain."*

I know all the toilets at each stop and each landing-stage. The attendant at the toilets on **Topçular** landing-stage has just finished her tour of duty and locks the door as I come out. The only solution for the other passengers on the bus is the open country! The toilet on the bus is simply unapproachable!…

Cheers and clapping as the new bus arrives. Order is restored. We are now prepared for any kind of stop. All that matters is that we are on our way!…

It is undoubtedly the infinite expanse of nature that nurtures and strengthens our hope. The infinite expanse seen from the hills is the

2

Gulf of Gökova. The blues and myriad greens of the sea penetrate into the broad valley.

Whatever the advantages, how could it ever occur to anyone to build a nuclear reactor in **Gökova!** For what possible future gain could one contemplate the destruction of the most fertile soil in Caria?…

Obviously the politicians are, as always, thinking only of our good!…

Most of the time we are utterly confused in our attitude to the future. We are perfectly ready to sacrifice for so-called progress beauty that has existed for thousands of years and that we should never be able to recreate in centuries to come…

"No problem in Marmaris."

I found this written on a postcard I received immediately on setting foot in **Marmaris**. The postcard itself was a sight for sore eyes: the sun setting behind the masts of a boat and on the left a topless lady with a champagne glass in her hand!… Another postcard had been taken in front of **Pamukkale** with a lady in green spangles and hands on hips…

3

I am convinced that my flight was absolutely necessary! The only recourse is to get on to the boat… The first thing is to take off our shoes and all other unnecessary garments. *"Make me a whisky on the rocks right away,"* I say to *Gürbüz. Gürbüz, Hüseyin* and *Feray* are the silent, hard-working members of the crew. *Erden* is the owner of the yacht, while *Muharrem* arrives in full glory as captain. *Captain Muharrem* is an expert in human relations and the blue seas. He has matured in salt water and the heat of the sun.

1

2

In some boats you find sailors with head-bands and ear-rings. In every market in **Marmaris** you'll find young men with bare chests, a scarf around their necks, gold bracelets, an ear-ring in one ear and and a coloured head-band. And in almost every every port you'll hear *Captain Erhan* exclaim, "God knows what's happened to our young people!"

3

1. Marmaris fishermen in Kadırga Bay.
2. Gerbekse Bay.
3. Ayşegül in Gerbekse Bay.

A sea voyage has absolutely nothing in common with a journey by land. It gives its captain, its crew and its passengers a privileged position. But the character of the "Blue Voyage" has changed since the days of the *Fisherman of Halicarnassus* and *Eyüboğlu*. There are even some people who boast of having done the trip by helicopter…

We are impatient to get away from the land as quickly as possible. Some of us go out shopping while we give the captain the list of ports of call. Our list of passengers resembles that of the **Argonauts**: the *Ayhan, Şeyda, Sevda Sarguner* group are given the job of seeing to our health. *Reşit* and *Nesrin Erzin* perform the function undertaken by **Orpheus** on the **Argo**!

361

1

1. Evening in Gerbekse Bay.
2. Gerbekse Church.
3. Fire altars on the Gerbekse-Tola road.
4. Water conduit hollowed out of the stone on the Gerbekse-Tola road.

Zeynep, Ayşegül and myself take over from Phineus the responsibility for prophecy. Or, to put it more plainly, playing the pedant in rummaging through books and maps and showing the way and recounting old legends!...

Captain Muharrem is the helmsman *Tiphys...* That's all very well, but did the **Argo** ever go down to the **Mediteranean**? No, it didn't, but we are all for enjoying ourselves. That's why, as soon as our boat sets sail, all of us, apart from the children, take refuge in *Dionysos'* warm embrace.

With his dark glasses, his generous paunch and a moustache that reminds one of *Zola, Captain Muharrem* stands looking out to sea with his hands clasped behind his back.

A man of few words, who never interferes with anyone, even by way of a joke, *Muharrem* is a captain who holds the whole responsibility of the vessel in his own hands and solves every problem entirely by himself.

He even faces storms standing astride with his hands still clasped behind his back.

I ask him why he speaks so little:

"I've been at sea for twenty-three years. I've seen so many passengers…
"Some eat on deck. Some eat in their cabins. If they all sit down to table togeth-
er you'll find that bosom friends won't be on speaking terms in a few hours.
The boat sometimes turns into a fashion show and everyone goes crazy.
"The best way is to keep well out of things.
"The sea is no place for fighting and wrangling."
Every cruise along the **Carian** and **Lycian** coasts is called a "Blue

Voyage". But the distinguishing feature of all these journeys lies in nature, history and civilization.

Merely bathing in the blue waters of the Mediterranean is not sufficient. You've got to feel the waters of civilization on your body.

Our first port of call was **Kadırga**, and after that **İnceada** and **Gerbekse**. Some say **Gerbek Kilise**. Others get out of it by saying **Gebe Kilise**.

There's nothing very special about **Gerbekse** as far as natural scenery is concerned, but when you wash off the dust of the journey in its salt waters you realize the true magnificence of nature. The only sound in your ears is the song of the cicadas. The lead-grey rocks of **Gerbekse** are covered with olive trees.

As day dawns over the water and the rocks, **Gerbekse Bay** changes to a sort of bottle green. The lead-grey rocks seem to be swimming in the water. Just at the end of the shore there is an arched building, and on the ridge to its right the remains of a church. You immediately set out in a rowing-boat for the shore. In the middle of the arched building you find a cistern. And there's another cistern behind.

You climb up the ridge on your right. Everyone makes his own way to the short path that leads through bushes and olive trees to the church. As soon as I look out of the mullioned window in the apse as daylight falls

(opposite page) Loryma/Bozukkale harbour, in which the Athenian fleet took refuge during the Peloponnesian War. (left) Sunset at Bozukkale.

over the sea I realize I that was mistaken. I have no idea what the sea-men of the **Byzantine** age worshipped when they looked out from this little church on to the beauty and magnificence of the olive trees, the lead-grey rocks and the glass green sea, but for myself, when I think of the urban hell in which I spend my everyday existence I believe my immortality resides in those two bays placed one beside the other.

We return to the boat to find a meal awaiting us worthy of *Dionysos* himself. But first of all I abandon myself to waters that foam from the tips of my fingers. Having consecrated myself in the waters of the **Mediterranean** I make my way to the head of the festive board…

Our ten days' cruise has one aim and one reason only: to enjoy the scenery and civilization of the **Mediterranean** and the **Aegean**. *Captain Muharrem* is well aware of this, but in planning our itinerary we pay full heed to the sea's whims and caprices. Nor do we forget our stops on the return journey.

Our third port of call is **Bozuk Kale** or **Loryma** between **Değirmen Point** and **Kale Point**. **Loryma** offers a safe haven in all sorts of weather. That is why the **Athenian** fleet took refuge here during the *Peloponnesian War*. On **Kale Burnu** (Castle Point) there is a castle with nine bastions, five gates and walls extending for 320 m. Some of the stones are more than 5 m long. **Loryma**, a city that deserves extensive archaeological investigation, is mentioned by a 10th century **Byzantine** historian.

As far as the *Carians* are concerned one should listen to what old *Herodotus* has to say:

> "The Carians came from the islands to the mainland. But the Carians themselves do not accept this. They claim that they originally belonged to the mainland and always bore the same name as they bear today."

And another quote from *Herodotus:*

> "In those days the Carians formed the most famous and most numerous of the various peoples. They invented three things that the Greeks later borrowed from them: they gave us the crest on the war helmet and the signs inscribed on the shields, and the grip for holding the shield was also their invention. Until that time shields were not held by means of a grip but were slung over the left shoulder by means of a belt around the neck."

Another feature of these shores is the number of unknowns, and it is the pursuit of these unknowns that complete the pleasure afforded by the sea and the table. And particularly if you are fed up with the trivial political discussions of the present day and of an environment in which self-interest rules and is generally accepted as the norm, these little adventures will lend some savour to life. That's what I do, as we set out to find the ancient city to which *Gürbüz* gives the name **Tola**.

(opposite page) Captian Muharrem looking like Zola.

KNIDOS AND APHRODITE

Tola mill, displaying highly skilled masonry work.

Whenever I set out on a trip, through the **Aegean** and the **Mediterranean**, I take with me everything I can find connected with myths and legends. The myths created by man thousands of years ago, their heroes, gods and goddesses, are the very stuff of life itself. Their quarrels, recriminations, jealousies, loves and fears serve to express what the people themselves cannot say outright. Cities are sometimes founded in their name. Festivities and works of art are dedicated to them.

When I heard the seaman *Gürbüz* talk about large buildings at a place called **Tola** there was no holding me back. **Tola** is about one and a half hour's walk beyond two ranges of mountains behind **Loryma**. According to *Gürbüz* and the captain there were mills, monasteries, fountains and houses in the ancient city.

I put on my hat, my boots and my trousers with all the pockets, and slung my camera and binoculars round my neck. *Gürbüz* put on his sandals and picked up a water bottle, and off we went.

We clambered up the side of the hills like goats. When I looked down from the first hill through my binoculars at our boat, the single-masted *Erden,* I felt a real joy at seeing it floating calmly on the dark blue and glass-green water.

Our journey went on over a second hill and then over a third. *"You see that hill over there with the clump of olive trees on it,"* says *Gürbüz, "It's just beyond that. Can you make it?"* Whereas, for my part, my mind is occupied with the chilled white wine I drank at noon. Wine and sun… It's a good thing I've got a hat moistened with water.

After an hour or so the effect of the wine gives way to the fragrance of

1. Tola mill.
2. An abandoned house in Tola.
3. Tola appears in front of us after an adventurous journey.

the mint and sage on the mountains. My mind and heart are at ease, but the road never ends. At last we come upon a fountain by the side of a few almond trees. The spout from which the water flows out, the round basin and the trough, four or five metres long, are all carved out of a single block of marble. Probably of the first millennium.

A spring that has continued to flow for thousands of years. My enthusiasm is whetted on seeing a three-tiered altar, also carved from a single block of marble.

Gürbüz is like a greyhound. In any case he's only half my age. But the hope of discovering the unknown keeps me going. And there isn't a soul in sight.

3

As we trudge along I can't help laughing as I remember the excavations carried out in **Kaleiçi** in **Antalya** by a group of archaeologists. One passage was excavated after another. More work with picks and shovels and yet another passage opened up to shouts of *"We've found it!"* Then a voice came from within: *"Two sweet coffees and one medium."*

Apparently they had been excavating a passage right over a coffee-house.

I shouldn't be at all surprised if the same thing happened to me!...

After that little adventure, and more mountains, peaks and valleys, we saw stone houses and a mill in the distance, as well as another harbour.

The harbour was a long way below. As for the buildings beneath the olive trees, they were not as I had dreamed. They had probably been abandoned a few hundred years ago. Nevertheless, the mill displayed very skilful stone workmanship. But what really amazed me was the large marble slab not far from the settlement with a fine spiral water channel, of which I have seen other specimens belonging to the old civilizations...

HİSARÖNÜ GULF. 1994.

Knidos and Karaburun have been guarding a gulf for thousands of years. And Simi Island lies right in the middle of it. The gulf is called Hisarönü… And on its skirts, towards Karaburun, there is Yeşilova or Sömbeki Gulf.

In her book *Blue Voyage* Azra Erhat describes the Gulf of Hisarönü in the following terms:

"The northern shore of Hisarönü Gulf is very irregular, with a great many coves and inlets. There are a number of bays, like Çiftlik Limani and Kuruca Bükü, where you can moor for the night, but the best place to stop is Kayıkaşıran. This is the narrowest point of the Datça peninsula. You can leave the yacht a little way out and get to shore in a cutter, and then make your way across hills and dales to the peak between the gulfs of Hisarönü and Gökova. Here you you look down over both gulfs to the most amazing view in the whole world, with a lacework of thousands of little coves by a deep blue sea.

"When you see Gökova at sunset or Hisarönü at sunrise you will find it hard to believe that anything so beautiful could exist anywhere in the world.

"Can this be the place where the they began to cut through the isthmus to protect Knidos from the Persians?

"The names Kaşıkıran and Balıkaşıran are rather interesting. It would imply that the people believed that both boats and fish could cross over from the one to the other."

Hisarönü, like Gökova, is absolutely full of a myriad pranks of nature.

From Datça, as you enter the deep waters at the end of the gulf, you will see many bays to choose from. One of these is Bencik Bay. This is a cool channel shadowed by pines that fills one with hope and exuberance. It reminds one of Kargılı Bay in the Gulf of Gökova.

Bencik Koyu is one of the bays of which the sailors say that "when the sea grows grey it also grows beautiful". The best thing to do in a gulf like this is to pontificate over the chart with a glass of wine in your hand.

Every inlet and blue patch will raise your interest to the peak, but be careful. Look at the depth contours. If you see figures like 3, 5 or 7, that means your yacht may find itself grounded. In any case, none of the captains would ever go into such places, and if you suggest it they may put you down in no uncertain terms!

Don't be content with a distant look at Orhaniye, Delikli Yol and Selimiye Bays. And you mustn't go on without spending a night at the little bay, with no name on the map, between Sığ Point, a little beyond Selimiye Bay, and Küçüven Point.

"What about bees?"

Bees will never leave you alone on any shore or any piece of water in the Aegean or NMediterranean. And what's more, they're quite unlike the usual honey bees. They have magnificent bodies and brilliant colours. Some people call them wasps because of their size but in my opinion there's no connection.

They have been here since ancient times, and can be seen in ancient jewellery and costumes.

As you sit drinking the captain will probably tell you that they love perfume, but don't forget that they also love the taste of your rakı and your wine. The only thing to do is to wait for them to go without making too much of a fuss. If more and more come along the best thing to do is to take the boat further off shore and anchor there.

"And if they come out there?"

In any case, by the time the bees get out there in the wind the glass in your hand will see to it that you aren't able to distinguish a mosquito from a wasp!…

Another beautiful place is the nameless bay beside Ağıl Point as you pass between Kamerya and Koca Island. After Atabol Point comes Yeşilova Gulf, and then you wind your way in a spiral through Tavşanbükü, Kızıl, Yeşil, Zeytin and Söğüt Islands. All there is to be said about Bozburun, Söğüt Limanları, Kızılyer and Ayasaranda is that it is here that you will find the beginning of your excape.

But nothing will be changed by your escape from the cities, your surroundings and even, perhaps, yourself. It all depends on where you escape to. Perhaps that is why the "eleven months flower", as they call the bougainvillea, is the flower of the Aegean and the Mediterranean. No one knows why there is one month when it doesn't bloom. They say it's because of the salt winds. A typical Dionysian explanation! As if there were no salt winds in the other months! It's my belief that it fails to bloom in one particular month so as not to tempt providence!..

Darkness was falling. We chose another path back; by goat tracks. Goats never take the steepest route. They clamber up and down by oblique paths. We were guided along the track by the little black beads the goats leave behind them! The adventure came to an end after about six hours. I started hallooing as soon as I saw the boat. No one paid

Datça.

any attention. Apparently they had agreed among themselves to completely ignore me! And for my part I kept quiet about **Tola** right to the end of the trip!…

We saved our evening enjoyment for the restaurant by the shore. They make very good *tandır ekmeği,* and on *Ahmet's* suggestion a kid is thrown into the oven. The roast goat-meat doesn't arouse much interest. Most of us spend the evening on bread, goat's milk cheese, salad, fried aubergine and peppers. *"You're dark,"* Ahmet calls out to the wife of the restaurant owner, *"and your husband's dark. How comes it both your daughters are fair?"*

"We are both sun lambs," she replies with a laugh, *"My daughters are shade lambs."*

What a wonderful definition!…

*Knidos. The southern harbour and
wooden landing-stage.*

On getting back to the boat we prepare another sort of meal for ourselves. The whole night is before us, and the stars, and the sea phosphorescent in the light of the moon...

I take a blanket and spend the whole night in the stern of the boat, joined by *Ayşegül, Şeyda, Ahmet, Ayhan* and *Sevda.*

Captain Muharrem usually sets out at four in the morning so as to avoid getting caught in a storm. Spray from the waves wake me just as we are passing **Kara** and **Kızıl Points**. We make a long journey through the straits between **Nimos** and **Simi Island** towards **Knidos,** in the vicinity of **Deve Boynu.**

1. *Knidos. The lighthouse and sunset.*
2. *Knidos. Pasture.*
3. *Knidos. An unknown carved in stone.*

We can see the church and white houses of **Simi**.
Knidos lies at the extreme end of the **Datça Peninsula**. According to *Strabo,* the famous ancient geographer, born in **Amasya** in 64 or 63 B.C.:*"The wines of Knidos are of very special excellence, both for the pleasure they give and their medicinal virtues."*

1

2

3

4

1. Knidos. The ruins.
2. Knidos, Roman remains.
3. Knidos. Marble decoration.
4. Sketch of the statue of Demeter.
Knidos, the sanctuary of Demeter.
C.T.Newton, 1862. "A History of
Discoveries of Halicarnassus, Cnidos
and Branchidae".

And it is also the city of *Aphrodite*. **Knidos** was famed for the nude statue of *Aphrodite*. carved by the sculptor *Praxiteles*.

You would be amazed at the offers made for this statue of *Aphrodite!* Some offered to pay off the whole debt of the city in return for it. Both **Knidos** and its nude *Aphrodite* were Caesar's favourites… But the citizens of **Knidos** remained unmoved, thus further enhancing their fame.

This was undoubtedly a victory for art. A wonderful beauty transformed into an artistic legend that every community in every age would do well to ponder.

But **Knidos'** fame is based on more than *Aphrodite* and delicious wines. The famous astronomer, physicist, mathematician and philosopher *Eudoxus*. was a native of **Knidos**. The sundial we noticed on a hill not far from the 4500 capacity theatre may have been a part of the observatory built by *Eudoxus* in the **Temple of Aphrodite**.

Knidos, with its odeons, temples, two large theatres, agora, statues, wall frescoes, floor mosaics and house terraces, all laid out according to plans prepared by *Hippodamos*, the celebrated town planner of the ancient world, requires a long visit and a thorough, exhaustive examination. A rapid tour of the city is quite out of the question.

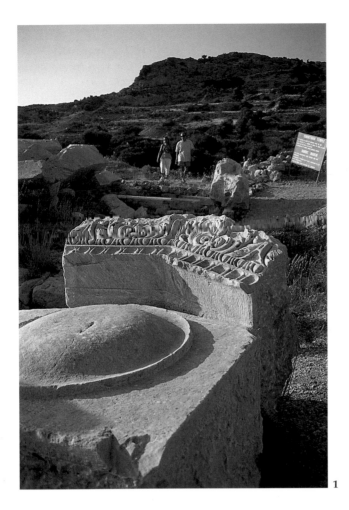

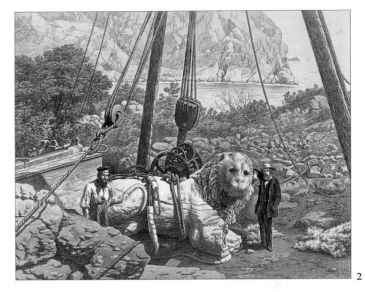

Knidos may have had its sometimes eccentric sometimes brilliant ideas, but its plans of campaign were often marked by guile and deceit. For example, a stone wall was built along the bottom of the great harbour so that hostile warships would shatter themselves against it .

The 2nd century B.C. writer *Lucian* mentions having seen *terracotta* vases and erotic figurines in the vicinity of the **Temple of Aphrodite**. Something else that never escapes the human tongue and ear.

On the one hand the nude *Aphrodite*, and on the other a wine that makes drunkenness a joy and the deep blue waves beating against the shore in the setting sun. Imagine climbing up half tipsy to the theatre by terraced gardens and stepped streets to see festivities dedicated to *Dionysos* under a starry sky. Life may be more than just beauty and intoxication, but what of it! Aren't these the qualities we try to recall, the qualities that enter our dreams?…

1. Knidos. The ruins.
2. Knidos. Sketch of the monumental lion. C.T.Newton, 1862. "A History of Discoveries of Halicarnassus, Cnidos and Branchidae".
3. Knidos. Tomb of Lykaethios. C.T.Newton, 1862. "A History of Discoveries of Halicarnassus, Cnidos and Branchidae".

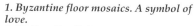

1. Byzantine floor mosaics. A symbol of love.
2. Knidos. Sundial.
3. Knidos. An inscription.
4. Knidos. The harbour as seen from the ruins.

On returning to the boat we begin talking about **Knidos.** *Captain Muharrem* says that *Aphrodite* used to swim here. *Reşit* is telling *Nesrin's* fortune in the coffee-cups, in his own inimitable satirical style: "Don't worry, all the cats are behaving themseves. Look, *Emil* and *Kesban* (*Nesrin's* cats) are sleeping in the armchair. But where is *Mini*?"

378

he says, with a meaningful look…

We arrange a supper in honour of **Knidos.** We open a bottle of chilled wine. As for the orfoz, that is entrusted to *Gürbüz's* skilled hands.

We set off once more at four o'clock in the morning. This time our journey is rather difficult. We are sailing non-stop from **Knidos** to **Yedi Adalar** (Seven Islands). There is no decent harbour where we could stop on the way. The sea is quite rough. As we leave the shore we begin to pitch and toss in the waves. I compete with the waves by playing works for clarinet by *Mozart, Rossini* and *Weber* that *Reşit* had recorded on cassette. I'm like a matador attacking a bull… Unable to withstand the grey-blue or black waves, tempests and storms, I leave it all to *Hera*, the wife of *Zeus!…*

Fishing for orfoz in the Gulf of Gökova.

But *Hera* can't manage it either. As the passengers begin to give way to panic *Captain Muharrem* turns back to **Knidos**. The captain goes into the bows of the ship and watches the sea till noon, when he is obliged to cast anchor. The storm has somewhat abated. We are relieved to see the light of day. After a six hours' journey we anchor at **Yedi Adalar** in the **Gulf of Gökova**. *Sevda* asks if there are any historical monuments here. *"There aren't any historical monuments,"* says little *Ayşegül,* imitating me, *"but there are some natural ones."*

And she's right. All the shores are covered in green. The grey soil and olive trees of **Knidos** are replaced here by thick pine forests. Another interesting phenomenon is that the sea is a different temperature in every bay. As a refugee from a great city I realize that it is impossible to remain far away from green, blue, indigo and the chorus of cicadas. And yet, in spite of all its blemishes and its tiredness and exhaustion, I love the indestructible profundity of **Istanbul**… But it has become a city of hucksters…

The joy and sorrow of birth and death are to be found in the waters of the **Aegean** and the **Mediterranean**. The only thing you won't find are crowds in pursuit of an ugliness and vulgar they nourish on honey and *börek…*

You won't find a trace of this pursuit of ugliness anywhere on these shores. Whereas "I told you so"s, vicious circles, deaths of friends in mosque courtyards and hucksters girding on ugliness wait for me at home.

I search for the very few, exceptional people who can hear the voice of nature and give ear to it.

Such a search is sometimes a very melancholy one.

As we sail through the bright, dark blue waters a dove suddenly falls on

THE FATE OF KNIDOS. 1994.

You may have already read about the "Aphrodite of the Knidians" in the impressions of the Blue Voyage of 1987, short notes that didn't go into too much detail. I returned to Knidos several times after that. My last trip there was in August 1994.

A full seven years have passed since I wrote those notes on Knidos. Nothing has changed there, apart from a decrease in the number of carved stones!…

But I can see a change in myself. That's why I open a window on Knidos, a city famous for its wine and Aphrodite…

In any case, I have a very good reason. In 1987 I wrote that *"you can't just take a quick look at a city designed by the town planner Hippodamos of Miletus."* No matter at what time of day you choose to sail into Knidos harbour don't expect to find yourself face to face with a striking natural landscape. The secret of Knidos lies in its art and culture.

Here, you won't see the monumental buildings soaring up to the clouds and the sky that you can see in other ancient cities. Knidos consists of ruins covered with grey earth. The theatre is probably the only thing that may arouse your interest.

Don't be lazy. If you have any books to hand, search through their pages.

Knidos is one of the essential stories of civilization.

And one important fact about Knidos is that all the boats anchor in the southern harbour. The northern harbour is open to the waves and the darkness.

If you make your way past the wooden quay in the southern harbour, the restaurant and the grocer's shop and turn to the right, a hundred or a hundred and fifty paces further on you will come under the spell of the ancient city. And if you turn towards the temple of Dionysus, even if you don't want to, you will feel forced to stop. And when you turn round you will see the two harbours, right next to one another, but on the worst of terms.

This visit should be undertaken, not when the sun is at its height, but one hour before the gates of the ancient city close for the night. The Knidos lighthouse and the shadows of the boats in the water are at their most most beautiful at sunset.

There are two things I have always recommended in the Aegean and the Mediterranean: sunrise and sunset…

In his book *Turkey Beyond the Meander* George Bean, a distinguished scholar who carried out research in the Aegean and Mediterranean and taught Greek for twenty-five years in the University of Istanbul relates the following story of the Knidos Aphrodite:

"Praxiteles is said to have "flourished" between 365 and 360; this may mean that he was then about forty years of age, or perhaps that he created his most famous work, the Aphrodite, around that time. In any event, when the Cnidians ordered their new statue of the goddess, it happened that the men of Cos also had just done the same; and it further happened that Praxiteles had two Aphrodites ready in his workshop, one draped and the other nude. The Coans were given the choice and took the former; the nude

accordingly remained for the Cnidians, and afterwards gained immensely more fame than the other, so that many people, as Pliny says, sailed to Cnidus simply to see it. Now the Coans too had moved the site of their city in 365 B.C., and it is hard to resist the conclusion that they and the Cnidians found themselves simultaneously in the same need to equip their new temples…

…

"A work entitled Love Affairs, passing under the name of Lucian in the second century A.D., gives an account of a visit to Cnidus. After admiring the gardens which filled the precinct, the party entered the temple and stood amazed before the beauty of the statue in the middle; then, wishing to see the back as well (for the statue was noted as being equally lovely in all aspects) they went round to the rear of the temple, where the door was opened for them by the old woman who held the key. The back of the statue proved indeed to be in no way inferior to the front; they noticed, however, a dark patch like a stain on the inner part of the thigh. At first they supposed this to be a flaw in the marble, and admired the skill of the sculptor in contriving that it should come in so inconspicuous a place; but the old woman explained that this was not so. There had been, she said, a young man who fell in love with the goddess and dreamed of marrying her. All his days he spent in the temple from morning to evening; and to estimate his chances he cast knucklebones (the ancient dice) in the hope of making the throw named after the goddess herself, when all four dice showed different faces. Finally, driven to desperation by his desire, he concealed himself in the temple one day and contrived to remain hidden when the doors were closed for the night. In the morning the mark of his passionate embraces was clear on the marble, and there it remained ever since."

This mad story of beauty and desire created its own legend. As well as beauty, the Knidians also sent their own special wine throughout the whole of the Mediterranean. And, besides wine and grapes, they were also famous for a vinegar that could rival that of Egypt.

So, what happened to this marvellous statue?

Some think that it was taken to Constantinople, where it was broken up and burned; others that someday it may be reborn!...

Of the temple of Aphrodite, which occupied a site dominating the peninsula, only the round foundations and some steps remain. An interesting point, in view of the story of the stain left on the statue of the goddess of beauty by her lover, is the discovery in the vicinity of the temple of a large number of erotic pottery fragments.

So there was probably something in the old woman's story! Herodotus, however, paid very little attention to such matters. The great historian had no time for mere gossip.

An interesting part of the history of Knidos concerns the doings of Harpagus..

Homer gives us some details about the city:

"Harpagus enslaved the Curians, who were unable to achieve any success, and the other Greek settlements in the region showed themselves to be no more heroic than the Carians. One of these was the Laodecimonian colony of Knidos. Their land looked out on to the sea, which is why it was called Triopion. It forms an extension of the Bybassos peninsula, the whole of Knidos territory being surrounded by sea apart from a narrow isthmus. To the north lay the Gulf of Ceraicos, to the south the Gulf of Syme and Rhodes. When Harpagus arrived in Ionia the Knidians began to cut through the isthmus, which was five stadia wide, with the intention of converting their territory into an island. They would thus have been able to withdraw completely on to their own land, because the section they were cutting formed the only connection with the mainland. A great deal of labour was expended on the work, but it was found that the splintering of the hard rock was injuring the faces and eyes of the workmen more than appeared natural. They therefore sent envoys to the oracle at Delphi for advice. According to the Knidians themselves, the god replied, in iambics:

> *The isthmus requires neither castle nor digging*
> *If Zeus had so desired he would himself have made*
> *this land an island.*

"Upon receiving this prophecy the Knidians abandoned work on the isthmus and on Harpagus' arrival surrendered without resistance."

Knidos, like so many ancient cities, is full of unknowns. Perhaps that is a rather commonplace remark, but the fact that the famous astronomer and mathematician Eudoxus, the sculptor Praxiteles and Sostratos, who built the lighthouse at Alexandria, were all natives of Knidos is a good enough reason.

Today we know so very little about the other works of this great scholar and creative artist! That is why Knidos still guards its secret.

That this city should still be full of unknowns after thousands of years is the fate of Knidos.

For those of our own generation, who look on all this only from a distance and take little or no interest in art or culture as they dip their adventurous hearts in the waters of the Aegean and the Mediterranean, there is so much to say!...

Perhaps, one day, they will encounter the wrath of Aphrodite!...

(above) Kargılı Bay.
(below) Şehir Islands and Cleopatra Bay.

The injured dove that fell on to our deck and spent three days sailing with us on our boat, and a sketch I drew under the impact of its death.

the deck. It must have been injured in some way…
We try to catch hold of it but it scurries away in terror.
We finally get hold of it in a corner of the boat. We stroke it. Its eyes are sad and melancholy. It trembles with fear. There's a purple band across its breast. A wound opens out beneath it. We put it in a box.
Everyone's eyes and ears are on the wounded dove.

(above) Karaca Bay.
(below) Remains of the Roman theatre beside the Cleopatra Beach.

We bathe the wound. But it's no good. We open its beak and feed it through a dropper.

It pecks away a little at the food in the box but it has very little strength.

For three days it accompanies us on our journey across seas and bays. It experiences all the different winds.

On the third day I wake up as the first rays of the sun strike my face. I lift the half open lid of the box. Its beak is half open. Its eyes are filled with the melancholy coldness of death. The blue and grey stripes on its wings rebel against its dying. It's as if the wings were about to wrench themselves away and take flight.

The gods of nature have summoned it.

*(above) Cleopatra Beach, for which
Antony is said to have brought sand
from North Africa for love of Cleopatra.
(below) Bencik Bay.
(opposite page) From the Şehir Islands.*

Gürbüz and I get into the boat and take it to the shore. We find a spot for
it below the pine and laurel trees. We cover it over with dry leaves.

It wasn't right for death to be so near in the blue of the **Mediterranean**.
We are a generation that thinks every ripple on the sea a storm and fal-
ters in the face of death.

Our only consolation was that our little dove didn't fall and die amid
the city crowds. It could well have been crushed and killed in the noise
and confusion…

We sail from **Yedi Adalar** to **Tuzla Bay**, from there to the gulf of **Gökova**
and on towards the **Şehir Islands**, where we spend three days touring
Karaca Bay and **Değirmen Bükü**. **Sedir** or **Sedrai Island** is quite unforgettable. It has seen the coming of the **Spartans**, the **Persians**, the **Romans**,
the **Knights of Rhodes** and *Alexander the Great*.

One can't pay a visit to **Şehir Island** without seeing the spot where
Cleopatra swam… It is said that, for love of *Cleopatra*, *Antony* had sand
brought to this shore from **North Africa**. It's a pleasant tale. As for the
sand, it is indescribably beautiful. It's as if coloured marble had been
ground to poppy seeds over thousands of years. The colour of the sea is
the colour of green glass… But the place is filled now with so many of
our own *Cleopatras* that there's no space left for dreams!…

We make straight for the little theatre surrounded by olive trees, leaving
our plump *Cleopatras* to their own devices!…

1. Serçe Harbour.
2. From Serçe Harbour.
3. Hisarönü Gulf.
4. Söğüt Köyü (Ayasaranda).

The shores of **Karaca Bay** are covered with myrrh trees, oleanders and pines.

As the day loses its brilliance, clouds begin to cast their shadow over the bay. There are two small restaurants on the shore, together with a grocer's and a few houses with gardens. White, green, blue and crimson painted, tall-masted vessels are reflected in the water. Impossible to describe the beauty and all the myriad shades of colour. That's why we prepared our table with due respect for nature. Even the passage of each sip of our drinks past our nostrils was carried out without undue haste... But round about midnight we were startled by a heart-rending cry. Not a cry really. More a shriek.

> *"Oy, oy, my Emine,*
> *What sort of beauty is this,*
> *Bracelets on your arm."*

There couldn't have been more than four or five customers in the restaurant. Goodness knows who they were playing this song to. We swore we'd never again anchor at any spot where there was even a single restaurant on the shore...

That's why we didn't stop at **Bodrum**. This time we made our way into several bays we had left specially for the return journey.

It is impossible ever to forget **Kargılı** or **Löngöz Bay** that stretches out like an enchanted corridor, **Bencik Bay** in the gulf of **Hisar** that fills your heart with hope, **Bozukkale**, that you reach after passing **Dirsel Bükü** and **Kara Point**, and finally **Serçe Harbour** and its waters.

Serçe Harbour also has a wreck and thyme honey... But I didn't want to talk about the harbour at **Datça**.

As you climb up to the theatre and the castle at **Amos** you will see how it dominates everything around it on sea and land...

Unfortunately, the cities of **Knidos, Loryma, Bybasos** in **Keçi Bükü** and

Amos have all been abandoned to the mercy of nature and the looting and pillaging of any passerby. Yet even the location of the small theatre has a message for our own age...

Beauty is an essential factor in binding people to the soil on which they

387

(above) Kumbükü Köyü from the slopes of the historical city of Amos.
(right) Gökova Bay.
(opposite page) The blue waters from the island near Keçibükü (Orhaniye).

live. Sea and sand is not enough. It is necessary, as I keep on repeating, to bathe in the same waters as the people of thousands of years ago. The still virgin bays and waters of the **Aegean** and the **Mediterranean** wait for us with a way of life preserved over thousands of years. But they have one condition. That unmannerly individuals intent on pillage should be sacrificed to *Hades,* the god of the underworld.

THE COUNTRY OF ALL THE TRIBES: THE SEAMEN OF PAMPHYLIA

(opposite page) The imposing Gate of Hadrian and the Kaleiçi houses in the heart of Antalya.

In ancient times the **Mediterranean** region around the port of **Antalya** was known as **Pamphylia**. This section of the polytheistic world was surrounded by **Lycia, Pisidia** and **Cilicia**.

The inhabitants of this region, which extends 118 kilometres from east to west and 30 kilometres from north to south, were described by *Herodotus* in the following terms:

> *"These Pamphylians were brothers in arms of Amphilocus and Calchas and descendants of those that dispersed on the return from Troy."*

Strabo, in praising the *Lycians,* also mentions the *Pamphylians:*

> *"The dockyards in Side, a city in Pamphylia, were open to the Cilicians and it was here that they sold their prisoners by open auction, in spite of the fact that they admitted that they were free men. The Pamphylians succeeded in extending their command of the sea as far Italy, but the Lycians conducted their lives in so civilized and refined a manner that they never made shameful demands and remained within their own sphere of influence in the Lycian League bequeathed to them by their ancestors."*

Very little information is available concerning the prehistoric period in **Pamphylia**, but there is said to have been some connection with the **Troy-Yortan** culture in the island of **Cyprus** in the 3rd millennium B.C. From the inscriptions, it would appear that the people spoke the language known as **Luwi.** In the 2nd millennium B.C. the *Hittites* referred to the region as **Mopsopia**.

From the coins and inscriptions of **Perge, Aspendos, Sillyon** and **Selge** it

of various shapes and sizes filled with goldfish. And from every pool a small water channel went under the wall of the neighbouring garden to the pool in the next courtyard. Just like the water channel that connected your own pool to the neighbouring pool on the other side.

The most remarkable thing was the number of fish.

There was a countless number. And there was no question of yours or mine!

When the water level was high one or two of your own fish would be swept down the channel under the wall into your neighbour's pool…

Every now and again the water in the pools in the **Kaleiçi** houses would quite joyfully experience this curious migration.

In every district, practically in every street, you would find sea-captains and their familes who had sailed to **Rhodes, Crete, Bodrum, Marmaris** and even the shores of **North Africa,** and there were nurses, mothers; and children who only saw their fathers and grandfathers once every three or four months…

Most of the boats in the harbour were wooden vessels or barges but now and again iron vessels carrying coal, cotton or timber would moor there.

The white passenger ships that anchored once a month offshore and which we could hear from a long way off were both our playthings and the substance of our dreams.

They were our dreams, because we could never ourselves have imagined such a ship.

They were our playthings, because as soon as we saw one anchor we would leap into the boat we had rigged up ourselves and make our way to its side. But not the port side. Right under the bow where they dropped the chain.

We played the craziest games. We would clamber with bare feet up the thick links of the chain for a ticket to the cinema or a paper cornet of sunflower seeds.

Clambering up was nothing. The most difficult thing was getting through the opening in the chain onto the deck.

If the chain had slackened just a stretch, we would have been done for! But once on to the iron deck, that made our day! A free cinema or a cornet of sunflower seeds.

The iron deck, burning in the scorching heat of the **Mediterranean** kept us hopping from one foot to the other. But what we feared most was being chased by the sailors. Then we would leap in terror into the sea. We couldn't get down the way we came up. Another frightening thing was the ringing in our ears as our bodies plunged deep down into the water.

What did it matter? It had made our day. We'd pile into our boat and head for the shore. Then past *Hadrian's* gate to find ourselves in front of **Karaali Park.** Three musketeers with sunflowers and the rattle of swords.

The coastal city of Side, one of the five cities of Pamphylia. The name 'Side', which means 'pomegranate', was a source of inspiration to artists. That is why the prizes presented in the races organized in honour of Apollo were in the form of pomegranates.

THE FIVE CITIES OF PAMPHYLIA

According to *Arif Müfit Mansel* very little is known of the early history of the city of **Side**, or 'pomegranate'.

In his book on the 1947-1966 excavations and researches in **Side** published in 1978, *Mansel* explains the meaning of the name **Pamphylia** as *"the country of all the tribes"*.

What a wonderful definition! And it's true! For in the course of the "Aegean migrations" tribes and peoples from every part of the country from the **Hittite Kingdom** to burning **Troy**, made their way, led by their prophets and soothsayers, down south to the province of **Pamphylia**. Did you expect them to be able to agree among themselves? What a hope!… They were all engaged in bitter economic and political rivalry. They earned their living from maritime commerce, agriculture and cattle-raising. And they became very wealthy.

Until the foundation of the city of **Attaleia, Side** was the only port.

Antalya and **Side** are quite near each other. According to *Mansel*, only 65 kilometres as the crow flies. From the mouth of the **Melas**, i.e. **Manavgat**, it is only 10 kilometres.

The city was founded some time in the 7th century B.C. but the exact date is uncertain.

1. *Antalya. Side harbour as seen from the theatre.*
2. *The shores at Side.*
3. *Side. Monumental columns.*
4. *Side. The monument and fountain of Vespasian.*

According to *Mansel* "Side may be regarded as the oldest city in Southern Anatolia".

As far as the name is concerned he adds that:

"Side is neither Greek nor Phoenician. It is purely Anatolian in origin."

And he goes on:

"Coins and inscriptions prior to the 6th century B.C., together with three stone inscriptions belonging to the 3rd-2nd centuries B.C. discovered at Side prove that the language spoken in Side very probably derived from

3

4

Antalya. Side theatre and corridor.

*an old Anatolian language (Luwi ?).and that until well into the
Hellenistic period it differed quite markedly from the Pamphylian dialect
employed in the vicinity. They also show the employment of a script quite
peculiar to Side."*

Side coins dating from around 500 B.C. bear representations of a
pomegranate and a fish. They are of very great beauty, and well worthy

of their **Mediterranean** origin.

The citizens of **Side** dedicated their festivals to *Athena* and *Apollo*, the festivals held in honour of *Apollo* being known as **"Pythia"**. The winners in the competitions were awarded a pomegranate, the symbol of the city, combined, of course, with a crown and the branch of a date palm. There was also. a competition known as *"themis"* for which money

A woman statue in Side Museum. According to Mansel the monuments and statues date from the 2nd and 3rd centuries A.D.

prizes were given. I have no idea which aroused the greater interest, but there is no doubt that in our own day the *"themis"* would have been the only competition to be held!…

Mansel confirms that the monuments, statues and imposing buildings were erected in the 2nd-3rd centuries A.D.

Irrigation facilitated the production of the olives and olive oil that constituted the most important produce of the region. At the same time a large part of the city's revenue was obtained from ship-building and fishing.

The city's prosperity was so obviously reflected in the houses, streets, water supply and environment that the city of Side was said to have no rival in this respect.

> *"When asked at a drinking party who were the most rascally of mankind, the famous harpist Stratonicus, who was famous for his ready wit, replied 'In Pamphylia, the men of Phaselis, in the whole world, the men of Side'."*

We don't know how the brawl provoked by this remark ended, but it would appear from their inscriptions that the citizens of **Side** always spoke of their city in the most laudatory terms.

With its theatre, streets, underground water channels, its temples on the shore, its agora, fountains and statues, **Side** is now both a fascinating ancient city and a very popular holiday resort.

The ancient baths have been converted into a museum with nude statues waiting for you in every corner. The water supply and heating system of the baths is both a source of amusement and food for thought.

Compare this with the present day, when there is not a single monumental building on the whole of the **Aegean** or **Mediterranean** shores that could possibly provide either...

The **Manavgat (Meles) River,** which is fed by the underground streams that pour down from the **Toros Mts.** and reaches its climax at **Manavgat** itself could well be described as nature's gift to the

A woman statue from Side Museum.

region. The citizens of **Perge** erected a 30 kilometre system for the transport of this water, parts of the old aqueduct and underground canals still remaining in use at the present day.

Perge, located 15 kilometres from **Antalya** and 2 kilometres beyond the present-day village of **Aksu,** is the second city in **Pamphylia.**

It is now an open-air museum.

You may want to stay in **Side** and visit **Perge** from there, returning to **Side** in the evening for a swim and a pleasant meal. If so, you will make us very jealous.

(above and right) Perge, the famous city on the plain, with its aqueducts, conduits and monumental buildings possesses all the features of an open-air museum.

After *Prof.Arif Mansel's* death in 1975, the excavations and researches at **Perge** which he had begun in 1946 and continued throughout the following years, were taken over by *Prof.Dr.Jale İnan,* who had always worked very closely with this very distinguished scholar. Later still, those who had been assistants or students in those early days were to commence work as scholars in their own right.

Strabo, our constant source of information, gives the following description of **Perge** and the neighbouring cities:

> *"Perge may be reached by sailing sixty stadia (10,980 m) up the river Cestros. On a neighbouring piece of high ground one arrives at the temple of Artemis Pergaea, the site of an annual festival. After that, some forty stadia further up, one arrives at the lofty city of Syllion, which is visible from Perge, then a large lake known as Capria, then the river Eurymedon (Köprüçay), and finally the populous city of Aspendos, founded by citizens of Argos. Just above Aspendos lies Petnelissos. Then there is another city and a number of islands at some distance from the shore. After that one arrives at Side, a colony of Cyme, with a temple to Athena, and, immediately beside it, the*

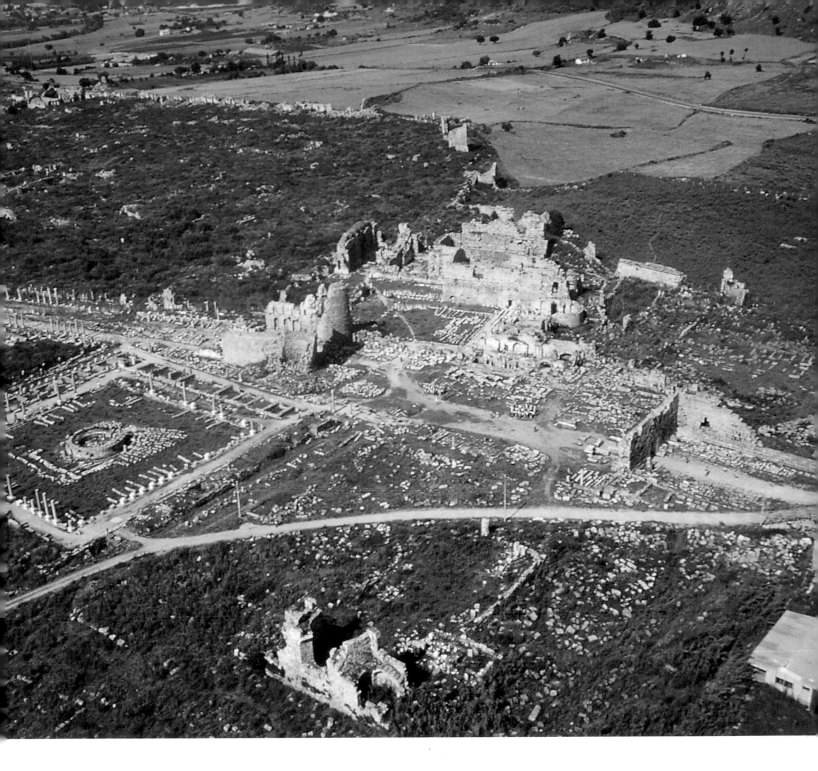

small shore of Cibyrates. Then comes the river Melas (Manavgat), then an anchorage and then the city of Ptolemais."

Prof.Dr.Ekrem Akurgal gives the following information regarding the foundation of the city:

"The appearance of the names Calchas and Mopsos in the inscriptions on the statue pedestals found in the oldest entrance gate of the city proves that the Pergaeans believed the city of Perge to have been founded by these Hellenic heroes after the Trojan war."

The Graeco-Roman theatre for fifteen thousand spectators contains effi-

1

1. Side. The stadium dating from the 2nd century A.D.
2, 3. The Perge theatre with seats for 25,000 was built in the Graeco-Roman style. The theatre contains monuments dedicated to the river god Cestros and Dionysus.

gies of the river-god Cestros and Dionysos, the god of rapture.

This theatre resembles that of **Side** in not, as was usual in ancient times, being built against the slope of a hill. Nearby lies one of the finest stadiums to have survived to the present day. It is thought to have been built in the 2nd century A.D. Below the tiers of seats are lodged rows of shops where the people could do their shopping after the games, which had been watched wih tremendous enthusiasm by the twelve thousand spectators. The most important thing about these shops was who sold what. That is why there are inscriptions on the walls giving the name of the shopkeeper and the type of ware sold.

This ancient city presents a truly monumental appearance with its twin towers, the statues in niches and its decorative elements.

Perge, the birthplace of the celebrated mathematician *Apollonius,* remained independent until the arrival of *Alexander the Great.* The absence of defence walls may have been a result of this type of independence.

A number of statues and other finds yielded by the **Perge** excavations are now exhibited in the **Antalya Museum.** The collection also includes a

2

3

409

large number of very interesting exhibits ranging from artistic artefacts of the Palaeolothic Age to 20th century objects of ethnographic interest. These include finds discovered in the **Karain** cavern excavations and marble, terra cotta and metal objects and icons from **Burdur-Hacılar, Elmalı, Finike, Xanthos, Perge, Side, Demre, Kumluca** and **Aspendos.** The museum also contains carpets and kilims reflecting local styles from the famous looms of the **Antalya** region. **Döşemealtı** and **Elmalı** are only two of these...

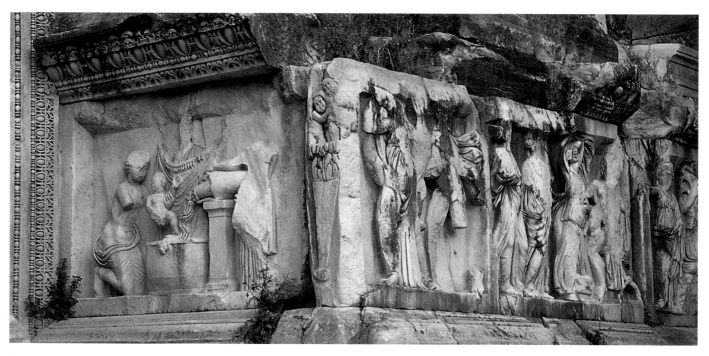

From Perge.

But it is in **Perge** that the greatest number of statues have been found, with imposing representations of gods, goddesses, generals, emperors. *Erotes* and dancers.

As you make your way from **Perge** to **Aspendos** you will see the city of **Sillyon** on a hill to your left.

Though rarely mentioned, **Sillyon** is of considerable importance from the architectural point of view and displays the distinguishing features of the Hellenistic age.

Mansel describes it as *"a chateau dominating the plain".*

The city of **Aspendos** on the banks of the **Köprüçay (Eurymedon)** is now famous for the theatre dominating the broad expanse of the plain and all its beauty.

Known to the local inhabitants as **Belkis,** after the nearby village, **Aspendos** was founded by tribes from **Argos.** It was the only city apart from **Side** to mint coins in the 5th century B.C. As *Prof.Akurgal* has pointed out, the present-day **Köprü Çay** penetrated right into the heart of **Aspendos** and provided anchorage for various fleets.

The river also facilitated an active trade in salt, oil and wool, and it was this rich commerce that inspired *Alexander the Great* with the desire to capture the city. On the citizens' refusal to surrender, he decided to occupy it by force.

This prosperity continued throughout the **Roman** period, during which a number of imposing buildings were erected.

The theatre for twenty thousand spectators built by *Theodoros'* son, the architect *Zenon,* has survived in an excellent state of preservation due to its continued used and maintenance throughout the **Seljuk** period. The brick repairs were carried out by the *Seljuks.* The columns in the arcades and the entrance wall built as a support also date from this period.

After these various cities situated on the sea-shore, the banks of a river or a plain, comes the mountain city: **Termessos.**

Why the citizens of **Termessos,** who settled on a level piece of ground on **Güllük Dağ** 30 kilometres from **Antalya,** should have decided to found a city 1050 metres above sea-level is a mystery.

Did the citizens of **Termessos** choose this spot, surrounded by steep paths and precipitous slopes, to escape from wars and migrations?

They were fully justified by events. There must have been good reason why *Alexander the Great*, although he laid siege to **Termessos** and laid waste the country around it, failed in his attempt to capture the city.

The reason for his failure lay in the city's situation on a geographical site unsuitable for pitched battle and with plenty of water to endure a lengthy siege.

In their inscriptions, the citizens of **Termessos** claimed that they were the descendants of the *Solymians,* an indigenous **Pamphylian** tribe. **Termessos** was at the height of its prosperity during the **Hellenistic** and **Roman** periods.

We are also told of a very interesting incident relating to the city.

Alexander's death was followed by a power struggle between his former generals in the course of which **Antigonus** seized control of the province of **Asia**. Thereupon *Alcetas*, one of *Alexander's* generals, formed an army with the support of the citizens of **Termessos**. Defeated in battle, he sought refuge in **Termessos,** but the elders of the city were unwilling to

Alexander the Great. Marble. Magnesia ad Sipylum (Manisa), Hellenistic period, mid 3rd century B.C. Found together with inscription containing the name of the sculptor "Manas".Istanbul Archaeological Museum.

*Antalya. Detail of the Aspendos theatre
for 20,000 spectators.*

give him asylum and *Alcetas* committed suicide. The elders surrendered the corpse to *Antigonus,* but the young men of **Termessos,** who had strongly supported *Alcetas* and were deeply ashamed of the treacherous behaviour of their elders, seized the body of the general who had preferred death to humiliation and brought it back to their own city. There they buried the body with all due ceremony in the soil of **Termessos.**

There is still a great deal of research and investigation to be carried out in this city, now located in the **Termessos** National Park amidst forests of pines.

It is impossible to sit on the steps of the theatre for 4,200 spectators without thinking of *Zeus.* The colour of the surrounding countryside and the clouds coming straight towards you carry you back thousands of years in a thrill of excitement.

You are able here to understand much more clearly why man, who created the myths of *Zeus,* was to choose such precipitous rocks as a refuge. They could have found a place like **Side**, with its fruits and vegetables and far more favourable climate.

It is said that in the 3rd century B.C. **Termessos** had a population of 150 thousand. Perhaps that is why tombs can be found scattered around the four corners of the city. **Termessos** is, indeed, an imposing city, with its temples to *Zeus* and *Artemis*, its colonnaded street, its agora, cisterns, odeon and gymnasium.

Termessos, the mountain city that Alexander besieged but failed to capture, was said to have had a population of 150,000 in the 3rd century B.C.

ALAIYE: THE CITY OF THE SELJUK SULTAN

K andeleri Point is the symbol of **Alanya**. Ever since the earliest times
successive communities have chosen it as a place of habitation.
Known to the ancient **Greeks** as **Coracesium**, to the **Byzantines** as
Kalonoros, the 'Fine Mountain', and to the medieval **Latins** as
Candelore or **Lescandelour**, in 1221 its name was finally changed by the

414

Seljuk Sultan *Alaeddin Keykubad* to **Alaiyya.** In popular speech this became corrupted to **Alanya** and the long narrow cape entered the relevant literature as **Kandeleri.** According to *Strabo*, **Coracesium** was a city built on a steep rock.

Its ease of defence and its sheltered harbour made it an attractive base not only for great kings and sultans but also for pirates. Attempts were made to capture it by one bold adventurer after another. Even during the Seljuk period it attracted the attention of both the Venetians and the Genoese.

The castle on **Kendeleri Point** was rebuilt by *Keykubad.*

This cape, with its superb location, its castle, mosque, church, market and dervish lodges, became an essential port of call for all travellers.

The **Red Tower** and dockyard on the left hand side of **Kandeleri Point** also date from the reign of *Sultan Keykubad.* The stonework, function and location of **Şara-psu** and **Alarahan** on the road connecting **Alâiye** to

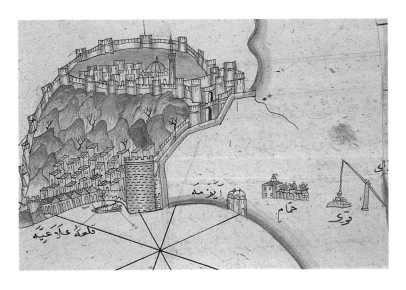

(opposite page) Alanya. The harbour, Red Tower and Castle dating from the reign of Sultan Alâeddin Keykûbad. (left) Kal'a-i Alâiyye. One of the maps of Piri Reis.

Konya also indicate a similar origin… The **Dockyard,** the **Red Tower** and the castle still preserve their original beauty. The same cannot be said of **Alanya** itself.

The article *"Time in the Eastern Mediterranean"* by the brilliant writer *Adalet Ağaoğlu* published in the periodical *"Skylife"* in 1994 offers a rather pessimistic view:

> *"The end of summer is a novel of longing. To be able to stop the passing of time for a moment, to put it down on paper… But to be quite frank, it is also a time of disillusion. For longing is the product of inadequate*

knowledge. Lives that pass too quickly are destined to be too little known.

"There are places you feel a certain thrill in remembering. Places that a photograph, a certain breeze, the opening and closing of a shutter arouses the desire to see again. A city, the top of a bridge, that stretch of shore…

"Places that make you say: 'If only I could be there!'

"I have seen the rapidity of the changes undergone in a certain period of time by the whole province of Pamphylia; by Side, Manavgat, Alanya and its environs, İncekum, Afsallar, Alara and even the lovely sea itself. It is as if the last twenty or thirty years had swallowed up the previous twenty or thirty centuries.

"Several places on the Mediterranean shores resemble women who have been the victims of a passionate but brutal love. A love that wounds, crushes and casts aside. A devouring and squandering of love.

"I could already perceive this in the 1950s. In the 60s I witnessed it more closely and confirmed my impressions. But the history and natural land-scape of this country have a strange way of attracting and holding one. Enchanted and enchanting shores…

"The eastern section of Antalya, in the days of the Lydians, the Persians, Alexander the Great, the Romans.

"Seljuk caravanserais, bridges, caravan routes. Ottoman mosques, cis-terns, baths…

"Pirate strongholds, natural harbours, conglomerates, pine forests… The pungent fragrance of rosemary and oleander… The passionate embrace of history and nature. A love plunged into fear and suspicion.

"A doubtful time. Doubtful shores. A doubtful history. Who knows, probably it is in this that its charm lies.

"At one time I used to go there very frequently. In those years it must have been just exactly the moment of equilibrium on the crest of the wave. The second between movement from one side to the other; the knife-edge of time. At every departure the same feeing would throb with-in me: Those days can never return… The days when, in the evenings, in our little house by the shore made from local stone, we would listen only to the song of the nightbirds and the cicadas and hear only the whisper-ing of the water nymphs.

"But did those days ever really exist?

"Every time I went down there I felt I was living all the epochs simul-taneaously. I strove to find a centre of gravity for all those ages heaped one on top of the other. I drew a line down the centre of the map of Turkey. For the region on the right hand side I would say, 'That's the Eastern Mediterranean'. Not the Mediterranean of the Aegean winds, of the Middle East or North Africa. The Eastern Mediterranean. Nothing has been written of the sea or the life of the sea, because since the Arabs there has been no life in the Mediterranean. It is as if the sea, with its fishermen, its pirates and its sailing-boats had simply never existed… Everything was as transitory as footprints in the sand washed away by

The Seljuk dockyard in Alanya.

the waves. And yet so many things have happened since that time.

"Alanya Castle. The lacework of the bastions against the blue of the sky. Remembering how 'offending slaves' were once thrown down from this height into the sea. Dark blue-green waters in the embrace of giant cactuses. Castle houses with bay windows looking out onto the harbour through windows with embroidered or crocheted curtains. To the west of Alanya, inland from Şarapsu and İncekum, you can find traces of the old caravans on the forest roads. And then a stone-arched Roman bridge. And some fifteen kilometres inland from Manavgat you will find the imposing building of Alara Han, constructed in regular stone masonry in the 13th century by Alâeddin Keykubad. And if we stroll a little further through history, we will find fires burning in spacious courtyards in the middle of rows of caravanserai rooms, lambs roasting over the fires and ice-cold water from the upland plateaux. Down below, fire-flies twinkling in the valley of the Alara rather than the headlights of an endless line of trucks and cars.

"Side, where Cleopatra would meet Antony, and the lagoons where they would bathe together. The entrance gate, the monumental fountain, the

Alanya. Houses in the Kaleiçi.

two broad streets, the market place, the temple, the baths, the cemetery and the theatre.

"In the 7th century B.C. a centre of piracy that before the Alexandrian and Roman periods had known both Lydian and Persian hegemony, Side was, during the Roman period, one of the main markets in the Mediterranean slave trade. Its name is derived from the word for 'pomegranate'. A pomegranate town. But in my opinion, it is not so much the slave trade of the past as the passionate but shameful manner in which the city is loved at the present-day that makes the pomegranates change from one colour to the other and makes their faces blush with shame. At sunset this motley colour is reflected on the marble and on the sands, and a variegated pink invests the ruined seawalls with all the appearance of a water-colour.

"Soon the boats will enter the harbour and hundred of Romans, their togas blowing in the wind, will make their way along the mosaic street to the agora and then set out for the theatre in two-wheeled carts.

"I too will huddle down in a cart and make my way to the amphitheatre for twenty-five thousand built in the 2nd century. Once again I am abso-

lutely amazed at the perfection of the acoustics in this theatre, built, not against the slope of a hill like the other theatres of the time, but on round piers. With the full moon turning the sea to silver on three sides I listen to the lyres of the musicians. The aqueducts stretch right across the plain catching the eye with the light on the water. At Side, one looks in bewilderment at the PET bottles filling the spaces between the marble remains. What age am I living in?

"There are faces whose expression changes from one moment to the next. The new face of the Eastern Mediterranean reminds you of one of those."

There's no limit to destruction. But in our own age the limits of creation are being reached. Beyond the limits, all vestiges are erased.

It is as if everything was being donated to **Hades**, the god of the underworld.

Here too, we have only a single witness: the mingling waters of the **Aegean** and the **Mediterranean...**

We are indebted to that for this long voyage. And for these beauties.

And nature has only one support in its struggle to protect itself against us: the god **Poseidon!**

When stirred to wrath the seas and their waters can whip up utter confusion with their storms and tempests. There can be rain and lightning, wiping all evil and all ugliness from the face of the earth. And that goes for the land too.

But there is one drawback as far as **Poseidon** is concerned. He has been the protector of many a city but he was always defeated in every competition he entered.

What he can do now in this rapidly growing world I really don't know!...

But the **Aegean** and the **Mediterranean** will hide their mysterious waters and create him anew.

The civilizations that have existed for thousands of years are our witness...

BLUE NOTES

THE INFINITY OF THE AEGEAN AND THE MEDITERRANEAN

Everyone has his own particular shade of blue; a blue that changes with the light, the mountains, the wind, the rain, the foam, the sunrise and the sunset.

Sometimes it approaches purple; sometimes green, sometimes white, sometimes grey, sometimes black, sometimes the mysterious gold of lapis lazuli…

Green too, like blue, has a myriad different shades.

Then there are the rocks, with their strange grey and their burnt brown.

Do the seas occupy more space, or the land? I really don't know! But however it may be, it is obvious that water everywhere infiltrates the land. Even on land, water might be said to establish a hegemony.

Without water, nothing on land can sprout or grow. Moreover, every piece of land owes its beauty to the paths traced by water and to the blossoming trees, the grass and the thousand and one animals it harbours. Moreover, many of the minerals extracted from its depths resemble water in their colour.

In other words, water dominates everything, everywhere.

But there's nothing very mysterious about all this.

What am I trying to get at?

The infinity of the Aegean and the Mediterranean…

For forty years I have been working and playing with colour. But ever since I started cruising in the Aegean and the Mediterranean I have found myself unable to define blue. I become quite bewildered on observing it.

That is why I have called this book *"Blue Civilization"*. Blue is not merely a shade of colour. It has established a warm friendship with the human races that founded cities in close harmony with the environment. Communities and societies that left their homelands to follow the paths of migration would come, whenever they could, and settle down by the side of water. Sometimes on the shore of the sea, sometimes on the banks of a river or lake.

The communities that for thousands of years have migrated to the Aegean and the Mediterranean have devoted themselves so passionately to art and science that they are now known as the "founders of civilization".

THE SEA AND THE TREE

The sailing-boat has always been the type of vessel by means of which the seas have dominated man and man has attempted to dominate the seas. That is why I have such a liking for the Bodrum *Goulette* .

I feel a particular sympathy for wood; not that I understand it. The various communities that have taken up their abode on this earth have used wood for everything you can think of, from house construction to musical instruments made from very special types of wood.

It would appear from the wooden boats that have survived to the present day under water in a remarkably fine state of preservation that the contours on the keel are all very carefully calculated.

Elm is used for keels, and rivets of wood and copper are made to hold it in place.

The *Goulette* is the product of just such a development. And what particularly attracts me is the smell produced by salt water on wood, pitch and varnish. And there is also the beauty of the veins that become ever lovelier as the wood is planed and the beauty of the sound of the wood cleaving the waves.

The sound of the waves striking the teak, of the wind against the broad stern and the music created by the hull as it meets the foam that slips in friendly fashion through your fingers might well have been produced by a lute-player. Perhaps the lines of the wood resembles the lines of the sea, like the lines of the staff in music.

Brown can never form a harmony with blue, green or grey. So how can we explain the fact that pine, cedar, teak and elm can all go hand in hand with blue and green?…

Perhaps none of them is pure and unadulterated.

Each one of them is a shade peculiar to itself and at the same time an infinity. The shade appears when in a state of motion or when the ripples are transformed into waves.

We all prefer calm waters when on a voyage by sea. But no one can deny the beauty of the salt spray that penetrates your marrow, the troughs of the waves and the foam scattered from their crests.

It is these that produce the real joy of the Aegean and the Mediterranean. That's when you realize the joy of calm after stormy seas.

I don't believe that anything easily obtainable can ever have true strength or beauty.

It was the infinite waters of the Mediterranean that gave birth to Aphrodite, but it is to the storms and breakers of the Mediterranean that she owes her limpid beauty.

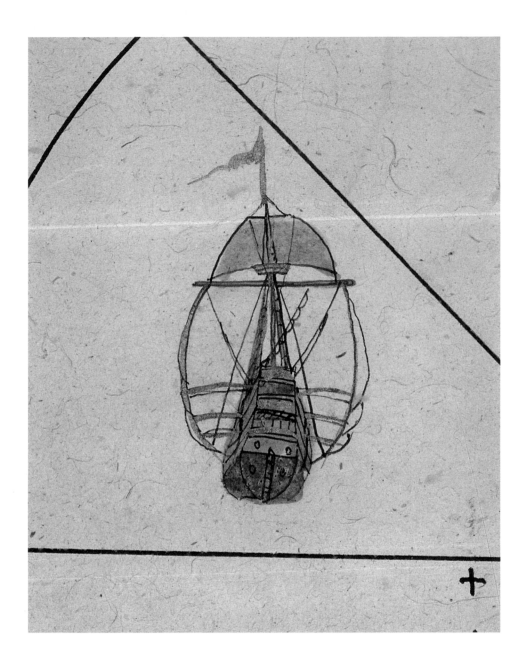

The simile may be rather crude, but life, like the groove opened by a carpenter's plane, is never absolutely straight. Bitter as it may seem, I don't believe that a life without sickness or disconfort can ever produce real happiness.

The eye and ear that cannot perceive change may build houses for themselves and adorn every part with precious stones. They may, as in the old legends, offer their guests wine in golden goblets.

But is that enough?

Who can adapt himself to the depth that approaches poetry and creates

poetry and music? Who will help us when we are surrounded by pain and despair, when we fall down into dry wells?…

This is truly the "depth" and nothing else. That is the sacred nature of waters, seas and trees. It cannot be explained by words like "peace" and "tranqillity".

4 July 1994 / Amos

FEAR AND GERBEKSE

We entered Gerbekse Bay in the wake of a swell. Gerbekse is a bay in İnce Island 4.5 sea miles south-west of Kadırga Point between Marmaris and Karaburun.

There was not a ripple on the water as we entered Gerbekse Bay and yet the wind was so strong that one single anchor wasn't sufficient and we had to cast a second.

But it never occurred to us to cast it at the stern.

The wind blowing from the land was as stiflingly hot as the air from an oven. We kept swinging backwards and forwards between our twin anchors.

The very bees were afraid to stay on our boat. They probably went off to find refuge in the trunks of the trees on the shore.

We were completely shrouded in the darkness of night.

The moonlight shone on the deep, dark blue water inflamed by the hot wind.

The green and red lights on port and starboard kept continually switching sides. There was no point in trying to sleep. The fear that something unpleasant might happen at any moment kept us wide awake.

What about the harbour? But ships had been known to collide and sink there as a result of sudden storms.

We began to receive signals from a vessel near the shore. Its lamp kept flashing. We weren't very near each other but the distance that separated us was only half what it had been when we moored earlier in the day.

The two foreign women sailing the yacht were probably terrified.

Captain Haydar came running from the helm but went back quite calmly. The distance between the arc traced by our boat as it swung between the two anchors and the path traced by theirs must have seemed to him to be quite sufficient.

It was five or half-past five in the morning. The scorching wind suddenly dropped.

As the darkness receded from over us the cicadas began to sing. It was as if someone was conducting the orchestra of nature in a polytheistic world.

No doubt, the cicadas had for thousands of years been perfectly familiar with all the possible changes in it.

What was happening?

Who was in charge of it all?

Who was it that had made the rocks the sea urchins were clinging to so attractive?

Perhaps sailors who were born to the sea will take no notice of what I say. They would doubtless just dismiss it with a laugh. For them, my

heart, bred on fear and suspicion, is probably quite incomprehensible. They will simply regard me as someone who is making his first acquaintance with the sea and its waters and is on the lookout for adventure.

But whatever the result, for one whole night I observed the various transformations of nature and found a vast amount of pleasure in so doing.

6 july 1994 / Gerbekse

THE LANGUAGE OF THE PLANTS

The production of dyes depends on the plants and the soil. And to produce a dye one must first of all be familiar with the plants.

Dyes were first produced in China in the 3rd millennia B.C. They are also known to have been produced and applied to fabrics during the Middle Kingdom in Egypt.

There has been a tradition of dye production in India, in the Indus Valley, since 2500 B.C.

Whatever the era under consideration, these facts provide evidence of a constant interest in nature and its plants.

The Aegean and the Mediterranean produced not only the goddess Aphrodite but also a thousand and one trees and flowers.

Few of us have any detailed knowledge of the trees that grow on these shores. We usually refer to anything that looks like a tree as a "pine". And yet the term "pine" covers so many different varieties of tree: *the pistachio pine, larch, Aleppo pine, Scotch pine, cluster pine, etc. etc.*

A position of infinite importance in the civilizations of the Aegean and the Mediterranean is occupied by the *cedar, the laurel, the olive* and *the pomegranate.*

In any archaeological museum you may happen to visit you are sure to find a gold crown with motifs based on the boughs, leaves, blossoms or fruit of the olive or myrtle.

Every piece of jewellery is inspired by the fruit of the trees or blossoms of the Aegean and the Mediterranean.

How does that come about?

In some cases because of their usefulness, in others because of their beauty. Natural forms can be traced in architecture, sculpture, murals, jewellery and garments.

This tradition is still carried on at the present day in places like Side, which means pomegranate, and in Caria, which suggests the walnut. In Anatolia you can find children with names such as *Çiçek* (Blossom),

Kiraz (Cherry), *Fidan* (Shoot), *Ilgın* (Tamarisk), *Yasemin* (Jasmine), *Çınar* (Plane) and *Defne* (Laurel). There are a great many people with names derived from flowers and plants.

And not only from flowers and plants. Children are also given names like *Deniz* (Sea), *Su* (Water), *Yunus* (Dolphin), *Yağmur* (Rain), *Bora* (Storm), *Güneş* (Sun), *Pınar* (Spring), *Bulut* (Cloud), *Damla* (Drop), *Çimen* (Grass), *Kaya* (Rock), *Lâra* and *Siren*.

The first production of natural dyes was a matter of pure chance combined with trial and error. It was all part of an attempt to make life more beautiful. They produced colours which cannot be produced by even the most modern industrial methods.

Mauve and *purple* are obtained from the shell-fish known as *Murex* and *Purpura* and are among the most difficult to produce. The natural colour is a pale yellow, but in the rays of the sun it becomes first of all *green*, and then *light red, crimson* and *purple.*

Purple dyes were of such rarity in ancient times that Julius Caesar forbade the wearing of purple togas by anyone except himself. The use of purple by senators attending meeting of the Senate was confined to a band along the hem of their garments.

The crimson obtained from the female insect on the Mediterranean evergreen known as the *kermes oak* is no way inferior to purple.

We find the following note in the account of the researches carried out by *Ü.Eyüboğlu, I.Okaygün* and *F.Yaraş*: *"Crimson made up a large part of the tribute paid to the occupying Roman armies"*. In the Old Testament, Exodus Chapter 25, we find the following passage: *"And the Lord spake unto Moses, saying: Speak unto the children of Israel, that they bring me an offering.... And this is the offering that ye shall take of them; gold and silver and brass, and blue, and purple, and scarlet, and fine linen, and goats' hair, and rams' skins died red..."*

Colours have acquired the same sacred quality as trees and plants.

Could you ever have expected to find commands regarding colours in the Bible?

The blue and indigo obtained from *Isatis tinctoria* is no way inferior to the dyes from *Murex* and *Purpura* and the *Kermes oak*.

It is to this *Isatis tinctoria* that we owe the deep sheen of the blues and indigos to be seen in the old Anatolian *kilims...*

There is a dye obtained on the shores of the Aegean. This dye, widely known as Turkish red, is generally referred to as *kökboya,* or madder. Madder is actually a plant with a hairy stalk used in dyeing fabrics. According to researchers, it achieved great fame after the 15th century. The manufacture and application of the dye was a closely guarded secret, and no one now knows the method by which the dye was extracted from the plant.

A yellow dye is obtained from the branches and leaves of the *sandalwood* to be found in the Mediterranean maquis. Yellow can also be obtained from both the tree and fruit of the pomegranate.

Two thousand years ago, Vitruvius, who was interested in everything in nature in any way connected with architecture, gave a detailed account of the production of dyes. Let me quote the passages concerned with the virtues of pitch pine and wine lees:

"Set fire to the chippings and other parts of the pitch pine. When they have burned to charcoal put out the fire and pound the charcoal in a large mortar. By this method a fairly deep black will be obtained suitable for fresco work."

"The wine lees is dried, baked in an oven and then pounded. The dye produced, when applied to a wall, is even more pleasant than the normal black."

The *henna tree* is an essential feature of Aegean and Mediterranean vegetation. As a means of dyeing hair, hands and finger-nails, the dye produced, which is of a reddish-orange colour, makes an indispensable contribution to every wedding ceremony. .

Plants are the source of innumerable spices, dyes, foods, drinks and jewellery. No civilization has ignored or rejected them. For example, young men of between eighteen and twenty years of age would practice boxing in the building known as the *Ephebeion* in Priene. In another room in the same building wounds were treated with olive oil,.

The wounds were cleaned by the application of olive oil and then cured by leaving a layer of oil on the body.

This treatment, which is still used in many parts of Anatolia, was known as *athletes.*

In those days olive oil was very expensive, but it was used extensively in connection with athletic competitions and games. That was why they always sought out a wealthy citizen to meet the needs of olive oil consumption. This benefactor was always a guest of honour at the competitions.

Scholars have the following to say regarding the taste of the fruit left to dry in attics or on flat roofs. *"It begins to spread out in waves as if newly plucked from the branches."*

On one of my travels along the Aegean and the Mediterranean coast my eye was suddenly caught by the sight of a blossom that had opened on a bare branch in a copse made practically inaccessible by thorns. I was fascinated by these leafless branches on which a purple blossom had opened as if just to spite me.

In the Aegean and the Mediterranean, as everywhere else in the world, the vegetation would appear to be full of unknowns.

But the way the ancient communities of the Aegean and the Mediterranean depicted their plants and flowers on stone, marble, metal, wood and fabric shows that the shores of these seas differ markedly from the mainland…

9 July 1994 / Manastır Bay

THE LEGACY OF ALEXANDER THE GREAT

There is one person it is impossible to avoid anywhere in the Aegean or the Mediterranean, a man by whom I myself have been accompanied throughout the course of all my researches. Few things have affected me so much as the extraordinary skill displayed by the marble bust of Alexander the Great in the Istanbul Archaeological Museum, while the funeral monument known as the *Alexander Sarcophagus* is unforgettable, not only for the skilful carving of the figures and decoration, but also for the remarkable skill displayed in the depiction of a scene of battle.

I am not interested in the question, "Who was Alexander the Great?"

That he was a master of warfare certainly enters into it, but what really interests me is that he was an emperor by the age of twenty and that in the course of thirteen years he had advanced as far as India, leaving behind him monumental works of art and architecture.

Some describe him as a Greek, others as a Macedonian. Yet others, like Prof.Dr.Arif Müfit Mansel, who base their theses on scholarly research, declare that *"...he inherited from his mother both his genius and all his ambitions and excesses, and his achievement of so much in so short a time was due to the fusion in one single individual of so many contrary moral elements"*.

His mother was the Illyrian princess Olympias.

He may have been impetuous. He may have defied all moral codes. But there is one thing no one can deny: that he possessed quite extraordinary qualities. Even in the midst of war and devastation he always had an eye for the minute detail…

You would like an example?…

Mansel informs us that before crossing to Anatolia Alexander marched on the Thracian tribes that were threatening Macedonia. As he made his way towards the Danube a rumour spread among the people in the Illyrian mountains that he was dead. This immediately gave rise to mutinies in Thebes and Athens, which had been under Alexander's rule. With forced marches of thirty kilometres a day he made his way with great rapidity into Greece, where he laid waste the whole territory. But on his own special wish the home of the poet Pindar was saved from destruction.

Alexander, who was born in 356 B.C., had Aristotle as his tutor.

It must have been from Aristotle than he obtained his knowledge of science, philosophy and art.

In the time of Alexander there was one kingdom with an irresistible power of expansion: the Kingdom of Persia.

The Persians arrived with a fleet of four hundred ships to conquer the Mediterranean. The Persian army was far superior to the Macedonian. It contained a number of Greek soldiers. Moreoever, the Persian treasury was crammed full of gold and silver.

In 334 B.C. the two armies met at Granicus (Bigaçay), where the Persians were overcome by the opposing forces.

Alexander's star was now in the ascendant. The Persians, looked upon as invincible throughout the Aegean, Mediterranean and Anatolia, had received their first shock. Alexander and the Persian King Darius, with their horses and war chariots, are to be seen depicted on mosaics in Pompei.

The Egyptian priests greeted him as "the son of Amon", thus investing him with divinity. The priests of Didyma, determined not to be outdone by the Egyptians, hailed him as "son of Zeus".

Everywhere he went he took with him his own system of administration, and as there were fewer administrators in Macedonia than in Persia he took a number of Persians into his employment. Sometimes he had difficulties with the Persian administrators, but he always managed to reach a consensus.

He was a leader who, quite apart from his skills in war, created his own administrative principles. By issuing his own currency he brought the commerce of the Aegean and the Mediterranean under his control.

An interesting aspect of his character is that he never regarded war and expansion as his sole aim. Wherever he went he would be accompanied by scholars, artists and architects.

He sent a group of researchers to North Africa to find out the reason for the

Head of Alexandre the Great. Marble. Hellenistic Period. II. century B.C. Cos (İstanköy). İstanbul Archaeological Museum.

recurrent flooding of the Nile. They decided that the flooding was caused by tropical rains in Ethiopia.

It was also at his suggestion that the Hippodamos system of town planning was implemented in designing the city of Alexandria.

His identification with Dionysos, Heracles and Achilles is one result of his exceptional qualities.

Historians mention his extraordinary power of imagination. They ascribe his affinity with artists to his keen sensitivity. But his redrawing of the map of the world, his foundation of some seventy cities, his development of a postal system, his initation of scientific research on cities, waters and seas and his proposal that Harpalos should grow Mediterranean vegetation in Babylon by creating a garden of plants is no small achievement for a life of only thirty-three years.

Strabo describes him as *"a passionate admirer of Homer, who kept a copy of Homer in a box that formed one of the most valuable objects in the Persian treasury."*

Alexander the Great, a man who knew how to kill and win battles, who was well aware of the superiority of force, who dismissed ten thousand mutinous soldiers and sent them back to their homes with gifts, who immediately formed a new army with which he gained new victories and new territories, remains, in my opinion, quite unique in the history of mankind.

Every city he captured or founded is remembered as a city of culture and commerce. He realized that civilizations cannot be created by military force alone. To keep the people contented and win their loyalty he made friends with their gods, their poets, their musicians and their sculptors.

They have said of him that "by organizing culture and commerce on lands extending from Gibraltar to the Punjab, he founded an empire open to social influences. He created a new world."

And then?

What followed is only too well known. Dynastic and power struggles, disintegration, new expectations, new hopes...

That is why the legacy of Alexander the Great in the Aegean and the Mediterranean is of such importance...

14 August 1994 / Gemiler Island

SIMENA AND KEKOVA

While we were mooring the boat to the grey, craggy rocks in Simena (Kale-Üçağız) Harbour behind Kekova, a boat approached us, skimming lightly over the glass-green water. The oarsman was a man of seventy or seventy-five. The Mediterranean sun shone on the spectacles that sat askew on his nose and which he had obviously bought from some street vendor.

"Would you like some sage or thyme", he asked us.

Then he started, without anyone asking him, telling us all about his children, his daughters-in-law and his grand-children. He adorned his short sentences in the manner of a village story-teller.

The smell of sage rose up from his boat and permeated the whole area around us. We bought a bunch and hung it up over the dinner table.

"I've got rich (?) friends like you in Sirkeci in Istanbul," said the old man of Simena as he finally left us. He seemed to have no idea of his age but was keen on raising as large a family as possible. *"They like making me talk. And I tell them whatever comes into my mind. There are two things about us locals: loads of children and loads of talk."*

I have never met anyone born on the sea-shore that was taciturn. The water seems to make them talkative…

Aspasia, who lived in the 440s B.C., was a friend of Pericles. She gave him lessons in the art of speaking. Aspasia worked in a brothel. She managed her beautiful women, and at the same time promoted the art of beautiful speech.

Pericles used to take his students to the brothel to listen to Aspasia and take lessons from her.

Of course, this may have been just an excuse on Perciles' part, who knows?

It is obvious that the Aegean and the Mediterranean stimulate the creation of beauty…

As soon as we left Üçağız and had moored our boat between Kale and Kekova Island we set out for the shore. We were all in such a hurry that none of us could wait for the boat to come back for a second trip and all eight of us piled in at the same time.

The reason for all the rush was our eagerness to see the sunset from Kale. And our haste was fully justified.

I have no idea what sort of a place paradise is. They say there are crystal streams, motley-coloured birds, beautiful girls, a thousand and one fruits and delicious drinks. They also say that these beautiful girls will offer you anything you could imagine…

I am not too keen on places like that. But Kekova is one of the few places on earth blessed by both God and Nature. For thousands of years it has watched over the nearby island where so many civilizations have cast anchor.

There is no such thing as a road on Kale. One has to make one's way over slippery rocks that are sometimes as jagged as the teeth of a saw, with thorn bushes between them. A goat's trail can pass through a courtyard as easily as a stable. Or through a fish restaurant.

All along these roads there were old women, young girls and children from Kale selling *yazmas* and necklaces made from insects dyed all sorts of colours. They were also eager to show us the way. Because if you go off on your own believing that you know the way or will easily find it you will end up having to climb the castle walls!…

A woman of seventy-five or eighty was selling *yazmas* in a large, shallow basket.

We walk on together. She shows us the way.

"I can't see properly any more," she says.

While I am climbing over the rocks in fear and trembling clutching desperately at every point of support, I see her hopping lightly along, as if she was walking along a perfecly flat road, talking away at the same time saying whatever comes into her head, just like the old man of Simena himself.

I couldn't help asking her how she could make her way over the rocks like that if she couldn't see properly.

"I use my mind, my son," she replied, *"I use my mind. I was born here. these rocks know me and I know them. The girls are no use compared with me. Ah, you should see my daughter-in-law, how she minces along the road. I can get along fine without being able to see. I know it all inside out!"*

Is the ability to see so essential to life?

Or is every stranger that comes along - whether he can speak her language or not - merely a voice?

Who knows?

There is no place for incongruities on shores washed by the sea. Nature will swallow up anything in any way incongruous. Sun, water and salt knead men, rocks, plants, moss and fish in the one great trough.

Where does the pine in Manastır Bay at Göcek that dips its needles like a fishing-line into the sea find its nourishment?

From the salt water.

Believe it or not. The roots of the pine stretch down into the salt water like so many fish.

Perhaps that is why the love of nature and civilization never dies in the mountain and shore cities of Lycia.

I wouldn't know. Is every beauty that exists to be associated with the word "love"?

We ought to find another word.

We ought to find another word to define the beauty of the sunset at Kale.

No one can decide what point to choose for the best view of the sunset. Everyone, locals or visitors, are staring dumbly out at some point or other.

Some have made their way to the Lycian tombs that have been lying for two thousand four hundred years under the olive trees. Others have settled down on the battlements of the castle, and sit puffing away at a cigarette.

Others, deeply in love, are unable to resist giving the friend they are embracing a Mediterranean kiss.

The whole beauty arises from the sunset that comes rolling down on to the sea over Kısıkbelen hill from the island of Kekova that gives shelter from the southern winds and the small islands of Topak and Kara Ada.

I hear *Ayşegül* calling. She wants to show me the sunset through a gap in the ruins of the castle wall.

Where was it?

At first I couldn't make it out myself. Then I realized it was a secluded part of Üçağız where we had moored that morning.

There are only two boats, at quite some distance from one another. Olive trees on both shores. The sea is lying asleep. I quite happily light a cigarette in spite of my promise to cut down.

This is surely a place that could never be described in poetry, painting, story or music.

But perhaps the dancers of Dionysos may wind their way down from the blue sky with their white garments blowing in the wind...

In 1979 Azra Erhat said that she was curious to know what might happen to Kale, but as a matter of fact not very much has happened in the close on twenty years that have elapsed since then. In fact, it is heartening to see how little has changed.

Erhat was overjoyed to find the local traditions continuing unimpaired. *"Every time we go there,"* she writes, *"we are met by children and young people that deluge us with gifts of carobs, almonds, honey, eggs and yoghurt, take us for trips in their rowing-boats and motor-boats without asking a penny, give us specimens of their home-made yazmas and kilims, entertain us to meals in their houses and send letters to our address. In Kekova we still find vestiges of the Golden Age."*

All those are joys that are becoming much rarer in our own day. Things have changed since twenty or thirty boats a day began to anchor in the harbour. In his book on the first philosophers George Thomason quotes a proverb current in the 7th century B.C. : *"Man is money"*.

Kale owes much to the Lycians and the Ottomans, but the main thing is the remarkable beauty of the countryside. All the local inhabitants have to do is to look after the narrow streets, the restaurants, the houses and the island itself as carefully as a mastic tree and not to allow any signs or notices to rival the colour of the bougainvillea. In short, not to turn their jewel into a flea market.

But now it's time to go back.

We leave Kale just as the sun is setting. There is a stone building on the edge of a cliff. This single-storey building with the stone court-yard and rooms with a view over an endless expanse is the village primary school.

If you can wait a little the philosophers of the ancient world may arrive to give their lessons in their white garments and sandals.

I would like to have been taught in a school like that, and to have taught in it.

My first lesson would have been on "blue".

My second lesson would have been on the love and friendship between blue and the water. For my third lesson I would have lined the pupils up in front of the window, towards the sea, with the mountains and clouds turning from blue and green to purple.

The next day my first lesson would have been on sunshine, light and darkness. I would have allowed them to wander around and play for a couple of hours in the courtyard. If they wanted, they could go home or to the theatre or the seashore.

For the first lesson in the afternoon I would ask them what they saw from the window. I would make each pupil answer one by one.

Then I would ask them to go out and take a careful look at the the-atre and the castle. Then we would continue with our game in the theatre. I would ask them to consider, not how the steps 50-60 metres away were used, but why they were made.

"You can all stand wherever you like on the steps," I would tell them. "and say out loud whatever comes into your head."

On the third day I would give them an exercise. "This time you're going to write about your dreams. Describe both your dreams and your day-dreams."

How could civilization ever exist where there were no dreams?…

The sea has its own voice and music.

Our lesson is on sounds…

Later I would have given my pupils a lesson on human voices and natural sounds. But perhaps it might be better to start off by talking about sound and silence.

Anyone who knew nothing of sound and silence could never be real-ly happy in the Mediterranean.

And what else would I have taught them?

Perhaps what unknowns are… Or the language of colours…

And after that?… I don't see any end to all this. One day a letter with an official heading would arrive: *"In view of his tendency to give lessons incompatible with the curriculum…"*

But there's one hopeful point. I am well out of their sight, and probably no one would take any notice of me. They might even forget me altogether.

One day I would throw discretion to the winds and go off with my pupils in a motor-boat to the unknowns in Kale and Kekova. It would be their turn to teach the unknowns, things I had never seen…

There is a story in Eduardo Galeano's *"El libro de los Abrazos"* connected with the virtue of being able to see.

"Diego had never seen the sea. One day his father, Santiago Kovadlof, took him to see it. They went south.

The sea was waiting behind high sand dunes.

When father and son, after a long walk, finally the reached the top of the dunes the sea suddenly spread out shining in front of them.

The child was struck dumb by the vast expanse of the shining sea.

When at last, stammering and trembling, he was able to speak, he turned to his father:

'Help me to see it', he said."

17 August 1994 / Kekova.

WORDS

While revising this book I noticed that there were certain words that kept cropping up in expressing the depths in nature in which sight and perception meet…

"Joy", "taste", "rapture", "mystery", "depth", "inspiration", "nature", "image", "endless" are only a few of these.

I smiled at myself, at my inability to find other terms, other words.

My only consolation is that words like joy, taste, rapture, mystery, depth, inspiration, nature, image and endless are terms used throughout the whole of life. I don't believe that everyday, monotonous days and nights can ever make life worth while.

Life lives in its details, and in its skills…

Life is sometimes defined as an "art". But art is the interpretation of what can be grasped within life itself. It is the reflection of the soot and sediment we gather upon us.

Nature, on the other hand, is the source of everything.

It is no easy matter to hear the myriad voices of nature or to comprehend the music of the human voice; or the voices of the Aegean and the Mediterranean…

Those who created Dionysos in their dreams and produced dance and poetry and colour were the heralds of civilization.

Who were the inventors of the flute, the drum, the cymbals and the lyre?

Undoubtedly those who could taste the true savour of life…

Perhaps it is all rather far from our shores, but the command of the Commagenian King Antiochus is a source of joy for our race:

"My birthday will be celebrated every month and every year as a holiday. In the ceremonies, the gods and the priest (on the strength of the authority generously granted by myself and the laws) will don on my behalf Persian costumes and will place gold wreaths on the statues of the gods and my ancestors. Loads of incense will be burned for each of us. If necessary, sacrifices will be offered. The sacred tables will be furnished with the finest food and wines. My people gathered here will eat their fill and make holiday."

Antiochus did a wonderful thing in dedicating his birthday every year to festivity and rejoicing. But how did they manage to celebrate his birthday every month? It is pretty obvious that Antiochus was on the lookout for an excuse for a celebration.

Life is celebrated with the finest jewellery, perfumes, garments, food and wine.

Again I find myself obliged to use the same word: the savour of life, the rapture concealed in the depth of nature.

Food and drink is a pleasure never to be despised, never at any time.

As for this word "savour" that I keep on using rather at random. Throughout all the millennia there has never been a community that rejected the pleasures of the palate. No better proof of this can be found than the spice road that runs from North Africa to the Mediterranean and from India to the West.

It is also evidenced by the pitchers of wine, the seeds and the exotic cereals found in the wrecks of the vessels that sank in storms off the coasts of the Aegean and the Mediterranean.

The transition from the cereal to the grape is of great importance. On the rock relief at İvriz, Tarhu, the god of storm and vegetation is holding a bunch of grapes in one hand and a sheaf of wheat in the other. King Warpalawas is depicted opposite paying homage to the god. This Late Hittite relief symbolises the choice made by the great cultures that extended from Anatolia to the Aegean and the Mediterranean.

When the mainland communities come in contact with the sea they also open themselves up to exuberance and rapture. The grape, the fruit of Tarhu, was also the fruit of Dionysos and Bacchus. This is the origin of the grape harvest festivals. The grape lies at the heart of life. We can never ignore the influence it has exerted on both art and religion. It altered the whole progress of poetry, music, dance and thought.

The culture and art that grew up around wheat, the olive and the grape is essentially an act of worship.

Moreover, rapture cannot be created out of nothing. It needs something to touch, to moisten the palate.

The Aegean and Mediterranean culture of which we are the tenants was kneaded with these, and washed and laid out in the sun.

There is a passage from "The Little Prince" by Saint-Exupéry that I have carried around with me everywhere for years.

"If the flower we love is to be found in just one of a million stars, that is enough to make the sight of the stars a joy."

I feel that that is always the way I shall look at the Aegean and the Mediterranean.

12 October 1994 / Istanbul

BIBLIOGRAPHY

AĞAOĞLU, ADALET. "Doğu Akdeniz'de Zaman", *Skylife*, No. 136, İstanbul 1994.

AKŞİT, İLHAN. *Batı Anadolu Mitolojisi ve Troya Efsanesi*, 1979.

AKŞİT, İLHAN. *Mavi Yolculuk (Akdeniz Kıyı Uygarlığı)*, İstanbul.

AKŞİT, OKTAY. *Likya Tarihi*, 1967.

AKURGAL, EKREM. *Anadolu Uygarlıkları*, İstanbul 1988.

AKURGAL, EKREM. *Eski Çağda Ege ve İzmir*, İzmir 1993.

ALPÖZEN, OĞUZ. *Türkiye'de Sualtı Arkeolojisi*, İstanbul 1975.

ALPÖZEN, OĞUZ. *Bodrum (Antik Halikarnassos)*, 1983.

ANADOL, NÜKHET. *Cennetin Rotası*, İstanbul.

AND, METİN. *Oyun ve Büyü*, Ankara 1974.

ANON. *Termessos Milli Parkı*, 1970.

ANON. *Anadolu Medeniyetleri I, II, III, (Anatolian Civilizations Exhibition Cakalogue)*, İstanbul 1983.

ANON. *Eski Yunan*, İstanbul 1987.

ANON. "Turquie Antique", *Geo*, March, 1987.

ANON. *Antalya Museum*, 1988.

ANON. "Turkei", *Geo*, (special number), February 1989.

ANON. *Hesiodos Eseri ve Kaynakları*, trans. S. Eyüboğlu-A. Erhat, Ankara 1991.

ANON. *Anadolu Kadınının 9000 Yılı, (Woman in Anatolia Exhibition Catalogue)*, İstanbul 1993.

ATAY, ÇINAR M. *Tarih İçinde İzmir*, 1978.

AYGEN, TEMUÇİN. *The Blue Paradise of Lycia*, İstanbul 1988.

AYGEN, TEMUÇİN-ÜSTÜN ÇELİKLER. "Ege'nin Eski İki Kenti", *Türkiyemiz*, No. 59, İstanbul 1989.

BASS, GEORGE. "Splendors of the Bronz Age", *National Geographic*, December 1987.

BAYBURTLUOĞLU, CEVDET. *Lykia*, 1981.

BAYRAKTAR, VEHBİ. *Pergamon*, İstanbul 1989.

BEAN, GEORGE E. *Aegean Turkey*, İstanbul 1967.

BEAN, GEORGE E. *Turkey's Southern Shore*.

BEAN, GEORGE E. "Knidos", *Tarih ve Toplum*, No. 20, İstanbul 1985.

BEAN, GEORGE E. *Turkey beyond the Meander*, John Murray, 1989.

BEAN, GEORGE E. *Lycian Turkey*.

BEKTAŞ, CENGİZ-SELMİN BAŞAK. *Bodrum*, İstanbul 1979.

BERGİL, MEHMET SUAT. *Doğada, Bilimde, Sanatta Altın Oran*, İstanbul 1988.

BRAUDEL, FERNAND. *La Mediterranèe, les Hommes et l'Hêritage Arts et Mètiers Graphiques*, 1988.

BRAUDEL, FERNAND. *La Mèditerranèe et le monde mèditerranèen a l'epoque de Philippe II*.

BOYSAL, YUSUF. *Arkaik Devir Heykeltraşlığı*, Ankara 1979.

CAMUS, ALBERT. *Denemeler*, trans. S. Eyüboğlu-V. Günyol, İstanbul 1960.

CANAV, ÜZLİFAT. *Cam Eserler Koleksiyonu*, 1985.

CARETTO, GIACOMO. *Akdeniz'de Türkler*, trans. D. Kundakçı-Gülbende Kuray, Ankara 1992.

CECAN, HALUK. "Sualtından Notlar", *Atlas*, No. 1, İstanbul 1993..

CERAM, C. W. *Tanrılar, Mezarlar, Bilginler*, trans. Hayrullah Örs, İstanbul 1969.

CHILDE, GORDON. *What Happened in History*.

ÇAPAN, CEVAT. *Sapho*, İstanbul 1972.

ÇAPAN, CEVAT. *Çağdaş Yunan Şiiri Antolojisi*, İstanbul 1982.

DANİŞ, TİMUR. "Ege", *Photo Globe*, March, 1994.

DARGA, MUHİBBE. *Hitit Sanatı*, İstanbul 1992.

DE CHARDIN TEILHARD. *La Place de l'homme dans la nature*, 1956.

DURU, ORHAN. *Mavi Gezi*, İstanbul 1986.

ECO, UMBERTO. *La definizione dell'arte*.

ELBE, HALUK. *Bodrum*, İstanbul 1972.

ERDEMGİL, SELAHATTİN. *Efes*, İstanbul 1988.

ERHAT, AZRA. "Marmaris'ten Antalya'ya", *Türkiye Turing ve Otomobil Kurumu Belleteni*, No. 337, İstanbul 1977.

ERHAT, AZRA. *Karya'dan Pamfilya'ya*, 1984.

ERHAT, AZRA. *Mitoloji Sözlüğü*, İstanbul 1972.

ERTÜRK, BANU. "Bafa Gölü", *Atlas*, No. 15, İstanbul 1994.

ERZEN, AFİF. *Eski Çağ Tarihi Hakkında Dört Konferans*, İstanbul 1984.

EURİPİDES. *Bakhhalar*, trans. S. Eyüboğlu, İstanbul 1944.

EYÜBOĞLU, İSMET ZEKİ. *Tanrı Yaratan Toprak, Anadolu*, İstanbul 1973.

EYÜBOĞLU, İSMET ZEKİ. *Cinci Büyüleri ve Yıldızname*, İstanbul 1978.

EYÜBOĞLU, İSMET ZEKİ. *Geçmişin Yaşama Gücü*, İstanbul 1982.

EYÜBOĞLU, İSMET ZEKİ. *Anadolu Uygarlığı*, İstanbul 1981.

EYÜBOĞLU, İSMET ZEKİ. *Anadolu İnançları, Anadolu Mitolojisi*, İstanbul 1987.

FELLOW, C. *Lykia*, 1840.

FRAZER, JAMES G. *The Golden Bough the Roots of Religion and Folklore*, 1890.

GOFFMAN, DANIEL. *İzmir and the Levantine World 1550-1650*, Washington 1990.

GÖKSEL, DOĞU. *Didim, Milet, Priene.*

HALİKARNAS BALIKÇISI. *Merhaba Akdeniz,* İstanbul 1962.

HALİKARNAS BALIKÇISI. *Ege'nin Dibi,* İstanbul 1952.

HALİKARNAS BALIKÇISI. *Anadolu Efsaneleri,* İstanbul 1954.

HALİKARNAS BALIKÇISI. *Anadolu Tanrıları,* İstanbul 1955.

HALİKARNAS BALIKÇISI. *Gülen Ada,* İstanbul 1957.

HALİKARNAS BALIKÇISI. *Anadolu'nun Sesi,* İstanbul 1971.

HALİKARNAS BALIKÇISI. *Hey Koca Yurt,* İstanbul 1972.

HALİKARNAS BALIKÇISI. *Ege'den,* İstanbul 1972.

HALMAN, TALAT SAIT. *Eski Uygarlıkların Şiirleri,* İstanbul 1974.

HASOL, DOĞAN. *Mimarlık Sözlüğü,* İstanbul 1975.

HEIKELL, ROD. *The Turquoise Coast of Turkey,* İstanbul 1988.

HERODOTOS. *Herodot Tarihi,* trans. Müntekim Ökmen, İstanbul 1973.

HOMEROS. *İlyada,* trans. Azra Erhat- A. Kadir, İstanbul 1967.

HOMEROS. *Odeysseia,* trans. Azra Erhat- A. Kadir, İstanbul 1984.

İNAN, AFET. *Eski Mısır Tarih ve Medeniyeti,* Ankara 1992.

İNAN, JALE. *Antalya Bölgesi Roma Devri Portreleri,* 1965.

KÜÇÜKERMAN, ÖNDER. *Cam,* İstanbul 1978.

LAROCHE, JANE. *Fethiye,* İstanbul.

LEVİ, DORO. *İasos Kazıları,* 1986.

LEVI-STRAUSS, CLAUDE. *Din ve Büyü,* ed. and trans. Ahmet Güngören, İstabul 1983.

LLYOD, SETON-D. STORM RICE. *Alanya (Alâ'ıyya),* trans. Nermin Sinemoğlu, Ankara 1989.

MANSEL, ARİF MÜFİT. *Ege ve Yunan Tarihi,* Ankara 1963.

MANSEL, ARİF MÜFİT. *Side Klavuzu,* Ankara 1967.

MANSEL, ARİF MÜFİT. *Side,* Ankara 1978.

MESSEQUE, MARURICE. *C'est la nature qui a raison.*

MESSEQUE, MARURICE. *Mon Herbier de Santé.*

NAUMANN, R. *Didyma Führer,* İstanbul.

NECATİGİL, BEHÇET. *100 Soruda Mitologya,* İstanbul 1969.

OHRİ, İSKENDER. *Anadolu'nun Öyküsü,* İstanbul 1978.

ÖNDER, MEHMET. *Türkiye Müzeleri,* 1977.

ÖNEN, ÜLGÜR. *Lycia,* 1984.

PAKSOY, NADİR. *"Bir Kaş, Bir Kekova, Üçağız",* *Atlas,* No. 15, İstanbul 1994.

PEKMAN, ADNAN. *Eski Çağda Bazı Anadolu Şehirlerinin Tanrı ve Kahraman Ktistes'leri,* İstanbul 1970.

PİRİ REİS. *Kitâb-ı Bahriyye,* İstanbul 1973.

PLUTARKHOS MESTRIUS. *Marcus Antonius,* trans. Dr. Mehmet Ozaktürk, Ankara 1992.

RADT, WOLFGANG. *Pergamon,* İstanbul 1973.

SAKAOĞLU, SAİM. *Anadolu-Türk Efsanelerinde Taş Kesilme Motifi ve Bu Efsanelerin Tip Kataloğu,* Ankara 1980.

SAYGI, EROL. *Gökçeada İmbros,* 1988.

SAYILAN FİRDEVS *"Akdeniz'in Eski Kentleri",* *Türkiyemiz,* No. 55, İstanbul 1988.

SÖZEN, GÜROL. *"Onbin Yıllık Kültür Anadolu Uygarlığı",* *Antur Magazine,* İstanbul 1985.

SÖZEN, GÜROL. *"Zeus'un Mavi Derinliğinde Bir Kent: Phaselis",* *Status,* No. 4, İstanbul 1986.

SÖZEN, GÜROL. *"Mavi Uygarlık",* *Güneş gazetesi,* 21-30 Ağustos 1986.

SÖZEN, GÜROL. *"Mavi Tatil",* *Güneş gazetesi,* 11-14 Eylül 1987.

SÖZEN, GÜROL. *"Blue Civilizations",* *Turkey,* 1987.

SÖZEN, GÜROL. *"Mavi Uygarlık",* *Türkiyemiz,* No. 55, İstanbul 1988.

SÖZEN, GÜROL. *"Ege'de Antik Gezi",* *Güneş gazetesi,* 25-28 Temmuz 1990.

SÖZEN, GÜROL. *"Bir Sonsuzluk Dionysos",* *Urart Kataloğu,* İstanbul 1990.

SÖZEN, GÜROL. *"Antik Kent Priene",* *Cumhuriyet gazetesi,* 29 Mayıs 1993.

SÖZEN, GÜROL. *"Bodrum Kalesi'nde İki Müze",* *Cumhuriyet gazetesi,* 15 Ağustos 1993

SÖZEN, GÜROL. *"Ege Kıyılarında Sanat ve Bilimin Gücü",* *Türkiyemiz,* No. 69, İstanbul 1993.

SÖZEN, METİN-UĞUR TANYELİ. *Sanat Kavram ve Terimleri Sözlüğü,* İstanbul 1986.

STRABON. *Coğrafya, Anadolu (Kitap: XII, XIII, XIV),* trans. Prof. Dr. Adnan Pekman, İstanbul 1987.

THOMSON, GEORGE. *Studies in Ancient Greek Society- The Prehistorie Aegean.*

THOMSON, GEORGE. *Studies in Ancient Greek Society- The First Philosophers,* 1955.

TOMPKINS, PETER-C. BIRD. *Bitkilerin Gizli Yaşamı,* trans. Sulhi Dölek, İstanbul 1983, (*The Secret life of plants* 1973).

TURANİ, ADNAN. *Sanat Terimleri Sözlüğü,* 1968.

TÜRKOĞLU, SABAHATTİN. *Efes'in Öyküsü,* İstanbul 1986.

UÇKU, SELÇUK. *"Assos",* *Türkiyemiz,* No. 70, İstanbul 1993.

ULUASLAN, HÜSEYİN. *Assos,* Çanakkale.

UMAR, BİLGE. *Trakya,* İstanbul.

UMAR, BİLGE. *Ionia,* İstanbul 1979.

UMAR, BİLGE. *Aiolis,* İstanbul 1980.

UMAR, BİLGE. *Troas,* İstanbul 1983.

UMAR, BİLGE. *Mysia,* İstanbul 1984.

UMAR, BİLGE. *Psidia,* İstanbul.

UMAR, BİLGE. *Türkiye'deki Tarihsel Adlar,* İstanbul 1993.

VİTRUVİUS. *Mimarlık Üzerine On Kitap,* trans. Dr. Suna Güven, Ankara 1990.

WÖLFFLIN, HEINRICH. *Sanat Tarihinin Temel Kavramları,* trans. Hayrullah Örs, İstanbul 1973.

WYCHERLEY, R. E. *Antik Çağda Kentler Nasıl Kuruldu,* trans. Nur Nirven- Nezih Başgelen, İstanbul 1986.

YOURCENAR, MARGUERITTE. *Memoires d'Hadrien.*

YÜCEL, ERDEM. *"Kuşadası",* *Türkiyemiz,* No. 60, İstanbul 1990.

453

INDEX

NAMES